ON REFERRING IN LITERATURE

ON REFERRING
IN LITERATURE

EDITED BY

ANNA WHITESIDE

AND

MICHAEL ISSACHAROFF

INDIANA UNIVERSITY PRESS
BLOOMINGTON AND INDIANAPOLIS

Manufactured in the United States of America

Library of Congress Cataloging-in-Publication Data
On referring in literature.
Bibliography: p.
Includes index.
Contents: Metafictional implications for novelistic
reference / Linda Hutcheon—The double bind: self-
referring poetry / Anna Whiteside—Bad references /
Gerald Prince—[etc.]
1. Literature—Philosophy. 2. Reference (Philosophy)
3. Reference (Linguistics) I. Whiteside, Anna.
II. Issacharoff, Michael.
PN49.05   1987   801   86-45748
ISBN 0-253-34262-7
ISBN 0-253-20437-2 (pbk.)
1 2 3 4 5 91 90 89 88 87

CONTENTS

PREFACE

The purpose of this volume is to show how reference is an integral part of (literary) interpretation. While much has been made, quite justifiably, of Jakobson's Theory of Communication, of speech-act theory, and of the sign in recent critical and theoretical works, the question of reference in literature remains a relatively unexplored domain. Those who have ventured to speak of it all too often equate it with mere reference to "real world" existents. But even then the issue is not as simple as it might appear; for what, one must ask, is this literary "real" world? Is it not, in fact, an artificial construct? If so, how is referential illusion created? This volume explores these problems and goes on to deal with other types of literary reference, showing what it is and how it works. Reference lies at the crossroads of reality and fiction, perception and interpretation being contingent on the way the referent and reference are construed.

Up till now, discussion of reference has been primarily philosophical and linguistic, with little contact between the Anglo-Saxon and European schools of thought. Although Ogden and Richards, as early as 1923 in *The Meaning of Meaning*, propounded their theory of the tripartite sign (Symbol/Thought/Referent), and though recent interest in Peirce, Austin, Searle, and Strawson has continued to underscore the validity of the referent as an indispensable third dimension of the sign, literary applications have been few. The European school, on the other hand, under the influence of Saussurian linguistics, has hitherto considered the sign as a binary entity (Signifier/Signified), while the referent was all but overlooked. Literary semiotics has tended to apply to its analyses the abstract Saussurian construct rather than the empirical Anglo-Saxon model. Yet the latter is, in fact, better suited to the specifics of literary interpretation.

These essays collectively pave the way to a marriage of the two schools and provide a series of essentially empirical applications of different aspects of the theory of reference (and hence of semiotics and linguistics) to a wide spectrum of major modern literary texts, comprising samples of drama, fiction, and poetry. We thus offer the reader a volume of practical semiotics focussing on the referent and reference in varied literary situations. The conclusion provides the theoretical backcloth for discussing and honing the multi-faceted concept of literary and, by definition, linguistic reference. It is our hope that these collected essays, given their empirical slant, will serve as the basis for similar applications in virtually any domain in world literature, in any genre, and thereby extend reference theory through the examination of literary praxis.

All the essays in this volume touch on types, ways, and modes of referring, as well as referentially determined meaning. The order in which they are presented is especially designed to reflect the ever-widening referential contexts they imply. For the way referring expressions and their referents (thus reference and ultimately meaning) are construed depends first and foremost on contexts and their interplay. The latter inevitably imply mode and mode-mixing (of "serious" and make-believe discourse, for example), help define types of reference (definite or indefinite, direct or opaque, unique or ambiguous), and obviously play an essential role in referential dynamics. For as anaphoric and cataphoric chains of reference evolve, they interrelate and so propel reference and coreference between contexts in a continually expanding and protean cross-referential network.

Accordingly, the first essay, by Linda Hutcheon, presents an overview of the four contextual spheres or levels: metatextual, intratextual, intertextual, and extratextual. Since her topic is "Metafictional Implications for Novelistic Reference" she arranges the levels according to their self-referential bias. Thus the "autorepresentational" or metatextual level is linked with the intertextual, since both are self-reflexive, while the extratextual and the intratextual are not. The essays that follow first elaborate reference within one contextual level, gradually widening to two, then three contexts, comparing and contrasting contextual interplay, and finally (in the last three chapters) embrace all contexts viewed in an ever-expanding framework of complementary contexts, reaching beyond them, opening up new referential horizons.

The second essay, by Anna Whiteside, limits itself to the metatextual context in self-referring poetry, discussing signs which are not only their own referents but also refer to their own process of reference and, thereby, of generating sense. Next Gerald Prince explores "bad reference" (in a Robbe-Grillet novel) which never succeeds in being extratextual or even intertextual, but remains intratextual and, in a sense, self-referential, since these apparently non-referring expressions ultimately refer to themselves as what they are: pure fiction. Jean Alter's "Waiting for the Referent: Waiting for Godot?" contrasts the virtual text as an intratextual entity and the performed text as an extratextual, ideological statement—one amongst a host of possible others, and so referring to the particular ideology it mirrors. In "Topological Poetics: Eluard's 'La Victoire de Guernica,'" Jean-Jacques Thomas also explores the opposition between intratextual and extratextual reference. He sees the extratextual evidence of the massacre of Guernica as a way of enhancing the irony underscored by this poem's internal system of opposition: victory versus the catastrophe the very name Guernica evokes. In the same vein, dealing with fiction, playscripts, and poetry, Françoise Meltzer, Michael Issacharoff, and Ross Chambers all develop the discussion of proper names: their status when, in literature, they refer extratextually to known existents such as Napoleon, Lenin, and Paris, and the altered status their intratextual use confers. Thus Napoleon is used to make fiction "realistic," Paris to trip the reader and so make him aware that in fact intertextuality (and not extratextual reference as it at first appears) is Baudelaire's dominant context, since his Parisian pictures refer first and foremost to other Parisian *pictures*. Michael Issacharoff uses reference within a play to Lenin and the quotation of one of his letters to show how different types of speech-act and the mixing of serious and non-serious modes determine reference, while at the same time contrasting extratextual and intertextual reference. Ultimately, as in the case of Guernica and Napoleon, it is the intratextual context which prevails. Michael Issacharoff goes on to contrast this intratextuality, prevalent in dramatic dialogue, with the play-script's "serious" extratextual instructions to real people (actors) about how to perform.

Intertextuality is explored by Bruce Morrissette in his analysis of Robbe-Grillet's device of slipping into and out of juxtaposed texts so that reference which initially seemed extratextual is only intertextually operative. It forms a series of intertextual mirrors and coreferential linkings. Recognizing these intertextual chains, and the codes to which they refer, is all part of a complex interpretational strategy.

Patrice Pavis, in "Production, Reception, and the Social Context," also focusses on interpretational strategies. In examining play productions as extratextually ideological statements (as do Jean Alter and Michael Issacharoff), he links interpretation to the intratextual whole, whose signs *mean* precisely through their internal reference and interplay. This intratextual level then affords a comparative intertextual interpretation and, finally, an ideological extratextual one as it incorporates superimposed levels of different ideologies. Wladimir Krysinski adds to these three contexts a metatextual one, thereby reminding us of the metatextual perspective of the first essay. But the focus is different, for what interests him is not so much the metatext mirroring the text (though inevitably it does) as texts which mirror their own creative process, and, whilst playing on extratextual and intratextual reference, point to their own process of becoming; that is, they refer autotelically. The final essay by Thomas Lewis on "The Referential Act" picks up this process and explores reference as an *act*. He opens the door to the ideological becomings of the text by showing how its ideology mirrors both those of other texts and the extratextual ideological projections of successive generations of readers. So reference, and the ideological interpretations it engenders, expands in ever-widening circles from the moment of a text's inception to the last syllable of its recorded readings.

Our warm thanks are due to all our contributors for their cooperation and patience; to Margot Dalingwater, to Manon Ames and McMaster University, and to Kitty Letsch and Johns Hopkins University for their help in preparing the typescript.

I.

METAFICTIONAL IMPLICATIONS FOR NOVELISTIC REFERENCE

Linda Hutcheon

The critical acceptance, not to say canonization, of contemporary metafiction—postmodernist, neobaroque,[1] or whatever it is eventually to be named—has led to a rethinking of many of the traditional assumptions about the novel as a mimetic genre. In other words, the actual forms of the fictions themselves have brought about a challenging of the theories that purport to explain them. For example, a self-reflexive form of fiction, one which in effect constitutes its own first critical commentary, has disturbing implications for concepts of novelistic reference. While the realist novel of the last century has usually provided the data base from which Marxist theories of reference[2] have developed, metafiction's *auto*-referential dimension complicates any attempt to conceive of fictional reference only in intratextual and extratextual terms. The major worry is probably that perhaps what metafiction has really done is to make explicit what is a truism of *all* fiction: the overdetermination of novelistic reference.

Of all the literary genres, the novel has had the most difficulty in escaping from naïve referential theories. Poetry was rescued from the myth of the instrumentality of language by the Symbolists, the New Critics, and a host of others. Part of the novel's problem is no doubt the result of the extended length of the genre. New Critical methods are not totally successful with larger verbal structures, partly because of the limitations of human memory: a novel is never one coherent spatio-temporal unit in the reader's mind, as a lyric poem might be. Critics, in discussing its language, must therefore decide whether they will isolate passages as subtexts for commentary, trace linguistic threads through a work, or use some other method.[3] Metafiction, in one sense, resolves this particular critical dilemma by bringing the formal language issue into the foreground of the fiction itself.

This kind of linguistic self-reflexiveness[4] can be overtly thematized in a text. Of course, the powers and limitations of language in both experiential and literary contexts are themes that are not the exclusive property of contemporary fiction. *Tristram Shandy*, not to mention *Don Quijote*, had raised the same questions about linguistic functioning in their narratives. What does seem to be more uniquely modern is the actualized or concretized version of these insights into language and the increased stress on the role of the reader. If words have the power to create worlds, for novelist and for reader, then novels can perhaps be generated from word play. Jean Ricardou, following the lead of Raymond Roussel, is only one of those who have investigated this possibility.

I.

If metafiction in general calls attention, overtly or covertly, to the fact that it is *text* first and foremost, that it is a human construct made up of and by words, then the traditional mimetic assumptions of novel criticism are explicitly being contested by the fiction itself. The "referential fallacy," when applied to this kind of fiction, becomes in a sense short-circuited. It is no longer, in Michael Riffaterre's formulation,[5] both the central obstacle to and the first step towards the reader's reaching the significance (semiosis) of the text. Instead, the fiction itself points to the fallacy as a fallacy, thereby preempting much of its status as necessity by presuming it as a given. What is immediately postulated as axiomatic in such fiction is the fictiveness of the referents of the text's language.

The clearest paradigm for this postulation is fantasy literature: here new, non-existent worlds must be created by using only the language of *this* world. But, of course, *all* novelists must convince the reader of the "existence" of their fictive universes, at least *during* the act of reading, and they must do so through language alone. Fantastic fiction, it might be argued, demands an increased effort on the writer's part because of the axiomatic imaginary character of its world. But perhaps the opposite is really true; that is, perhaps the reader's expectations as he reads a fantasy novel facilitate the task by also making axiomatic the fictiveness of the referents of the language. No one seems to demand that Tolkien's Middle Earth be a counter to our empirical world, just that it be an intratextually coherent universe. Tolkien himself wrote that the successful story-maker creates "a Secondary World which your mind can enter. Inside it, what he relates is 'true': it accords with the laws of that world. You therefore believe it, while you are, as it were, inside."[6] This would be true of even more radical fantasy worlds such as that of Ambrose Bierce's "The Damned Thing," where there are colours human eyes cannot see and sounds human ears cannot hear, or in David Lindsay's land of Tormance (in *A Voyage to Arcturus*) where Maskull, the human hero, has to grow non-human organs to cope with the geographical and emotional peculiarities of each region.

Fantasy literature manages to evade the demand for extratextual reference that plagues more traditional, especially realist, narrative. The self-conscious thematization of this very issue in metafiction acts as a marker of fictionality (like "once upon a time") and suggests that the referent of the language of *all* fiction is likely not the same as that of non-literary language. Prose may also be the form of our newspapers and our letters, but there is one important difference in context between my letter to my parents and that of Richardson's Pamela to hers. My letter will be judged by informational or expressive criteria (the accuracy and interest of its details, my sincerity as writer), but both the details and the form of Pamela's letter have an intratextual structural function in the plot and character motivation of the novel, *Pamela*. They have, in addition, no necessary reference at all to any extratextual reality.

Jean Ricardou feels that the main problem of the kind of realist poetics that would deny this last statement arises from a naïveté about extralinguistic reference that results in a confusing of the signified of a literary sign and its referent: "I think of all those people who, when reflecting on a novel, say: if I had been that character I would have done something different. . . . Well, one could say that those people are transposing a character from the domain of the signified to that of the referent."[7] But, despite the convenience of this distinction, it is not quite accurate. Surely, in strictly linguistic terms, the signified of a word in my letter and of the same word in Pamela's would be the same, that is, if they were taken in isolation. Their different contexts, however, would demand different referents. Therefore one could say that it is the nature of the referent itself that changes when a fictive universe is posited.

This kind of thinking underlies much of the recent work in pragmatics, semantics, and logic[8] on alternate or possible worlds, especially theories derived from Frege's distinction between sense and reference (or, in Ricardou's Saussurian terms, signified and referent).[9] Frege argued that in ordinary language usage a sign could have a sense and yet no reference if the latter did not "demonstrably" exist in our empirical world. In *literary* discourse, however, this idea of truth-value reference ceases to have much value or meaning, and Frege's own solution is not very satisfying. In an epic poem, he argues, "we are only interested in the sense of the sentences and the images and feelings thereby aroused. The question of truth would cause us to abandon aesthetic delight for an attitude of scientific investigation." If literary texts do not denote but only seem to denote, as Frege claims, then perhaps the notion of reference has to be expanded—not denied—to include such pseudo-denotative processes by which readers create fictive worlds. Recently pragmatic theories of "fictionality," as the regulative principle dominating all semantic operations in literary communication, have offered one way of opening up the concept of novelistic reference to make room for the implications of metafiction that explicitly or implicitly teaches its reader how to create its universe out of words, how to actualize a possible world through the act of reading. The fictions of Robert Coover, John Barth, Julio Cortazar, John Fowles, and others encode the fictiveness of their worlds directly into their texts, thereby implicating both the agent (the reader) and his or her world model in the creation of a new world.

These novels all suggest that what would be useful would be an expanded notion of referentiality that would make possible distinctions between real and fictive referents. One such theory was offered by Georges Lavis in response to a Frege-like claim that literary texts lacked referents.[10] At the level of *langue*, Lavis claims (using Saussure's definition of reference), there can be real referents which are either physical ("table," "forehead") or non-physical ("honesty"). There can only be fictive referents which are physical ("unicorn") or non-physical ("ubiquity"). At this level of *langue*, fictive referents are not real because they are nonexistent in empirical reality. On the level of *parole*,[11] the issue is more complex and more relevant to our discussion of literature. Referents can again be real, as in most ordinary language usage, or fictive (physical or not). Here, however, they are fictive either because they are lies (false referents) or because the objects are imagined. Obviously this latter case is of interest here, for two reasons. First, the denigration of fiction in earlier periods as ''lies'' can be seen to have its root in this question of false and fictive referents. Second, in the literary text, one could argue that there are no such things as real referents for the *reader* at least: *all* are fictive—''table,'' ''forehead,'' ''unicorn,'' ''honesty,'' ''ubiquity''—because their context would be an imagined world. Readers accept this as a given when they accept the fact that what they are reading is a fiction, that is, an imagined construct.

This acceptance is what Norman Mailer plays upon in *The Armies of the Night* when he divides his book into two parts: the novel as history, and history as a novel. Genres are more than mere classificatory devices for literary critics; they also enable readers to orient themselves and to understand the context in which they must situate the referent. ''In the novel,'' wrote Maurice Blanchot, ''the act of reading is unchanged, but the attitude of the person reading makes it different.''[12] It is very relevant to the reading experience whether or not the referent is believed to be real or fictive, that is, whether one is reading about the real world or one is creating an imaginary possible world oneself. This is not to deny referentiality, as we shall see, but rather to reconsider its dimensions.

Metafiction today challenges that reification which made what is essentially a temporally limited period-concept of realism into a definition of the entire novel genre. The result of this realist imperialism had been the implied positing of the referent of fiction as *real*, with the underlying assertion (and apologia for the novel) that if something ''really happened,'' or could be made to seem to, it was therefore its own justification and verification.[13] But this referential illusion could be said to destroy the integrity of the sign, almost cancelling out the signified by presuming direct collusion between referent and signifier. This establishes a kind of incomplete denotation (sign/referent becomes signifier/referent) in order to create what Barthes called an ''*effet* de réel.''

Yet even early and traditionally realistic novels have thematized this effect as mere effect. Don Quijote and Emma Bovary are literary examples of what happens when the referent of fiction is presumed to be real and operative. Emma is the most serious of realists, for she truly believes that art, even the romantic literature she reads, is a vehicle for experiences which really exist or can be made to exist in her own world. Her belief raises the question of how both ordinary and literary language can ever correspond to the precise nature of non-verbal realities. It is not that Emma reads the wrong books, as some have suggested, but that, like Don Quijote, she reads believing the referents to be real.

It is now an accepted truism of much contemporary criticism that literature cannot lay claim to truth value in a philosophical sense, and that in effect it derives its autonomous ontological status and value from this very fact. We can now see that the linguistic reason for this autonomy is that a truth claim would demand a real referent, not a fictive one. At the level of *parole*, lies and imaginary objects lack real referents. It is the fictiveness of the language's referents that effects the freeing of the reader from what Georges Poulet has called his ''usual sense of incompatibility between [his] consciousness and its objects."[14] It is the *objects*, which he or she now creates, that have changed their level of reference. Fictive referents[15] project a fictional universe, one which is aware always of its verbal reality.

One warning ought to be issued at this point: in fiction, the fictive referent and the signified ought never to be confused, in the sense that the former lies outside the Saussurian linguistic sign. Its focus is the imagination of the reader: hence Ricardou's refusal to acknowledge the different kinds of reference. Within his structuralist critical framework, the referent is, in fact, irrelevant. In the act of reading a novel, however, especially a metafictional one, it is too relevant to ignore. This is not in any way to place the referent above the sign itself in importance for textual analyses. Two signs may have the same referent ("mutt" and "dog") but, since the signified marks the distinctive features of the sign, the pejorative connotations of "mutt" are revealed through it and not through the referent that both signs share. In cancelling out this important role of the signified, realist dogma implicitly postulates a common real referent that all readers share, despite individual ideolects. In doing so, one could argue, a realist poetics actually mitigates the possibility of a "vivid" imagining of the text's universe.

II.

When a reader first picks up a novel and begins to read, one could say that at this early stage s/he can *only* read in such a way as to refer words to his/her own linguistic and experiential knowledge (which, since it includes his/her past reading experience as well, is in no way limited to his/her actual practical experience).[16] This is the realm of the Peircean "secondness," of "object," which exists prior to the sign. It is that with which the reader and author must presuppose an acquaintance in order for communication to take place at all. Gradually the words read by the reader take on their own unity of reference and create a self-contained world that is its own validity through its own contextual ideolect. Although this created world is total and complete, novel reference itself is never so. This is the difference between a novel and a film. In other words, the reader busily fills in the gaps in reference, guided by the text's encoded instructions,[17] actualizing a new possible world but doing so, at first, by means of his/her linguistic and empirical knowledge of his/her own world. The metafictions of Jorge Luis Borges, for one, stand as allegories of this, the reading (as well as writing) side of *poiesis*. The fictive referents gradually accumulate during the act of reading, thereby constructing a "heterocosm"—another cosmos, a second ordered referential system. This fictional universe is obviously not an object of perception, but an effect to be experienced by the readers, in the sense that it is something created by them and in them. Yet here *is* a link to real life.

Criticism today accepts that the novel is not a copy of the real world; nor does it stand in opposition to it. It seems to be less generally acknowledged, however, that the novel is, in fact, related to life experience in a very real way *for the reader*: that is, the novel is a continuation of that ordering, decoding, naming, fiction-making *process* that is part of the reader's normal coming-to-terms with experience in the real world. And it is this fact that theories of novelistic reference ultimately have to take into account, given the self-conscious narrative and linguistic thematization of it in metafiction itself.

For instance, in John Barth's novel, *The End of the Road*, the mythic world-creating or story-telling capacity of the mind is thematized overtly as the basis of what in the novel is called "mythotherapy." In life, as the doctor explains to the hero, Jacob Horner, "there are no essentially major or minor characters. To that extent, all fiction and biography, and most historiography, are a lie. Everyone is necessarily the hero of his own life story . . . we're the ones who conceive the story, and give other people the essences of minor characters."[18] For Barth, the narrative "heterocosmic" impulse is related to human choice and existential freedom. "So in a sense," continues the doctor, "fiction isn't a lie at all, but a true representation of the distortion that everyone makes of life."

Jacob, who is a teacher of the English language—the means by which he creates his fictions—is in the grip of a Pirandellian relativity paradox. To turn experience into linguistic speech, he reflects,

> —that is, to classify, to categorize, to conceptualize, to grammarize, to syntactify it—is always a betrayal of experience, a falsification of it; but only so betrayed can it be dealt with at all, and only in so dealing with it did I ever feel a man, alive and kicking. It is therefore that, when I had cause to think about it at all, I responded to this precise falsification, this adroit, careful *myth-making*, with all the upsetting exhilaration of any *artist at his work*. When my mythoplastic razors were sharply honed, it was unparalleled sport to lay about with them, to have at reality. (pp. 112–113; italics mine)

Jacob perceives two important things here: that language, by its creative power, is the key to this myth-making, and that, by its structures, language is the means to the only lucidity one can ever know. *Metafictions such as this which show a character looking at—that is, creating through words—the novelistic world, mime the mind's ordering and naming processes of coding and decoding, ciphering and deciphering.* And the essence of literary language lies not in its conforming to the kind of statement found in factual studies, but in its ability to create something new, a coherent, motivated "heterocosm." Svevo's hero in *La coscienza di Zeno*, thinking that he can be the novelist of his own life, learns that to recapture the past is to structure it, to falsify it; in short, to invent it as if it belonged to someone else. Later, in "Il vecchione," the only part of the past that Zeno actually can recall as real is what he wrote down, which is in part invented due to his linguistic limitations. A native Triestine-speaker, Zeno can only relate in Italian, and in writing, those parts of his world for which he has sufficient vocabulary.

This idea of a linguistic "heterocosm" of fictive referents that the reader and the writer co-create is not merely a concept of just *another*, possible world. The *cosmos* is "the world or universe as an *ordered* and *harmonious* system" (*O.E.D.*). Even in classical mimetic theory, mirrors are seen to create worlds even as they imitate (as Plato explains in the *Republic* X). In most metafiction today, literature remains a self-sufficient aesthetic system of internal relations among parts that aim at an Aristotelian harmony which the reader actualizes. But along with coming to terms with the ordered and self-informing characteristics of the novelistic universe (as created in the act of reading), the reader must also come to terms with that fictiveness which we have been examining. Since fiction is not a way of viewing reality, but a "reality" in its own right, the fictive "heterocosm" will have its own rules or codes of which the reader becomes gradually aware as he proceeds.

As well as being ordered and fictional, the "heterocosm" is, as we have seen, constructed in and through language, and both author and reader share the responsibility for this creation. Literature has a particular context created by relationships between words which are activated by the reader. Furthermore, the actual referents of those words are not real in the context of empirical reality. The result of this dual removal from the real is the liberation of the reader from the world he knows only through the senses. This does not deny a mimetic referentiality in the sense of a semantic, pragmatic, or psychological accumulation of reference, but it does relegate it to second place. The fictiveness of the referents of the novel's signs is responsible for this freeing of language from being just a counter to any reality outside fiction. It would be simplistic to claim, as indeed some have, that detective stories are "unrealistic" because, although full of murders, no one really dies. Surely, this is true of all fiction: no one fictional event is more or less real than any other.

In a very basic sense, all reading, whether of literature, history, or science, is an escape, for it involves a temporary transference of the reader's mind from his empirical surroundings to things imagined rather than perceived. The bridge from the real world to the other one of fiction is often explicitly provided by the narrator. For the reader, the narrator's living in that world is simultaneous with his writing of it: "as long as I live or write (which in my case means the same thing)," comments Tristram Shandy. The narrating "historian" of Gabriel García Márquez's Macondo, in *Cien años de soledad*, presents to the reader real, that is historical, events (the Colombian civil wars) as if lived for the first time in his fictive world where fantastic things occur equally logically. Time and space have no meaning (certainly no reference, in Frege's sense) outside the text itself.

It is thus only by the gradual cumulative constructing of the "heterocosm" through its (acknowledged) fictive referents that readers can be said to share in the creation of a text or a possible world. Though in actual fact the novel has no ultimate responsibility to the real, there are still retired cavalry officers who write to Claude Simon that they lived the events of his *La Route des Flandres*, the novel Ricardou claims is not at all representational. When this question arose at Cerisy in 1971, Ricardou's reply was typically dismissive because to him, and possibly to Simon, such real, personal reader experience is irrelevant: "What Simon gives are the referents of fiction: in no way does this mean that the fiction obtained by the text is the equivalent of the 'documentary' referent."[19]

This consciousness of the possible tension in the reading experience between real and fictive referents is perhaps most clearly seen in the novelist's use of real place names in novelistic settings, as many critics have pointed out. Robbe-Grillet admits that he has used Hong Kong and New York as explicit locations for the action of his fiction, but he perhaps rather naïvely adds: "I knew, though, that it could no longer be a question of representation, and I could name a real city while still producing a perfectly imaginary city by my own text."[20] Lest this appear to be a new and radical stand, it is worth recalling Kafka's vision of Prague. In his Preface to *Roderick Hudson*, Henry James even wrote that he actually felt that the naming of a real place in the novel, instead of being economical and realistic as intended, was limiting and unnecessary.

The autonomy of the referents of literary signs in relation to real referents is, therefore, not a modern radical realization of recent *criticism*. And even modern, self-informing, self-reflexive metafiction merely points self-consciously to what is a reality of the novel genre, a reality that has also been singled out indirectly by linguistic philosophers of this century, who worked to end the confusing of the meaning of a name with the bearer of a name, and to suggest that the final interpretation of art is justified by its internal, not external, relations. All language is experience, and not merely a store of easily extractable meaning. Yet there does seem to be a difference in the reader's imaginative process, an increase in the active element of that experience, if the referents are acknowledged as fictive—by the word "novel" on the book's cover, or even more overtly and textually, through metafictional thematization.

In summary, these fictive referents form an increasingly complete "heterocosm" of fictively referential totalities by means of a process of semantic accumulation. Nothing is in these referents that has not been expressed, explicitly or implicitly, in the text itself (or in the reader's filling in of gaps guided by the text). Therefore both the ontological and epistemological natures[21] of the "heterocosm" (of its characters, events, and so on) are in this sense fundamentally different both from those of the real world and from those of other texts. No matter how "prosaic" the language, no matter how close to banal reality the story, the language of fiction is transformed because it invites the reader, in Blanchot's words, "to make the words themselves render an understanding of what is happening in the world being proposed and whose reality is to be the object of a tale."[22]

It is the reader's genre expectations and his imaginative creating of the fictional universe through the referents of the language, and *not* the subject matter or any supposedly real referents, that determine the validity and even the status of the novel's world. In John Fowles's novel, *The French Lieutenant's Woman*, Sarah's "true story" is revealed to be fictional, and it is through the very realization of both that fictiveness and its validity that Sarah can free Charles at the end of the novel—in a *mise en abyme* of the liberation of the reader by the novelist.

III.

Metafictions such as Fowles's, which acknowledge their fictiveness textually and thematically, do not represent the death of the novel as some critics and reviewers insist. Rather, like fantasy fiction, they become emblematic of what begins to look like a literary reality of the novelistic form. All fiction retains the representational orientation of words, largely because this remains outside its control—that is, in the reader. But fiction also creates a new "heterocosm" through those words because the representation is of fictive referents, as the reader soon realizes. A second system comes into being, one which increasingly predominates in his act of reading. Although we move beyond the purely mimetic in reading, we never manage to eradicate it completely. A house in a novel can exist because it exists in the real world, or rather in our perceptual and linguistic experience of the real world. But this is never the point at which the reader stops. The theories of possible worlds and fictive referents permit a broadening of the concept of reference in reading fictive texts. They do so by allowing room for the positing of distinctions, distinctions that bring to light what is really an overdetermination of novelistic reference.

In fact, at least four separate but complementary levels of reference can be isolated in metafiction. Two of these, the most commonly overlapping, have already been discussed in detail: the inner (intratextual) reference is to the "heterocosm" in all its coherence and fictiveness, and the necessary outer mimetic reference is to the world outside the novel, in the sense of that first and inevitable presupposed knowledge that makes the "heterocosm" possible. It is crucial to keep in mind that we are still dealing on this level with fictive referents and that even if the author of a determinedly naturalistic novel should choose (for reasons of economy) to draw upon his/her reader's knowledge of extraliterary realities, he/she can do so in the sense of his/her text's having an "analagon"[23] to the world outside it. One could argue that such a relationship is, strictly speaking, almost metaphoric rather than referential, especially if by referential we mean, with Frege, having a real referent. The inner reference is also to fictive referents, of course. Here fantasy literature is the paradigm, for one hopes that vampires, unicorns, and hobbits only exist in words. Only language can conceive of the absent, the unreal, the supernatural.[24]

There are, however, at least two other levels of reference that metafiction specifically displays: an autorepresentational (the text as text) and an intertextual reference.[25] Certain current theories argue that intertextuality is a modality of perception in literature in that, through recognition of it, the reader identifies the structures which actually make the text a work of art. In Michael Riffaterre's terminology, it is in the "intertext" that this process operates. The loose and flexible limits of the "intertext" are those of the corpus of texts which a reader can legitimately connect with the text s/he is reading. (The legitimacy is determined by Riffaterre by the restriction that the connections must be made between variants of the same structure.)

Without disputing these complex and convincing theories, we should note the simple fact that metafiction again makes overt the intertextual reference of perhaps all fiction. Sometimes a particular text (or set of texts) is backgrounded (intended intertext) as is the Victorian novel, for example, in Fowles's *The French Lieutenant's Woman*. The modern novel here consists of a conscious superimposition of the new and the old. It incorporates the techniques and structures of fiction as written by George Eliot or Thomas Hardy, but there remains a critical distancing

between the backgrounded and the foregrounded texts that still allows us to call
this device parody, although the judgment is not always at the expense of the so-
called parodied text.[26] Sometimes in metafiction it is not a text but a set of literary
conventions, such as the journal or epistolary novel, that is the object of intertextual
reference. At other times a particular stereotyped narrative structure will be used.
One of the most common of these employed by metafiction is that of the detective
or mystery novel, itself a self-reflexive variation of the puzzle or enigma form.
Highly codified, the detective novel actually possesses *as conventions* overt and
covert modes of self-consciousness: there is often a writer of detective stories embedded within the fiction, just as there is inevitably a discussion about the novel's
events happening as if in fiction, not life. On a more covert level, the detective
plot itself, the following of clues by the detective, is a hermeneutic allegory of the
reader's act.

The ready adaptability of this particular narrative form to metafictional intertextual
reference is probably a result of these latter autorepresentational traits. The fact that
a text can refer to itself as a text, as language, is not particularly new, but perhaps
what is new, as suggested earlier, is the textual level at which it can do so.[27]
Furthermore, what metafiction's autoreferentiality appears to do is *not* what one
might expect it to, that is, to divert readers from making other references and to
limit them to a narcissistic textual formalism. Instead, autoreference and intertextual
reference actually combine to direct readers back to an outer reference; in fact, they
direct the readers outside the text, by reminding them (paradoxically) that, although
what they are reading is only a literary fiction which they themselves are creating
through language, this act itself is really a paradigm or an allegory of the ordering,
naming processes that are part of their daily experience of coming to terms with
reality. Instead of there being a textual dialectic between fiction and reality, as
Robert Alter has suggested,[28] there is a conflating of the two poles by the overdetermined reference demanded by the act of reading metafiction. The two most
self-reflexive modes of reference point directly towards the least so and, from there,
outside the text's boundaries. It is true that the extratextual level reached here is
one of *process*, the process of reading, and not one of an "analagon" with external
reality as a *product* (as fictive referents or represented objects). But the reified
notion of mimesis as product representation is one of those nineteenth-century
novelistic throwbacks (admittedly one aided by Auerbach, Watt, and other important
novel critics) that metafiction challenges.

The overt encoding of the ɗ   der in these texts forces open the Jakobsonian
concept of the self-focussing message in its "poetic" function and demands that
the addressee enter as *part* of that self-focussing process, not as part of an additional
function (conative). Literary discourse then becomes, in Ricoeur's terms, an *event*.[29]
The frequent metafictional use of detective plots and journal and epistolary conventions points to the importance of the event of reading as having a role in literary
creation, a role as significant as that of writing. It is the metafiction reader's perception of these superimposed levels of reference that directs him/her into, through,
and *out of* the text, the text as language. In other words, in metafiction, the only
way to make any mimetic connection to *real* referents, as I have defined them here,

would be on the level of *process*, that is, of the act of reading as an act of ordering and creating. The encoding within the text itself of the decoder and his/her role acts as a set of instructions to the *reader who exists in the real world* and who, though implicated directly by the existence of this narratee or surrogate addressee *within* the text, is actually an existing being, an interpreting, deciphering being, outside the work of art. The reader can read (or actualize or bring to life) the "heterocosm" of fictive referents only through an act that is the *same* as, and not the "analagon" of, the decoding process s/he engages in constantly in coming to terms with experience of all kinds. If we insist on wanting to speak of fiction's real referents, which by Frege's definition must exist in the real world, metafiction teaches us that it is going to have to be on another level: the *process* may indeed turn out to be "referential" in this sense, and in a way that the *products* can not be.

NOTES

1. The postmodernist label has recently been given the sanction of John Barth himself in "The Literature of Replenishment: Postmodernist Fiction," *The Atlantic* (January 1980), pp. 65–71. "Neobaroque" is the term used to describe the particular version of this phenomenon that arises in Latin America out of the Spanish tradition. See Severo Sarduy, "El barroco y el neobarroco" in César Fernandez Moreno, ed., *America Latina en su Literatura* (1972; 2nd ed., Buenos Aires: Siglo XXI, 1974), pp. 167–84.

2. See Thomas E. Lewis's interesting attempt to combine Marxist and semiotic approaches to the referent in his "Notes Toward a Theory of the Referent," *PMLA* 94, 3 (May 1979), 459–75.

3. See, for example, Ian Watt, "The First Paragraph of *The Ambassadors*," *Essays in Criticism* 10 (1960), 250–74; David Lodge, *Language of Fiction* (New York: Columbia University Press, 1966), p. x; Roger Fowler and Peter Mercer, "Criticism and the Language of Literature," *Style* 3 (1969), 45–72.

4. There is also a narrative or diegetic form of this. See Linda Hutcheon, "Modes et formes du narcissisme littéraire," *Poétique* 29 (février 1977), 90–106.

5. In his course on "The Semiotics of Poetry" at the International Summer Institute for Semiotic and Structural Studies, University of Toronto, June 1980.

6. J.R.R. Tolkien, "On Fairy-Stories," *The Tolkien Reader* (New York: Ballantine, 1966), p. 37.

7. "Je songe à tous ces gens qui pensent à propos de tel roman: moi, à la place de tel personnage, j'aurais fait autre chose . . . Eh bien, ces gens font en quelque sorte passer un personnage du domaine du signifié à celui du référent." In *Nouveau Roman: hier, aujourd'hui*, II, ed. J. Ricardou et F. van Rossum-Guyon (Paris: U.G.E. 10/18, 1972), p. 43.

8. For example, in the volume edited by Teun A. van Dijk, *Pragmatics of Language and Literature* (Amsterdam and Oxford: North-Holland Publishing Co., 1976), the following articles are of interest: Teun A. van Dijk, "Pragmatics and Poetics," pp. 23–57; David Harrah, "Formal Message Theory and Non-formal Discourse," especially p. 72; S.-Y. Kuroda, "Reflections on the Foundations of Narrative Theory from a Linguistic Point of View," pp. 107–140; and Siegfried J. Schmidt, "Towards a Pragmatic Interpretation of 'Fictionality,' " pp. 161–78.

9. See Frege's "On Sense and Reference" in *Translations from the Philosophical Writings of Gottlob Frege* (Oxford: Blackwell, 1952), pp. 56–78. For the signified/referent par-

12   On Referring in Literature

allel, see the argument of Oswald Ducrot in O. Ducrot and T. Todorov, *Dictionnaire encyclopédique des sciences du langage* (Paris: Seuil, 1972), pp. 319–20; translation, *Encyclopedic Dictionary of the Sciences of Language* (Baltimore: Johns Hopkins University Press, 1979), pp. 249–50.

10. Georges Lavis, "Le Texte littéraire, le référent, le réel, le vrai," *Cahiers d'analyse textuelle*, No. 13 (1971), 7–22; his attack is upon Arrivé's article in *Langue Française*, No. 3 (septembre 1969).

11. Frege does not make this crucial *langue/parole* distinction.

12. "Dans le roman, l'acte de lire n'est pas changé, mais l'attitude de celui qui lit le rend différent." In "Le Langage de la fiction," in *La Part du feu* (Paris: Gallimard, 1949), p. 82.

13. See Roland Barthes, "L'Effet de réel," *Communications*, No. 11 (1968), 88: "The *having-been-there* of things is a sufficient principle of words" ("*l'avoir-été-là* des choses est un principe suffisant de la parole").

14. "Phenomenology of Reading," *New Literary History* I (Autumn 1969), 55. Poulet, of course, attributes this change to different causes entirely.

15. Paul Ricoeur calls these referents "non-ostensive" ones, but retains a similar definition. See his "The Model of the Text: Meaningful Action Considered as a Text," in *Social Research* 38 (1971), 536. Ricoeur links the concept further to Heidegger and Wilhelm von Humboldt.

16. See Maurice-Jean Lefèbve, *Structure du discours et du récit* (Neuchâtel: La Baconnière, 1971), p. 108, on this point, although his final signified/referent distinction is not in accord with the one presented in this paper.

17. See Wolfgang Iser's *The Act of Reading* (Baltimore: Johns Hopkins University Press, 1978), pp. 135–59.

18. (1958; Garden City, N.Y.: Doubleday, 1967), p. 83. All further references will be to this edition and page numbers will appear in parentheses in the text.

19. "Ce qui est donné par Simon, ce sont les référents de la fiction: cela ne veut nullement dire que la fiction obtenue par le texte est l'équivalent du référent donné à titre documentaire." In *Nouveau Roman: hier, aujourd'hui*, I, p. 30. Note the contradiction to the remark quoted above to the effect that this involved instead a signified/referent confusion. Here he seems to have slipped outside the rigid linguistic structure.

20. "Je savais désormais qu'il ne pouvait plus être question de représentation, et je pouvais nommer une ville réelle tout en produisant par mon propre texte une ville parfaitement imaginaire." *Nouveau Roman: hier, aujourd'hui*, II, p. 166.

21. See Lubomír Doležel, *Narrative Modes in Czech Literature* (Toronto: University of Toronto Press, 1973), pp. 5–6.

22. "Réaliser sur les mots eux-mêmes la compréhension de ce qui se passe dans le monde qu'on lui propose et dont toute la réalité est d'être l'objet d'un récit." In "*Le langage de la fiction*," p. 84.

23. See Claude Duchet, "Une écriture de la socialité," *Poétique* 16 (1973), 450. See also, however, Paul Ricoeur's hermeneutic perspective on this level of reference in "Writing as a Problem for Literary Criticism and Philosophical Hermeneutics," in *Philosophical Exchange* 2 (1977), 10: ". . . to understand a text is to interpolate among the predicates of our situation all the significations which make a *Welt* out of our *Umwelt*. It is this enlarging of our horizon of existence which permits us to speak of the references opened up by the referential claims of most texts."

24. See Tzvetan Todorov, *Introduction à la littérature fantastique* (Paris: Seuil, 1970), p. 87. Trans. R. Howard: *The Fantastic; a Structural Approach to a Literary Genre* (Cleveland: Press of Case Western Reserve University, 1973), p.82.

25. See the early theory of Julia Kristeva in *Semeiotiké: recherches pour une sémanalyse* (Paris: Seuil, 1969), p. 255, and also more importantly, Michael Riffaterre, "The Semiotics of Poetry" course at the I.S.I.S.S.S.,1980.

26. See Linda Hutcheon, "Parody Without Ridicule: Observations on Modern Literary

Parody," *Canadian Review of Comparative Literature* 5, 2 (Spring 1978), 201–211, and also "Ironie et parodie: structure et stratégie," *Poétique* 36 (novembre 1978), 367–77.

27. This is the implication of Ricardou's interdimensional (i.e., fiction/narration) distinction between "autoreprésentation *expressive*" (pejorative) and "autoreprésentation productive" (modern and acceptable) in "La Population des miroirs," *Poétique* 22 (1975), 212.

28. *Partial Magic: The Novel as a Self-conscious Genre* (Berkeley: University of California Press, 1975).

29. "Biblical Hermeneutics," *Semeia* 4 (1975), 29–148; and "Structure, mot, événement" in *Le Conflit des interprétations* (Paris: Seuil, 1969) or the English translation "Structure, Word, Event" in *The Conflict of Interpretations*, ed. Don Ihde (Evanston: Northwestern University Press, 1974).

II.

THE DOUBLE BIND
SELF-REFERRING POETRY

Anna Whiteside

The purported prototype of self-referring expressions is Epimenides' Cretan paradox: "All Cretans are liars," said the Cretan. Since then, many others have also tried their hand. Quine's English rendition of Gödel's[1] mathematical homage to Epimenides is probably one of the best known: " 'Yields falsehood when appended to its quotation' yields falsehood when appended to its quotation." Other examples abound: "The sentence on the other side is true"; the other side of the page says "the sentence on the other side is false." Recently a similar round paradox appeared[2] (see fig. 1). Then there is "This sentence no verb," referring to that very lack by omission, and David Moser's story:

> *This Is the Title of This Story, Which Is Also*
> *Found Several Times in the Story Itself.*
> This is the first sentence of this story. . . . This sentence regretfully states that up to this point the self-referential mode of narrative has had a paralyzing effect on the actual progress of the story itself, that is, these sentences have been so concerned with analyzing themselves and their role in the story that they have failed by and large to perform their function as communicators of events and ideas that one hopes coalesce into a plot, character development, etc., in short, the very *raisons d'être* of any respectable, hardworking sentence in the midst of a piece of compelling prose fiction.[3]

Logicians are not alone in their fascination with self-reference. In the arts the very characteristics of the aesthetic function of an art form are this same ambiguity and self-reflexiveness of the message.[4] A host of examples springs to mind: Bach's and Hindemith's fugal and mirror writing,[5] Magritte's and Escher's art, literature's delight in *mise en abyme* and metacommentary, figures of speech such as palindromes,[6] chiasmas, paragrams, or hypograms,[7] and, most obviously perhaps, concrete poetry and its related forms. Although it is the latter which particularly interests us here, all poetry has a self-referential tendency. For poetic discourse (including the subversive prose-poem) goes beyond diegetic representation, beyond mimesis

Figure 1

too, and in fact, as Michael Riffaterre argues in his *Semiotics of Poetry*, represents nothing but itself.

The types of poetry we will be considering fall into three categories. The first is the ideogramme, the second concrete poetry, the third what I will call, for want of a better term, the sound icon. There also exist various permutations which take up and interweave the perennial loose ends of all three.

The ideogramme, stemming from the Hellenistic *technopagnia*, appears initially to refer extratextually. Apollinaire's "Il pleut" ("It's Raining," figs. 2a, 2b), with rain dripping down the page, or his "La Colombe poignardée et le jet d'eau" ("The Stabbed Dove and the Fountain," figs. 3a, 3b),[8] who flutters (or rather does not) above the fountain's spray of words, are typographical mimetic representations of the rain, in the first case, and a bird and fountain in the second. In "Il pleut" the streaming rain is metaphorically converted into bonds or chains falling away, so that although the title provides context to endow the vertical signifers with a signified, they refer not so much to rain as to themselves as a semiosical chain of semantic polyvalence. The dove and the fountain are referentially more equivocal because the proper names inscribed in the wings of the dove refer (proper names being the truest of referring expressions) to women Apollinaire knew. The fountain's stream of names of his male friends likewise corroborates an impression of extratextual reference. But here again reference is primarily intratextual, as is obvious from the typically Apollinairian female (dove) and male (fountain) symbols[9] and their visually suggested relationship to one another. It becomes clear that, though the names indeed refer to existents, their function as mentions is not so much that of a definite referring expression to this woman or that man ("'individuals,'" according to Strawson) as to the two classes "women and men Apollinaire has known," and thus to representative women and men. The two groups refer, as do their symbols here, to their relationship to each other, and the ambiguous lips with the round circle in the middle reiterates the essentially reciprocal nature of the two signs foregrounded by the title and commented on by the labial epigraph. Here, then, the icons of the dove and the fountain cannot seriously be deemed to refer to any particular dove or fountain. If reference there is, it seems rather to collide with

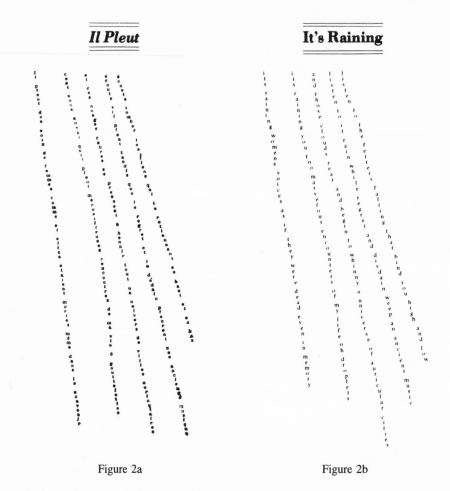

Figure 2a   Figure 2b

the poetic (or aesthetic) function as a visible demonstration of implied ambiguity and intratextual reference.

Concrete poetry is far less preoccupied with any pretence of mimetic extratextual reference for the simple reason that it is much more obviously self-referential. Called variously "*lettrisme*," "typewriter poems," "*spatialisme*," "physical poetry," or "thing-poetry," it fulfills what Ezra Pound advocated when he called for a visual poetry akin to ideographic writing in which we seem "to be watching *things* work out their fate."[10] Hiro Kamimura's "Water and Ice" (fig. 4)[11] shows both Pound's "haecceity"[12] and visible dynamics admirably. Here the "things" are the very signs themselves, and their opposition (forty-eight "ices" to one "water" completing the seven-line diamond square) is visually stated in terms analogous to their semantic relation to one another. Just as ice is water in an altered state, and *vice versa*, so the square's presentation is altered to a diamond and this diamond ensconced in the outer framing square. The single water character is surrounded by

La Colombe Poignardée et le Jet d'Eau

The Bleeding-Heart Dove and the Fountain

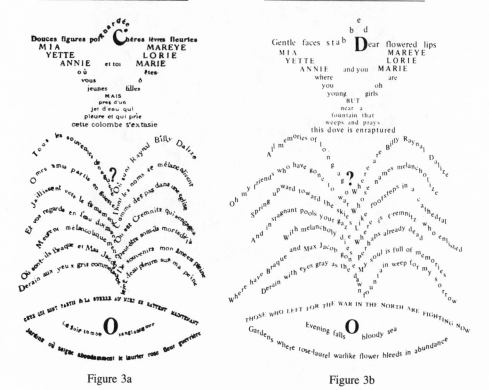

Figure 3a   Figure 3b

"ice" and, beyond, by what might be construed as the water's missing dot multiplied in the four corners of the non-ice non-water field, which thus refers to the marker of the difference between the conflicting signs and concepts, whilst reminding us that, apart from this dot, they are the same. Sameness and difference are stated in white on a dark field—two more concepts represented physically as mutually defining and so mimetically referring to the complementary contradiction of the difference.

In a reversal of concrete poetry's usual letter- or type-centered compositions, Henri Chopin's "Il manque toujours l'y" ("The y is always missing," fig. 5)[13] appears to "refer" to absence. It does this in several ways. The title "refers" to what is not there (and indeed it is not, since the row of y's is missing); but immediately after the two incomplete alphabets and the statement that the y is always missing, there follows an isolated row of them. So, though it is missing in the alphabetical system represented here in assorted typefaces, it is present outside the system. It is there (y means "there" in French) in more senses than one. It is visible not as a printed letter, but as a space all through the alphabet—once back to front—a

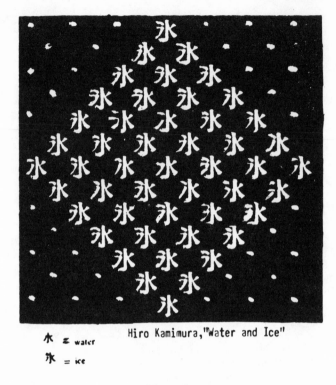

木 = water

冰 = ice

Hiro Kamimura,"Water and Ice"

Figure 4

mirror image of the reader's enlarged why (and "y," since it is conspicuously *not* "there") and, once more, in fragmented form. These fragments could be construed as *y*'s absence being about *y* since the upper left fragment can be seen as an inverted *i* with a long dot, which, in turn, could be a fragment of a distorted capital iota (⌐: doubly distorted because not only is it fragmented, but the angles of this z-like letter should be oblique and not acute). In this case the pivotal dot-cum-iota fragment refers to and relates the two forms of iota, the "*i grec*" (French for *y*), neither standing up straight, and both upside down in relation to each other—perhaps corresponding to the righthand *y*'s inversion.

   Indeed switching around, ambiguity, and being left out are the historical fate of this letter. Used in Latin to transcribe the Greek *upsilon*, it was an abused *iota*, as the lexicalized interpretation of *S* and *U* (Chopin's only upper case letters in this otherwise lower case alphabet) corroborate, by asking "est-ce *U*" (pronounced as the letters *s u* are in French)—is it *U*? The ambiguous answer to the doubts raised by this switching around: "Quelle importance" ("what does it matter" or "what importance," since there is no question mark), merely echoes the ambiguity of this letter in French: both yod and *i*, it is half vowel, half consonant; it is both letter and word. As a word (which appeared in French in 842) or, more precisely, as a pronoun, it can refer to many words left out or places not seen; as a letter, it is all

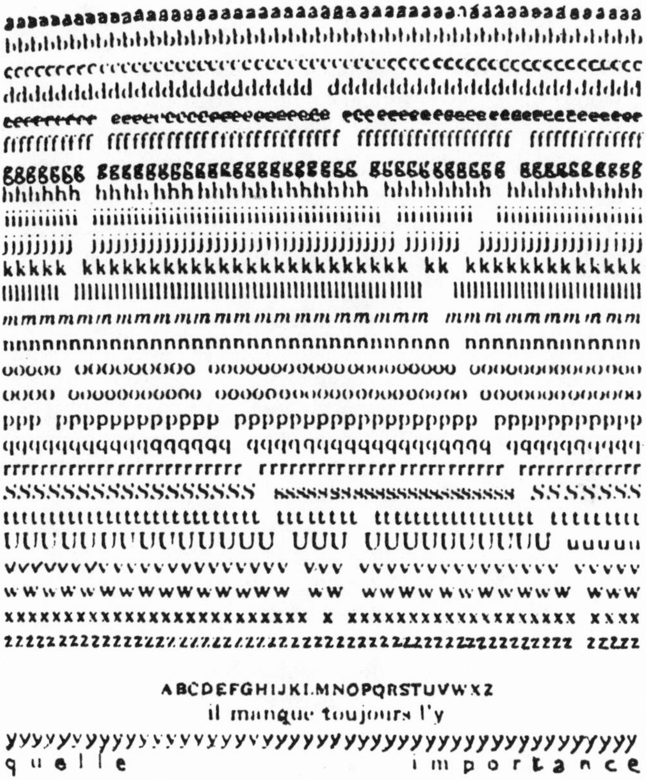

Figure 5

but left out of the French alphabet since with the exception of "y," all lexical items beginning in *y* are not French.[14]

So, what at first seemed to be a concrete poem not so much about letters as the spaces between them, is, in fact, about one particular letter referring to others, the better to refer to itself and its own ambivalence. Again, as in "Water and Ice," referring expressions (the signs singled out and their associated parts) and their referents a) are mutually referring, and thus entirely intratextual, b) create the dynamics of reference from opposition and ambiguity contained within themselves.

This creating or recreating of the pure referent, divesting it of all its fixed connotations, this attempt to "de-cliché" and thus resuscitate it, is and ever has been the aim of literature and, *a fortiori*, of poetry, which, unlike fiction and drama, has little or no representational pretensions, or preoccupation with *"l'effet de réel."* Since clichés arise from ossifying repetition in stereotyped contexts, let us see how concrete poetry, though restricted by its epigrammatic economy, liberates these frozen fossils. In a sense "Water and Ice" does this by setting one in opposition to the other. A similar example is Michael Gibbs's thirty-three identical reiterations of the three-in-one-word line ("treestreetree") where the word "tree," or its plural, is repeated in a long column down the page (fig. 6).[15] This monotony of tripled repetitions is suddenly broken at the bottom by "AVENUE"—different in meaning, appearance, and typography. The difference refers contrastively to the monotony of the rest, whose sameness is further emphasized both by the coalescing of the usually discrete lexeme "tree" into "treestreetree" and by the numerically suggested phonetic resemblance between threes lazily pronounced "trees" ("treetree" or 3, 3, that is, 33). Thus "treestreetree" could be vague enough to have *no* precise meaning since it could be construed as an ambiguous acoustic image of "trees" or of numbers. With the surprise contrast of "AVENUE" sameness evanesces, and

treestreetree
treestreetree
treestreetree
treestreetree
treestreetree
treestreetree
treestreetree
treestreetree
treestreetree
treestreetree
treestreetree
treestreetree
treestreetree
treestreetree
treestreetree
treestreetree
treestreetree
treestreetree
treestreetree
treestreetree
treestreetree
treestreetree
treestreetree
treestreetree
treestreetree
treestreetree
treestreetree
treestreetree
treestreetree
treestreetree
treestreetree
treestreetree
treestreetree

AVENUE

Figure 6

meaning is reborn as a "street," lined with trees on both sides, springs to life, reminding us that this is no longer a mere street, but a distinctive type whose arboreal difference is marked by its very name "avenue." Paradoxically it is still a type of street, but it now seems quite different as the eye oscillates between the two readings of the lines: unmarked clichés juxtaposed with marked non-clichés differentiated and rejuvenated. Thus "AVENUE" triggers a vertical reading (aligned "street" betwixt two rows of trees) which is projected on and transforms the hitherto undifferentiated horizontal one, as first the micro-referring expressions (tree, street, tree), then the macro-referring expression (the overall image) refer to their own representation of difference.

In poetry which uses sound icons, clichés are also unmarked and rejuvenated. Unfortunately the best examples I have encountered are virtually untranslatable. However, since the phenomenon shows language referring to empty language, that is, a mere sound signifying nothing—or anything, practically—a minimal commentary should suffice. Robert Desnos's "Rrose sélavy, etc." (figs. 7a, 7b)[16] refers to Ronsard's oft-quoted seductive *Carpe diem* ploy used in his poems to the various ladies whose charms he sought to exploit. The usual formulation involved the ephemeral rose to be plucked quickly ere tomorrow it wither and fade. As everyone knows, this rose is life. Now Desnos's title is a lexically distorted and contracted "clichéified" version of "rose c'est la vie" ("rose, that's life"). By its very (meaningless) form it refers to itself as an empty sign, referring in turn to the cliché as an equally empty sign. However, the rest of the poem refers . . . to the title—the title which, as an empty cliché, can be used to mean anything that corresponds to the same sounds. So that each line refers phonetically both to the title and to each and every other line, with a syncopated reiteration at the end:

> Rrose est-ce aile, est-ce elle?
> Est celle
> AVIS

Like a needle stuck on a record, it reminds us that this could go on indefinitely—as its co-referent *etc.* in the title has already indicated. The variation—the added *e* or "et" ("and") in lines 5 and 9–12, which splits the cliché into two, each half joined by an "and" or its approximate phonetic equivalent, merely reinforces the cliché's emptiness—it seems each half of the cliché can be used as two equally empty wholes. But the hole is not so wholly empty as at first appears, for in fact these self-referring expressions show the cliché for what it is and at the same time rekindle its erotic meaning in a new anti-context within, as it were, the old shell: a new context where the thing (the rose and the cliché symbol) is converted into a proper name, one which refers indefinitely, that is, atypically, not so much, one feels, to a particular Rose[17] as to a class—to any Rose, to Rose being Rose being Rose.

Desnos's *Langage Cuit* (literally "cooked," that is, dead language) abounds in reference to clichés of all sorts and in particular to ordinary discourse's idiomatic

Rrose Selavy, etc.

Rose aisselle a vit.
Rr'ose, essaie là, vit.
Rôts et sel à vie.
Rose, S, L, have I.
Rosée, c'est la vie.
Rrose scella vît.
Rrose sella vît.
Rrose sait la vie.
Rose, est-ce, hélas, vie?
Rrose aise héla vît.
Rrose est-ce aile, est-ce elle?
        Est celle
                AVIS

Figure 7a

[Rrose Zatslyffe, etc.

Rose armpit has prick.
Rr'dare, try there, it lives.
Roast and salt for life.
Rose it is, she, have I.
Rosy, dew, that's life.
Rrose clasped tightly to have seen.
Rrose astraddle to have lived.
Rrose now knows life.
Rose, is that, alas, life?
Rrose happy, hailed it, the better to live.
Rrose is it a wing, is it?
        It is
                WARNING]

                                (Approximate literal translation)

Figure 7b

expressions. On the one hand words are reduced to mere empty sounds and referred
to as such by their de-lexicalisation; words become mere letters which, when spoken,
are acoustic icons of the words: mutually referring symbols *qua* symbols.

Aime haine	[Love hate
Et n'aime	And loves not
haine aime	hate loves
aimai ne	I loved not]
M N	
N M	
N M	
M N[18]	

A more colourful example is his "Langage Cuit I." Ruth Amossy[19] has called this non-referring discourse, and it is true that, like most surrealist and nonsense writings, it very obviously makes no attempt to refer extratextually, nor even to represent any recognisable situation. But in fact it does refer. By blocking our usual representational interpretation strategies, discourse becomes self-referring and immediately opens up a new reading strategy: one of constant cross-reference to a cliché-ridden palimpsest.

Langage Cuit

I

Ce vieillard encore violet ou orangé ou rose
porte un pantalon en trompe d'éléphant.

Mon amour jette-moi ce regard chaud
où se lisent de blancs desseins!

Portrait au rallongé de nos âmes
parlerons-nous à coeur fermé
et ce coeur sur le pied?
Ou jouerons-nous toute la nuit à la main froide?

[*Cooked Language* I

This old man still purple or amber or pink
is wearing elephant-trunk-trick (lit. in the shape of an
                                    elephant's trunk) pants.

My love throw me over that hot look
in which one reads white scheming!

Toe-nail (lit. "long") sketch of our souls
Shall we talk closed-heartedly
and wear this heart on our knees (lit. "foot")?
Or shall we play all night long at hands off
                    (lit. "cold hands"—a play on the game hot cockles)?][20]

Youth is normally suggested by "green" but the substitution of *violet* points to the strangeness of the literal image of green men, a strangeness enhanced by the alternative colours. Flared trouser legs are cut "en patte d'éléphant" ("like an elephant's leg") but here the trunk ousts the leg, making us laugh at an expression whose elephantine arbitrariness we accepted unthinkingly till now. In the fourth line the cliché "black" or "dark" scheming is evoked by its harmless white opposite—harmless indeed since read in a lover's eyes. This bifocal reading next opposes the "long sketch" to the standard abridged one ("portrait au rallongé," here rendered as a toe-nail sketch to evoke the usual thumbnail one). The closed heart (l. 6) should be open, for in French one speaks "with an open heart" and one wears one's heart on one's hand ("avoir le coeur sur la main") instead of the English sleeve, whereas here it's on the foot; in French lovers traditionally play

hot cockles all night ("jouer à la main chaude") with hot hands and not with
Desnos's cold ones. So here language, cooked and otherwise, refers to language,
and its bizarre referring expressions which were almost empty of meaning refer to
their bizarrerie in a contrapuntal way as reference is established between the cliché
distorted and the distorting cliché, as well as to language as a string of clichés;
"cooked" language indeed—no longer the instrument of communication, but the
overdone product of impoverished phatic intercourse.

The creation and destruction of meaning is obviously not just a culinary matter;
it depends on context as does the referential function. In Michel Leiris's *Glossaire
(Glossary)*, words, apparently without context, are referred to as words—an as-
sembling of letters—by a "definition" which reinforces this quality:

<blockquote>

h-o-m-m-e: à chaud aime et meut[21]

[m-a-n: in heat loves and moves]

</blockquote>

Unfortunately the translation is incapable of rendering the phonetic effect of the
definition's exact echo of the letter sounds in this example of what Genette calls
"lexicalized spelling." In this case the lexeme's insertion in a glossary suggests
semantic context, whilst the way the lexical items are listed (each letter separated
from the next) suggests the more mechanical context of their graphic and phonetic
codes of representation—the letters and sounds that compose them. So that this
Glossary's entries refer to the role of context in deciding what the referent is: a
seme, a series of letters, or a series of sounds. Once again, an essentially bifocal
perception is in order (since the mediating graphic elements are subsequently subordinated to their phonetic equivalents): the referent is not one or the other, but
both. Reference obtains on the one hand between the two halves of each expression:
1) *homme* + definition, and 2) the sounds of the letters h-o-m-m-e and their lex-
icalization. On the other hand, co-reference obtains between both versions, one
jousting with and at the same time enhancing the other, as language's "double
articulation"[22] is brought to the fore. Coincidentally, reference is circular, since
each half of both versions may be seen as glossematic referring expression *and*
referent.

This use of different contexts to create contrapuntal polyvalence is best seen if
we return to concrete poetry. Ian Hamilton Finlay's sails and waves (fig. 8)[23] show
at a glance the effect of contextual anchors (verbal here) and their role in perception.[24] At the same time *Sails/Waves* suggests graphically a continuum of undifferentiated, that is, non-discrete signs which only cultural conditioning allows us
to "read" discretely.[25] Here then is written language referring to itself as a signifying system, with its own rules for encoding and decoding within a cultural
context, and another quasi-representational language (the curves) referring to its
own polysemic possibilities.

Finlay elaborates this bilingually in *Vague* (fig. 9)[26] as two codes of graphic
symbols interplay—alphabetical and proof-correcting symbols—whilst at the same
time interchanging French ("*vague*"; "wave") and English ("vague") codes and
cultural contexts,[27] so that wave and vague become confused—a fact attested to

Figure 8

Figure 9

by the wavy misspellings. This polysemy is enhanced by the physical context of the concrete wall bearing the inscription set against the curving cobblestone pattern beneath it, and also by the title of Finlay's subsequent postcard photograph of the inscription: ''The Battle of the Atlantic.'' This title foregrounds the less evident French code (given that the site, Livingston New Town, is not by the sea)—though the ∿, enhanced by the generous curve of the *g*, is in itself a sufficiently obvious representation of waves and counter-waves. Double meanings here serve to enhance

Figure 10

a duplicitous concrete referent which is vague both in its form (the wavy line gropes its way back through the misspellings) and in our perception of it (which oscillates between contexts and codes), so that both come to refer to one another and these distinctive self-referents seem, paradoxically, to merge.

Frames and titles constitute another sort of context, as René Magritte eloquently shows in his "Ceci n'est pas une pipe" (fig. 10).[28] Here the fact that the words are within an ornate painted frame, and so part of the picture rather than outside it, ironically refers to the painting as painting—to this pipe's representational but *non-referential* status and, perhaps equally ironically, to perceptual and interpretive conventions: particularly that of equating the signifier (the painting here) with its referent (an actual pipe, an existent).

Paul de Vree's "Eros" (fig. 11)[29] provides an excellent example of similar play on frame and title. For the title is very literally the frame of reference, but this frame is divided into its two parts *er-* and *-os*, and the reader must couple *er-* printed outside all four sides of the text and *-os* printed in the centre along four axes so that each is opposite and linked with one *er-*. Each signifier or half-signifier points to its other half, as mythological (intratextual) reference is completed by the reader. At the same time the reader finds himself in a central labyrinth, constituted by the four geometrically shaped *o*'s and *s*'s of *-os*, which provides the mythological context needed to identify recognisable (though sometimes distorted) referring expressions: five proper names—Er*os*, Daidal*os*, Knoss*os*, Icar*os*, Min*os*, and, given the mythological context these establish, one definite description—taur*os*, the Minotaur. Thus the final *-os* completes recognition of the referring expressions and, by relating them, reference—both intratextual and intertextual. But, more important,

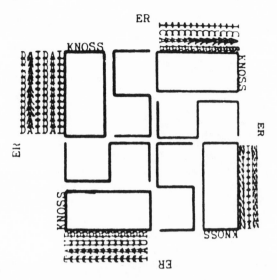

Figure 11

this -*os* relates these five referring expressions to and in Eros, lying as they do between its two parts, and to the a-mazing complexities we associate with these characters and their errings in these places (Minos's mother Europa and his wife Pasiphae both having been seduced by a bull, for example). The coupling of Eros from within and without—for the frame is both on the outside and on the inside— activates what might be considered a second frame of reference: a gnostic one derived from the coupling of Knoss-os (also spelt Gnossus, Cnossus, and Knosos), and so to the process of gaining knowledge: knowledge in its primal, Biblical sense, knowledge as a holistic linking of parts. What is particularly interesting in de Vree's dynamic linkings is that he shows how literary titles and proper names can sometimes share a similarly ambiguous role, both being simultaneously referring expressions *and* referents in a dynamic dipole which ultimately creates the text—for the title is indeed an integral part of the text.

Emmett Williams's "Thomas Stearns Eliot" (fig. 12)[30] plays entirely on a single proper name which is title, text, and context. It too is segmented, but here segmentation isolates not syllables but letters, each letter of the name-title constituting an immutable grid as the exact position of each letter of the extratextual referring expression's syntagm is reproduced in its vertical paradigmatic development. Thus, by the very act of reading, we activate the poetic function (defined by Jakobson as the projection of the paradigmatic axis on the syntagmatic axis[31]) as we read first the syntagm, then the paradigm, and, in the process, refer back to the syntagm of the name-title. Echoing this self-referential movement (name referring to name *qua* name) the text refers semantically not so much to the person as to the literary *persona* adduced from his texts' effect and religious connotations. But though one moves from an initial suggestion of extratextual proper-name reference through

t h o m a s   s t e a r n s   e l i o t

Figure 12

intertextual reference, here again the dominant referential level is intratextual. Despite an apparently static form, the act of reading paradoxically shows reference to be dynamic by activating the recreation of a poetic function, whose two axes our reading brings together—a process that the change in direction and axis of "alas" (written left to right, right to left and diagonally rather than horizontally) seems to emphasize just before the eye returns to the title.

That the poetic and referential functions merge in the examples shown—and most obviously in this last one—is hardly surprising, given the self-referring overstatement of this type of text. Their merging echoes that of the signifier and referent (be they graphic, linguistic, or acoustic) in these examples of indisputably triadic signs. In fact, contrary to Ogden and Richards's representation, the link between signifier and referent is stronger than those between signified and signifier or signifed and referent. Beyond these two aspects of concrete, ideogrammatic, and iconic sound poetry's self-reference lies a third: reference itself. For in fact these self-referring texts refer also, and, I suggest, above all, to reference as an act, an act of linking—refer, that is, to the dynamics of reference itself in which the act of reading functions as shifter—and thus brings out the parallels between graphic creation and interpretive (re)creation.

Emmett Williams's chiasma-like reversal in "sound sense"[32] emphasizes this co-reference (and cross-reference):

```
SENSE SOUND
SONSE SEUND
SOUSE SENND
SOUNE SENSD
SOUND SENSE
```

Here he plays on the principle of Lewis Carroll's "doublets" in which one word is transformed into another by letter substitution, so turning "head" into "tail":

```
HEAD
heal
teal
tell
tall
TAIL
```

or, as when he introduces Walrus to Carpenter, by syllable substitution:

```
WALRUS
peruse
harper
CARPENTER[33]
```

In the process of William's reversal, sound sense is itself transformed into a more literal sound sense as we hear the different sounds and see different senses or "non-senses."

One of the most economic (self-referring) expressions of the dynamics of the process of reference in process is Pierre Garnier's five-letter poem:[34]

o

m t   m t

In this ball-game one "word" or "*mot*" creates another as the *o* is tossed backwards and forwards—coincidentally referring to the process of writing (and reading) as words generate more words, one word leading to another and back again as the text's co-referring expressions link up anaphorically and cataphorically. This movement is graphically expressed by the *o*'s position: not central but either nearing or leaving the empty "*m-t*"—moving between the two, linking these co-referring and self-referring images, and caught in the very act of reference to itself as an act.

In fact, if we reconsider any of the examples given, we realize that beyond their obvious self-referring anamorphosis (a referring expression as pure form referring to form)[35] lies self-reference, shown for what it is: an act in process, a dynamic linking. "Il pleut" shows the act of raining, referring to the act of literary semiosis, whilst the present action ("it *is* raining") refers to becoming as it suffers a rain-change into its own metaphoric metamorphoses (voices communicating, chain

fetters, links). "Water and Ice" refers to the act of becoming and the tenuous-
ness of ice versus water—to the imminent and immanent becoming, the transformation of either state into the other. "Il manque toujours l'y"—in appearance as
static as "Thomas Stearns Eliot"—is also referring to its act of referring, in a three-
dimensional way, as we look everywhere and then find it magnified in the spaces,
its reversed and inverted images graphically recounting the dynamics of its diachronic metamorphoses. For here y refers to itself in the act of referring to its other
symbols as it leads the eye through its transformations: from y to i to $\backsim$ to U.

The dynamics of *self*-reference as an act is also reinforced, as in y, by reading
strategies (quite physically) in, say, *Vague*, where the letters led us from right to
left and the $\sim$ from left to right, both colliding, or rather eliding, as they move
towards one another. Reference moves in a mysterious way—forwards and backwards—as we know from reading any text. "Eros" forces us to read around the
square by turning it (or ourselves), and it takes us with it through its own labyrinthian
co-referential linking.

Even the sound icons force us to read in two different ways (in the case of
lexicalized spellings and "Langage Cuit"), and in many ways in "Rrose Sélavy."
In the latter many anamorphoses force us to undo the new-found segmenting and
hear it as the original form, this form itself hiding another (the Ronsardian prototype). From there we juggle contrapuntally, unleashing a grand stretto, as we play
them all together.

So a double bind does indeed exist. On the one hand, these three types of poetry
exaggerate literary discourse's tendency to refer to itself within itself; on the other,
literary discourse is at the same time referring to itself referring to itself. The paradox
(returning to Epimenides) is that whilst these examples refer to their process of
becoming, they are themselves in the process of becoming, for we the readers are
(re)creating them.

NOTES

1. The English paraphrase of which has been translated thus: "All consistent axiomatic
formulations of number theory include undecidable propositions." Douglas R. Hofstadter,
Gödel, Escher, Bach: an Eternal Golden Braid (Hassocks, Sussex: Harvester Press, 1979),
p. 17.
2. See the letter from L. N. Godbole in "Letters," *The Economist*, vol. 282, no. 7224
(Feb. 13, 1982), p. 6.
3. In Douglas R. Hofstadter, "Metamagical Themas," *Scientific American*, Jan. 1982,
12–16. This article reproduces two other interesting examples of self-reference. The first,
by Beverly Rowe, describes an *Errata* page in a hypothetical book, which reads thus:

(vi)
Errata
Page (vi): For "Errata" read "Erratum."

The second, which appears in D. R. Hofstadter's "Metamagical Themas," *Scientific American*, Jan. 1981, 34–41, is slightly more complex: "This sentence has three errors."

4. Cf. Umberto Eco's statement: "Les caractéristiques de l'image esthétique d'une langue sont l'ambiguité et l'autoréflexivité des messages." In "Langage artistique, segmentation du contenu et référent," *Degrés* 3 (juillet 1973).

5. Perhaps the most striking example is in Hindemith's *Ludus Tonalis*. Here the "Praeludium" and the "Postludium" are mirror images of each other, not only on a horizontal axis—the "Postludium" being a complete reversal of the "Praeludium"—but also vertically, so that the "Postludium" is the "Praeludium" both back to front and upside down.

6. Sometimes called Sotadics after Sotades. One of the most familiar examples in Greek is "nipon anomemata me monan opsn" (wash my transgressions, not only my face), often found inscribed in monastery or church fonts. There is another variety of palindrome in which each component word is also a palindrome: "Odo tenet mulum, madidam mappam tenet Anna, Anna tenet mappam madidam, mulum tenet Odo."

7. The distinction being that the paragram's matrix is lexical or graphematic, and derived from fragments of the key words scattered along the sentence, each embedded in the body of a word. The hypogram, as Riffaterre explains, "appears quite visibly in the shape of words embedded in sentences whose organisation reflects the presuppositions of the matrix's nuclear word." *Semiotics of Poetry* (Bloomington and London: Indiana University Press, 1978), p. 168. The example quoted is: Tibi vero gratias agam quo *clamore*? Amore more ore re (My emphasis).

8. *Calligrammes* in *Oeuvres poétiques* (Paris: Gallimard, 1965), pp. 203 and 213, respectively. Trans. Anne Hyde Greet: *Calligrammes* (Los Angeles and London: University of California Press, Berkeley, 1980), p. 123.

9. See particularly the *Poèmes à Lou* which may be seen as a key to the erotic nature of many of Guillaume Apollinaire's poems—particularly *Calligrammes*. See also my article "Poèmes de guerre et d'amour . . . ou la double chevauchée d'Apollinaire." *French Review*, vol. 54, no. 6 (May 1982), 147–172.

10. Ernest Fenollosa, *The Chinese Written Character as a Medium for Poetry*, ed. Ezra Pound (San Francisco: City Lights Books, 1936), p. 9.

11. Reprinted from *Speaking Pictures*, ed. Milton Klonsky (New York: Harmony Books 1975), p. 279.

12. This is C. S. Peirce's term which he uses (when explaining his three categories) to describe the second, the idea of "brute and obstinate existence . . . something *there*, a datum, a singular *this*." See David Savan, *An Introduction to C. S. Peirce's Semiotics*, Part I (Toronto: Toronto Semiotic Circle, 1976), p. 7. His "object" (our referent) is related to this class further on in the elaboration of his evolving triadic system.

13. Reprinted from *An Anthology of Concrete Poetry*, ed. Emmett Williams (West Glover, Vermont: Something Else Press, 1967), no pagination.

14. "Yeuse" (ilex) is from the old Provençal.

15. *Connotations* (Cardiff: Second Aeon Publications, 1973). No pagination.

16. *L'Aumonyme* in *Corps et biens* (Paris: Gallimard, 1953), p. 67.

17. Later in *Rrose Sélavy* (also in *Corps et biens*, a collection of epigrammatic phonetic echoes), Rrose Sélavy is a character who, despite the author's note (p. 31) is an Everyman's Everywoman cast again in a context of lexicalised sounds and whose definite reference is subordinated to semantico-phonetic games.

18. "Élégant cantique de Salomé Salomon," *Langage cuit*, in *Corps et biens*, p. 77.

19. Ruth Amossy et Elisheva Rosen, *Le Discours du cliché* (Paris: SEDES, 1982); see in particular the last chapter.

20. *Langage Cuit*, p. 72.

21. *Glossaire j'y serre mes gloses* in *Mots sans mémoire* (Paris: Gallimard, 1969), p. 93.

22. André Martinet, "La double articulation linguistique," *Travaux du Cercle Linguistique de Copenhague* 5 (30–37).

23. Reprinted from Groupe μ (Jacques Dubois *et al.*): *Documents de Travail et pré-publications: Trois fragments d'une rhétorique de l'image*. (Urbino: Università di Urbino, Centro Internazionale di Semiotica e di Linguistica, serie F, nos. 82–83, March-April, 1979), p. 42.

24. For a discussion on the vital role of contextual anchoring and how the latter determines interpretation, i.e., perception, see E. H. Gombrich, *Art and Illusion: A Study in the Psychology of Pictorial Representation* (Princeton: Princeton University Press, 2nd ed., 1969), in particular his discussion in the first chapter of the ambiguous cartoon (which had also fascinated Wittgenstein) of a shape we can interpret as either a duck's or a rabbit's head. Charles Chastain discusses aspects of the same problem in relation to primary and secondary reference in "Reference and Context," *Language, Mind and Knowledge*, ed. K. Gunderson, *Minnesota Studies in the Philosophy of Science*, no. vii (Minneapolis, 1975).

25. See Jean Piaget, *Les Mécanismes perceptifs* (Paris: P.U.F., 1961) for a full discussion of the role of segmentation versus continuum and the role of cultural conditionings in the process of isolating and interpreting forms.

26. Reproduced from Francis Edeline, *Ian Hamilton Finlay: Gnomique et Gnomonique* (Liège: Atelier de l'Agneau/Yellow Now, 1977), p. 12.

27. In fact, as Stephen Bann shows in his article "Le talon de saint Thomas," *Revue d'esthétique* (Paris: Union générale d'éditions, 1977), five languages are involved.

28. Reproduced from Suzi Gablik, *Magritte* (London: Thames and Hudson Ltd., 1970), p.128–137, Fig.111.

29. *Chicago Review, Anthology of Concretism*, ed. Eugene Wildman (Chicago: The Swallow Press, Inc., 1968), p. 129. First published in *Chicago Review*, vol. 19, no. 4 (1967).

30. *Selected Shorter Poems:1950–1970* (New York: New Directions Publishing Co., 1975; 1st ed., 1958), p. 122. Reprinted by permission of New Directions.

31. "The poetic function projects the principle of equivalence from the axis of selection into the axis of combination." "Linguistics and Poetics," in *Style and Language*, ed. T. Sebeok (Cambridge: M.I.T. Press, 1960), p. 358.

32. *Selected Shorter Poems: 1950–1970*, p. 25. Reprinted by permission of New Directions.

33. See Francis Huxley, *The Raven and the Writing Desk* (London: Thames and Hudson, 1976) on Carroll's logical games. In chapter III he discusses "Doublets" and their rules. The two examples may be found on pp. 49 and 51.

34. *Jardin japonais* (Paris: André Silvaire, 1978). No pagination.

35. On the subject of sound icons and anamorphosis see Mireille Calle-Gruber, "Anamorphoses textuelles," *Poétique*, no. 42 (1980), 234–249.

III.

BAD REFERENCES

Gerald Prince

They told me you had been to her,
And mentioned me to him:
She gave me a good character,
But said I could not swim . . .
—*Alice in Wonderland*

Of all the factors which make certain works of fiction difficult to process,[1] perhaps the most remarkable are the perturbations occurring in the referential system, in the set of references through which a (fictional) text constructs the model of a world and thanks to which we can know what the text is about.

I will not attempt in what follows to determine the ontological nature of fictional referents, of objects, entities, concepts, or states of affairs identified in a work of fiction through referring. Nor will I attempt to describe and explain their relation to referents in the real world.[2] I am more interested in the fact that a work of fiction makes use of reference and that the objects it refers to can be talked about (Roquentin lived in Bouville and Madame Bovary in Yonville; Sherlock Holmes solved the Case of the Speckled Band; Anna Karenina had a black velvet dress). In other words, I am interested in the fact that fictional discourse says certain things about certain entities rather than in the status of these entities.

I should point out, however, that students of reference have often insisted on two (possible) differences between fictional worlds and the real world. First, whereas the latter is said to be complete, the former are considered incomplete: for each entity a in a fiction and some relevantly applicable predicate F, it will normally be the case that neither "Fa" nor " $\sim Fa$" is true (what is Roquentin's weight? what is Meursault's date of birth? what are the exact dimensions of Jean-Baptiste Clamence's room?). Second, whereas the real world is taken to be consistent, fictional worlds are sometimes inconsistent: in Ray Bradbury's "A Sound of Thunder," for instance, Keith is elected president in 2055 and Keith is not elected president in 2055; and in Roger Martin du Gard's *Jean Barois*, the protagonist's daughter is eighteen years old in 1913 but also in 1910 and 1916. Of course, fictional worlds need not be inconsistent: there is no inconsistency in Perrault's *Little Red Riding*

Hood or in something like *John was unhappy, then he met Mary, then he became very happy*; moreover, it may well be that faith in the consistency of the real world is just a matter of faith. Of course too, fictional worlds need not be incomplete: "it might be possible to so write a story that every statement about its characters would be decided. For example one might write 'and everything not explicitly stated or implied here is false.' "[3] Besides, without invoking entities that no longer exist in our world (did Racine have an ingrown toenail? what was Shakespeare's weight?) and with respect to existing entities, it may well be impossible, given some predicate F, to determine whether or not F is true of an entity a. The differences between a fictional world and the real world may thus not be that easy to establish; but it is certainly less difficult to live with a lack of consistency and a lack of completeness in fiction, and writers—especially modern writers—have taken full advantage of this fact.

Instead of focusing on the referent in (a) fiction, I will discuss reference, that is, the relation holding between a given series of signs (the referring expression) and what the series stands for on particular occasions of its use.[4] Reference can be singular (when the signs refer to some specific entity) or general (when they refer to a class of entities). It can be anaphoric (backward-looking) or cataphoric (forward-looking). Most importantly, it can be correct (if what the referring expression says of the referent is true) or successful (if the referring expression allows for the identification of the referent) or both.

Consider *La Jalousie* [*Jealousy*],[5] which I take to be exemplary of modern fiction (at least in its handling of reference). It starts out pretty well; innocuously, at any rate, for what could be more innocuous than its title? The first word of the text proper is a deictic: *now*. It must be related to an "I." Patience is the only thing required and surely that "I" will appear. Many entities, perhaps too many, are introduced in the first two or three pages through definite descriptions: *the shadow, the column, the roof, the terrace, the flagstones, the sun, the walls, the gable*, and so on and so forth; but this is not unusual in fiction: after all, such definite descriptions help establish "what is (already) there" in the world represented. Very quickly, however, the start turns out to have been a false start (does a title come at the beginning or the end? isn't any *now* always tied to a past?) and the novel proves to be—among many other things, no doubt—a treatise on how not to refer successfully, a catalogue of bad references.

The first real difficulty occurs on page 11: "Mais le regard qui, venant du fond de la chambre, passe par-dessus la balustrade, ne touche terre que beaucoup plus loin" [page 40: But from the far side of the bedroom the [look] carries over the balustrade and touches ground only much further away]. What does the initial referring expression (if it is one!) refer to? Whose look is "the look"? That of anyone who would be in the back of the room (the familiar "observer" of nineteenth-century fiction)? that of the "I" announced by the liminary *now*? or that of A . . . who has entered the room on page 10? We will never know for sure. Several referents could satisfy this referring expression just as several can satisfy other referring expressions in the text. There are three different ships that something like *the ship* could refer to: the one anchored in the harbor, at the edge of the wharf; the one represented on the calendar; and the one mentioned in the African novel discussed by Franck and A . . . ; there are at least two lamps that *the second lamp* might designate; there are several windows evoked by *the corner window*, and several sheets of paper corresponding to *the sheet of paper*; and there are numerous stains in harmony with *the stain*: the stain left on the wall by the crushed centipede, the stain on the tablecloth, the stain on the blue letter paper, the oil stain in the courtyard, the red stain (is it blood?) under the window, the paint stain on the bannister, and more. In fact, there seems to be a stain everywhere:

> La tache est sur le mur de la maison, sur les dalles, sur le ciel vide. Elle est partout dans la vallée, depuis le jardin jusqu'à la rivière et sur l'autre versant. Elle est aussi dans le bureau, dans la chambre, dans la salle à manger, dans le salon, dans la cour, sur le chemin qui s'éloigne vers la grand-route. (p. 141)

> [The stain is on the wall of the house, on the flagstones, against the empty sky. It is everywhere in the valley, from the garden to the stream and up the opposite slope. It is in the office too, in the bedroom, in the dining room, in the living room, in the courtyard, on the road up to the highway. (p. 102)]

The innocuous title itself could designate a feeling (that of the mysterious "I," of course, but also that of Christiane who has every reason to be jealous, and even that of Franck or that of A . . .) just as well as it could refer to an object (but which of the many blinds would it be?). It is emblematic of the problems of reference in the novel.

Obviously, I do not mean to suggest that, for reference to be successful in *La Jalousie* (or any other text), the class of *potential* referents for every referring expression must be a class of one. I do not mean to imply that there should be one and only one ship, one and only one lamp, one and only one stain; nor do I mean to imply that, in case there are several ships or several stains, each should be named differently. Given any natural language and given any world but a singularly impoverished or heterogeneous one, it is impossible to have a different sign for every entity. Besides, it is not necessary. If, while eating a hamburger, I say to my dinner companion *The hamburger is delicious*, I can be pretty sure that the reference will be successful; and if I write to my wife who is away on vacation *The roof is leaking*, I think that she would understand which roof I am talking about. What is needed for reference to succeed is not so much referent uniqueness as referent uniqueness in context.

Sometimes, of course, a certain degree of linguistic precision, a few more specifications can help. Thus, instead of simply telling my friend something like *The guy asked me to check his car*, I would tell him *The guy you introduced me to yesterday asked me to check his car*. Now, *La Jalousie* is often very precise, not to say excessively or exhaustingly so:

> La main droite saisit le pain et le porte à la bouche, la main droite repose le pain sur

la nappe blanche et saisit le couteau, la main gauche saisit la fourchette, la fourchette pique la viande, le couteau coupe un morceau de viande, la main droite pose le couteau sur la nappe, la main gauche met la fourchette dans la main droite, qui pique le morceau de viande, qui s'approche de la bouche, qui se met à mastiquer avec des mouvements de contraction et d'extension. (pp. 111–112)[6]

[The right hand picks up the bread and raises it to the mouth, the right hand sets the bread down on the white cloth and picks up the knife, the left hand picks up the fork, the fork sinks into the meat, the knife cuts off a piece of meat, the right hand sets down the knife on the cloth, the left hand puts the fork in the right hand, which sinks the fork into the piece of meat, which approaches the mouth, which begins to chew with movements of contraction and extension. (p. 88)]

In fact, from the very "beginning," the text multiplies the specifying elements in its definite descriptions or resorts to metalinguistic explanations: "Maintenant l'ombre du pilier—le pilier qui soutient l'angle sud-ouest du toit" (p. 9) [Now the shadow of the column—the column which supports the southwest corner of the roof (p. 39)]; "Le côté droit (c'est-à-dire aval) n'a plus que treize bananiers" (p. 34) [The row on the right (that is to say the lower) side has no more than thirteen banana trees (p. 51)]; "Par devant brillent aussi le parallélogramme que la lame dessine et l'ellipse en métal au centre de la gomme" (pp. 137–138) [In front of it shines the oblong of the razor blade and the metal ellipse in the center of the eraser (p. 100)]. Yet, regardless of the number of specifying elements or metalinguistic explanations, *La Jalousie* is often not precise enough and its (potential) decoder can become as perplexed as someone listening to Franck and A . . . discuss an enigmatic novel: "Il est à présent question d'une jeune femme blanche—est-ce la même que tout à l'heure, ou bien sa rivale, ou quelque figure secondaire?—qui accorde ses faveurs à un indigène, peut-être à plusieurs" (p. 194) [Now they are talking about a young white woman—is it the same one as before, or her rival, or some secondary character?—who gives herself to a native, perhaps to several (p. 126)]. Indeed, by and large, no amount of precision turns out to be sufficient because the decoder does not know the context in which the references apply. If, in the middle of a race, I tell one of my competitors *The big, juicy, medium-rare hamburger is delicious*, he will probably feel that I am very tired; and he will feel the same way if I describe the quality of the meat in even more detail. What makes for bad references in *La Jalousie* is, above all, the impossibility of finding the appropriate context for many of the referring expressions. Fiction, it has been said, provides only a distant context. Robbe-Grillet's novel provides no context at all or, at best, a most distant and uncertain one.

In the first place, such questions as Who speaks? or Who sees? only find ambiguous answers. It is not quite enough to claim that everything is presented in terms of a protagonist, "I," one who is, if anything, radically incomplete, one who never appears as such yet who, like Flaubert's invisible novelist, is everywhere. We cannot be sure that what the text presents are the perceptions of this "I" rather than his thoughts, his memories, or his hallucinations. Besides, many passages could be attributed to an omniscient narrator, a kind of unsituated voice of truth:

"A . . . , sans y penser, regarde le bois dépeint de la balustrade" (p. 14) [A . . . absently stares at the paint-flaked wood of the balustrade (p. 41)]; "pour se rendre à l'office, le plus simple est de traverser la maison" (p. 48) [To get to the pantry, the easiest way is to cross the house (p. 58)]; "La nuit ensuite n'est pas longue à tomber, dans ces contrées sans crépuscules" (p. 137) [The night does not take long falling in these countries without twilight (p. 100)]; and many seem explicitly related to A . . .'s point of view: "A . . . écoute le chant indigène lointain mais net encore, qui parvient jusqu'à la terrasse" (p. 105) [A . . . listens to the native chant, distant but still distinct, which reaches the veranda (p. 85)]; "La voix grave du second chauffeur arrive jusqu'à elle" (p. 119) [The low voice of the second driver reaches her (p. 92)]. The ambiguity is further compounded by the extraordinary number of verbs used intransitively: "Le gris du bois y apparaît [à qui?], strié de petites fentes longitudinales" (p. 11) [The gray of the wood shows through *[for whom?]* streaked with tiny longitudinal cracks (p. 40)]; "Il serait difficile [pour qui?] de préciser où, exactement, il néglige quelque règle essentielle sur quel point particulier il manque de discrétion" (p. 23) [It would be difficult *[for whom?]* to specify exactly in what way he is neglecting some essential rule, at what particular point he is lacking in discretion (p. 46)]; "Vu de la porte de l'office le mur de la salle à manger paraît [à qui] sans tache" (p. 51) [From the pantry door, the dining-room wall seems [*to whom?]* to have no spot on it (p. 59)]; and by the numerous definite descriptions— the eye, the gaze, the ear, and the fingers—which function just as well generically as specifically (pp. 11, 13, 28, 70, *et passim*, or pp. 40, 41, 48, 68 in the translation). The problem of origin in *La Jalousie*, like the problem of destination (how would the textual addressee be described?), must remain a problem.

The time of events is undeterminable. The many temporal deictics used throughout the novel cannot be related to a given "I" with any certainty and they cannot be ordered chronologically. A centipede is squashed perhaps before a trip taken by Franck and A . . . , perhaps during that trip, and perhaps after it.[7] *Maintenant* is *maintenant* is *maintenant.* The text itself makes clear that *now* does not constitute a good answer to *when?*: "A une question peu précise concernant le moment où il a reçu cet ordre, il répond: 'Maintenant', ce qui ne fournit aucune indication satisfaisante" (p. 50) [To a vague question as to when he received this order, he answers: 'Now', which furnishes no satisfactory indication (p. 59)]. The present tense, which is used almost exclusively, provides little help: in French, as in English, the use of the present does not necessarily imply that the event or situation described is contemporaneous with the act of description. As for the prepositions and conjunctions of time (*after, next, as soon as, after a few minutes or a few seconds*), they can apply either to several well-defined contexts or to none at all. As with many other features of *La Jalousie*, "plusieurs solutions conviennent, par endroit, et ailleurs aucune" (p. 52) [several solutions seem possible at some places, and in others, none (p. 60)].

If the time of events is baffling, so is the space in which they presumably occur. Granted, the text not only abounds in detailed descriptions of objects and of their spatial relations but also manifests a remarkable affinity for demonstratives. Thus, we get "Il se dirige . . . vers la petite table, s'empare de celle-ci et . . . dépose

le tout un peu plus loin'' (p. 110) [He walks . . . toward the little table, picks [*this*]
up and . . . sets the whole thing down a little farther away (pp. 87–88)], instead
of "s'en empare et dépose le tout un peu plus loin'' [picks it up and sets the whole
thing down a little farther away], and "Entre cette première fenêtre et la seconde''
(p. 121) [Between this first window and the second (p. 93)] instead of "Entre la
première fenêtre et la seconde'' [Between the first window and the second]. Sometimes, the affinity for demonstratives leads to passages which would be most welcome in a book of French grammar for beginners: "Quand aux oiseaux eux-mêmes,
ils ne se montrent pas . . . restant à couvert sous les panaches de larges feuilles
vertes, tout autour de la maison. Dans la zone de terre nue qui sépare celle-ci de
ceux-là . . .'' (pp. 78–79) [As for the birds themselves, they [*do not show themselves*] . . . remaining in hiding under the clusters of wide green leaves on all sides
of the house. In the zone of naked earth which separates [*it from the former*] (p.
73)]. Sometimes, it even leads to infelicities: "puis il se lève de sa chaise sans
bruit, gardant sa serviette à la main. Il roule celle-ci (la main?) en bouchon et
s'approche du mur'' (p. 63) [Then he stands up, noiselessly, holding his napkin in
his hand. He wads it (*the hand*?) into a ball and approaches the wall (p. 65)]. What
the demonstratives point out or point to, however, what they designate, what they
"demonstrate,'' often remains elusive because of numerous and sudden changes in
scenery.[8] Anaphora and cataphora are confused (pp. 56, 99, 124, 126, *et passim*).
Here is no different from *there*, *this x* is no different from *that x* and, like *now*,
they constitute poor answers. For all its apparent precision, geography becomes
chaotic and many events—not to say all events—are so difficult to situate spatially
that they do not seem to take place.

"Où maintenant? Quand maintenant? Qui maintenant?'' [Where now? When now?
Who now?][9] If I do not know who, when, and where, I cannot know what. It is
difficult to specify what happens in *La Jalousie* because Robbe-Grillet's novel
contains little, if anything, that is firmly rooted.[10] Whereas the hallmark of most
texts is certainty, *La Jalousie* lives in uncertainty. It is astonishingly hesitant about
what happened, what is happening, what will happen, what might happen: "une
tache noirâtre marque l'emplacement du mille-pattes écrasé la semaine dernière, au
début du mois, le mois précédent peut-être, ou plus tard'' (p. 27) [a blackish spot
marks the place where a centipede was squashed last week, at the beginning of the
month, perhaps the month before, or later (p. 47)]; "Combien de temps s'est-il
écoulé depuis la dernière fois qu'il a fallu en rétablir le tablier?'' (p. 103) [How
much time has passed since the bridge underpinnings had to be repaired? (p.84)];
"Il rentre en scène aussitôt—ou un autre à sa place—et rétrécit bientôt son orbite''
(p. 148) [It immediately returns to view—or another returns in its place—and soon
[*narrows*] its orbit (p. 105)]. *La Jalousie* does not institute certain constants—save
inconstancy!—which could be assimilated. It does not propose a body of knowledge
which is to be acquired and shared. It consists, in large part, of ambiguous statements, and the possibly unambiguous ones are all contaminated. It is amnesic,
forgetting what it has or has not yet established, resorting to indefinite articles when
definite ones are expected and vice versa (pp. 115, 197, 216, *et passim*, or pp. 90,

128, 137 in the translation), assigning contradictory predicates to what may be the same entity and the same predicates to different entities (pp. 108 and 109; 27, 61 and 211; 216; *et passim*, or pp. 87, paragraphs 2 and 4; 47, 64 and 135; 137, in the translation). Untotalizable, unsummarizable, defeating memory and anticipation, defying spatio-temporal distinctions and hierarchies (in *La Jalousie*, we never know what to skip!), the novel disintegrates the scene of reading.

Consider, for instance, the passages describing or alluding to the partial squashing of a centipede on a wall (pp. 27, 63, 64, 97, *et passim*; or pp. 47, 65, 82, in the translation). If I take them to refer to one and the same referent, I have to deal with inconsistencies in the information I process: the insect is such that it can be squashed repeatedly, at different times, in different places, with different results. In other words, I cannot, until the very last page of the novel, take anything for granted and relax. I cannot assume that I know what there is to be known about the squashing. I cannot trust the conclusions I reach after any one set of descriptions. I cannot presume that what new information I gather will confirm or conform to the information already gathered. I cannot foresee, from what I learn, what may or may not happen. At any point in the novel, regardless of the context, the squashing of the centipede may occur in circumstances that I can neither predict nor expect. Suppose I try to eliminate inconsistencies by taking contradictory passages to refer to different places.[11] I would still be faced with the same problems. Once again, at any point, a new squashing of a centipede may occur. Once again, what I learn from the text does not allow me to expect or predict, even in part, what will or will not happen. Once again, it is a case of "le possible à chaque instant" [What is possible at each instant].

To try to account for the text by saying that it is basically about a husband jealous to the point of insanity (or that it illustrates the crumbling of colonial mastery) does not solve the problem either. It is merely another way of recognizing that the text is mad (schizophrenic: it is not modeled in terms of a receiver), that the language used is referentially inadequate, and that the novel cannot be processed and digested in conventional, sane, masterful ways.[12] There is no world I can abstract from *La Jalousie*, no material with which I can fill its gaps and plug its holes, no algorithm in terms of which I can distinguish what is said from what it is said about. *Here* must be *here, at this point in the text. Now* must be *now, at this moment in the text. It* must be *it, here and now in the text,* whatever *it* may be.

By subverting reference (and thus rejecting linguistic transparency as well as metaphoricity), *La Jalousie* places itself out of any communication circuit. It does not transmit. It is. The requisite distinctions for the construction of a world related to the "real world," the distinctions between likely and certain, same and different, old and new, before and after, here and there, are impossible to make. By multiplying bad references, *La Jalousie* multiplies potential meanings while destroying meaning and it aspires to pure fiction; that is, not merely what does not refer (directly) to events and existents in our world but what refers poorly to any world, what shows without showing, designates without designating, speaks without speaking; in a word, writes.

NOTES

1. On legibility and textual processing see Philippe Hamon, "Un Discours contraint," *Poétique* no. 16 (1973), 411–445; and Gerald Prince, "Questions, Answers, and Narrative Legibility" in *Retrospectives and Perspectives: A Symposium in Rhetoric*, ed. Turner S. Kobler, William E. Tanner, and J. Dean Bishop (Denton: Texas Woman's University Press, 1978), pp. 75–90.

2. On this problem, see John Woods, *The Logic of Fiction* (The Hague: Mouton, 1974) and "Formal Semantics and Literary Theory," ed. John Woods and Thomas G. Pavel, *Poetics* VIII, 1–2 (April 1979).

3. This was suggested by Dudley Shapere to John Heintz. See John Heintz, "Reference and Inference in Fiction," *Poetics* VIII, 1–2 (April 1979), 91.

4. John Lyons, *Semantics*, vol. I (Cambridge: Cambridge University Press, 1977), pp. 174–229, provides a helpful introduction to the problems of reference. M. A. K. Halliday and Ruquaiya Hasan, *Cohesion in English* (London: Longman, 1976) contains many interesting examples.

5. Alain Robbe-Grillet, *La Jalousie* (Paris: Les Éditions de Minuit, 1970). Translations are taken from *Jealousy* in *Two Novels by Robbe-Grillet: "Jealousy" and "In the Labyrinth,"* trans. Richard Howard (New York: Grove Press, 1965). All references will be to these editions. Any italicized words within square brackets in the translated version are my interjections or the editors' more literal translation.

6. I said *exhaustingly* because defamiliarization through detailing can be exhausting.

7. Cf. M. Mouillaud, "Le Nouveau Roman: Tentative de roman et roman de la tentative," *Revue d'Esthétique* XVII (août-décembre 1964), 228–263.

8. In *Les Romans de Robbe-Grillet* (Paris: Editions de Minuit, 1963), p. 131, Bruce Morrissette writes: "tous les changements de scène sont amorcés en début de paragraphe, à l'exception peut-être de ce 'fondu enchaîne' où le regard du mari passe d'une terrasse de café à la photo de A, puis à la terrasse réelle de la maison" (p. 126). This is not entirely correct. To give but one example among many, *la table* on page 110 (page 88 in the translation) may designate the little terrace table (first mention) and the dining-room table (second mention).

[Editors' note: The difference between this quotation and Morrissette's subsequent English translation, p. 134 in *The Novels of Robbe-Grillet* (Ithaca and London: Cornell University Press, 1975), is perhaps indicative of Morrissette's own doubts as to the accuracy of his original statement. The translation of the above runs thus: "almost all the transitions between scenes occur at the beginning of a paragraph. The rare exceptions pass almost unnoticed except on the most minute reading and represent only very brief alternates between tightly linked elements."]

9. Samuel Beckett *L'Innommable* (Paris: Editions de Minuit, 1953), p.7 [*The Unnamable* (New York: Grove Press, 1970), p. 3.]

10. In this respect, at least, *La Jalousie* is very similar to the novel read by Franck and A . . . as it is described on page 216 (137 in the translation).

11. Such a solution is hinted at (then seemingly rejected) by the text on page 171: "Combien de fois s'est répété le choc léger contre les dalles? À peine cinq ou six, ou même encore moins. . . . La chute d'un gros lézard, depuis le dessous du toit, produit souvent un 'flac' étouffé de cette sorte; mais il aurait alors fallu que cinq ou six lézards se laissent tomber l'un après l'autre, coup sur coup, ce qui est peu probable" [How many times was the faint impact repeated against the flagstones? Barely five or six, or even less. . . . The fall of a big lizard from the eaves often produces a similar muffled "slap"; but then it would have taken five or six lizards falling one after another, which is unlikely p. 115].

12. I do not mean to suggest that Bruce Morrissette, *The Novels of Robbe-Grillet*, and Jacques Leenhardt, *Lecture politique du roman: "La Jalousie" d'Alain Robbe-Grillet* (Paris: Editions de Minuit, 1973), are hopelessly wrong. Indeed, I have found both works excellent

and I have profited enormously from them and from Barthes's superb preface to Morrissette, just as I have profited from Jean Alter, *La Vision du monde d'Alain Robbe-Grillet: Structures et significations* (Genève: Droz, 1966), Olga Bernal, *Alain Robbe-Grillet: le roman de l' absence* (Paris: Gallimard, 1964), and Stephen Heath, *The Nouveau Roman: A Study in the Practice of Writing* (London: Elek, 1972).

IV.

WAITING FOR THE REFERENT
WAITING FOR GODOT?
On Referring in Theatre

Jean Alter

To deal cogently with *referents* in *theatre*, it is essential to clarify the meaning of both terms as well as the manner in which I shall be using them. Both concepts have given rise to considerable confusion and misunderstanding. The fact that my approach will be semiotic (in contrast to that of most previous studies on this topic) may further explain why, in this preliminary discussion, I must question and largely discard some current definitions, and replace them with more workable ones.

I. Theatre

In theory, a semiotic definition of theatre does not present any special problem. Here (as elsewhere), I take theatre to mean the entire process which culminates in a theatrical performance, and involves both internal and external factors. Theatre may thus be defined as an iconic representation of events by means of a number of codes and corresponding systems of signs. The latter are either text or stage signs. The interaction between the two categories during the theatrical process, the resulting transformations, further subdivisions of signs, and so forth, are all matters that can be conceptualized and even formalized.[1]

However, moving from the safe ground of theory into praxis, one is caught in a triple bind resulting from the ephemeral nature of the theatrical performance. As no two performances are ever identical (even of the same play on two successive nights), nothing guarantees that the choice of a particular performance for study will yield more than contingent observations. Furthermore, since the performance lapses into non-existence at the very moment it comes into being, there is no opportunity either for a second look at a specific feature or for a reproduction of the entire experience for purposes of verification. Finally, in the absence of a reproducible performance, any statement made about its stage signs must first translate them into verbal signs, with resulting semiotic confusion and risk of subjective bias.[2] It is possible that in the future, as progress in video, laser, and computer recordings leads to the establishment of vast *theatre archives*, the elusive character of performance may be overcome. If so—some problems will still remain—it will affect future scholarship only. At present, a theory which postulates the unity of the entire theatrical process from text to performance (within a specific cultural framework) cannot justifiably draw its illustrations from all the significant steps in that process, simply because not all are available or acceptable as evidence. Of course, critics can and do recreate performances from memory, notes, or photographs, but, in so doing, they are making personal statements which must be taken on faith, at best as second-hand accounts of authentic impressions. For purposes of analysis, discussion, and scholarship, such accounts are largely inadequate, however persuasive and stimulating they may be. One is reluctant to reject them, especially when they express one's own experience; but ultimately one must come back to the written text which alone allows for meaningful communication. Such a strategy has its own risks, but most can be avoided if the text of the play is clearly conceived as only one step in the entire process, and the work on that text inscribed in this process. Hence, when testing my hypotheses about the theatrical referent on Samuel Beckett's *Waiting for Godot*, I shall rely primarily on the written text of the play. Beckett's text, however, will not be considered as an autonomous literary work, but as an initial set of verbal signs intended to generate additional sets of stage signs and, after some transformation, to become part of a performance.

II. The referent

Defining the referent is by no means easy. While the notion may seem clear, its applications to the semiotics of theatre are far from being so. Obviously, the referent is "that which is referred to" (Webster), but what is meant by referring? A great deal has been written on the problem—from Meinong to Russell, Frege, and Austin, and other speech-act theoreticians such as Strawson or Searle. The referent has been central to the concerns of philosophers, logicians, formal linguists, and semanticists, interested in and working with ordinary language (utterances, acts), rather than with fictional discourse or other semiotic systems.[3] Much controversial ink has been spilled over the conditions of true or false referring, with the temptation to restrict reference to objects *existing in the actual world*.[4] And when a new generation of philosophers of language finally undertook the analysis of reference in fiction, their efforts were channelled by constraints of tradition into contrived and contradictory explanations of the aberrant practice of referring to non-existent objects: fascinating but inconclusive theories of possible or fictional worlds, story operators, "say so" authority, guises, etc.[5] Some of their points can be adapted, *mutatis mutandis*, for the semiotics of theatre; in particular, I am indebted to their notion of the "incompleteness" of fictional referents[6] and to the image of "in the mind's eye" representation.[7] But not much of this scholarship is directly relevant to the study of *theatrical* (text or stage) signs.

More specifically semiotic studies are not very helpful either, since they do not provide *much* semiotic discussion of reference, referring, or referents. Semioticians who deal with these notions are often unclear and many are heavily influenced by linguistics. If Ducrot and Todorov, for example, accept the concept of the referent, as a complement to the Saussurean theory of the sign, they add (cautiously) that the former, "in the easiest to imagine case," is a "real object" with which the sign is "linked"; referring is equated with denoting; and the single illustration of the process links the word "apple" to "real apples."[8] There is little difference between their supposedly semiotic definition and the frankly linguistic one offered by Dubois *et al.*, where the referent is "that to which a linguistic sign refers in extra-linguistic reality,"[9]—a restrictive notion which excludes fictional referents. A similar emphasis on verbal *reference* is apparent in Michael Issacharoff's decision to restrict the referent to "its properly linguistic meaning," based on Strawson and Searle.[10] But he qualifies this by citing a more semiotic source, Ogden and Richards, for whom the referent is "whatever we may be thinking of or referring to," that is, much more than a "material substance," and where, by inference, the referring may be done by signs other than words.[11] Patrice Pavis, in his recent *Dictionnaire du Théâtre*, also alludes to Ogden and Richards, but is somehow sidetracked by Benveniste's distinction between semiotics and semantics, with the result that the referent is reduced either to a material object on stage, to an illusion thereof, or to what it could have been at the time the dramatic text was written: an unnecessarily confused entry.[12] A much broader definition of the referent in theatre appears to be given by Anne Ubersfeld, who holds it to be "an image of the world," possibly an idea or an ideal embodied in a specific reference; but further analysis shows that this embodiment always requires an initial reference to some material object, and that the entire process attributes to both signs and referents an impossibly dual presence on the stage and in the world.[13] In all these instances, recent scholarship on reference in theatre seems to err in its hasty acceptance of often incompatible concepts. The theoretical bases require rethinking and would benefit from systematic reformulation.

It is evident, in that perspective, that the study of theatre must retain Saussure's split of the sign into its material manifestation, the signifier, and its coded meaning, the signified. Peirce's sign/referent relationship, especially the distinction among the icon, the index, and the symbol, can also be of use (though most of his other material may be discarded in the name of methodological austerity). Ogden and Richards proposed an attractive tripartite system: Referent/Thought/Symbol, but at the price of discarding the signifier/signified duality, which is essential for stage signs.[14] The Prague School's contributions came close to a workable synthesis of their predecessors, but tension between aesthetic and social concerns, inherited from Russian Formalism, stood in the way of a simple theory.[15] Instead of attempting to develop (and betray) any of these approaches, I am proposing to use Occam's razor and borrow from all of them in such a way that the triad Signifier/Signified/Referent may simply, sufficiently, and efficiently account for referring in theatre. Hence my definitions:

1) *The Signifier*: The material manifestation of a sign (graphy, sound, color, facial expression, costume, light, etc.), coded in the appropriate semiotic system as signifying by conventional association with:

2) *The Signified*: The definitional concept provided in the code, such as a dic-

tionary, or an internalized cultural code, consisting generally of essential or class properties,[16] which, in an existential discourse, may receive:

3) *A Referent*: A particular manifestation of the signified, conceived of or perceived as having a unique individual existence, real or fictional.

The first two definitions are standard. The third requires further comment.

(i) *Ontology* of the referent: I am postulating that the referent can be anything at all: real or fictional persons, objects, events, feelings, ideas, and combinations thereof, provided that they are perceived as having a unique real or fictional existence;

(ii) *Identification* of the referent: It may be assumed on pragmatic evidence that any semiotic referential discourse supplies not only the concept of the referent, as coded by the signified for a given signifier, but also at least one more property and possibly many more, and that the identification of the referent by receivers is made possible at some *sufficient level of specificity* dependent on the number or type of these properties;

(iii) *Incompleteness* of the referent: However specific, a reference can never be assumed to be complete, that is, to comprise all possible additional properties that may be attributed to the referent "in the mind's eye" of the sender or the receiver of the semiotic discourse; namely, those which the referential sign may trigger, in the form of a "display of internal representations," from among the complex network of latent representations recorded in memory and adding up to the internalized Representation of Reality;[17]

(iv) *Identity* of the referent: Strictly speaking, the referent therefore cannot be identical in all points for the sender and the various receivers of the semiotic discourse even when there is easy agreement on its identification. In practice one may assume, however, that either because of a high degree of referential specificity in the discourse, or because of a high degree of correspondence between internalized representations in each memory, a properly identified referent, however different it may be in each "mind's eye," will be perceived with a sufficient number of overlapping properties to insure, under normal circumstances, a similar understanding of its function in the discourse by the sender and the various receivers, regardless of the real or fictional nature of that discourse.

III. Literary referents in *Waiting for Godot*: primary and secondary referents

In order to see clearly how these concepts work as well as to explore the basic problems of *Godot*, it will be useful to start with a "literary" reading of the play, the one accessible to most people who forget that it is theatre. In this sense, *Godot* yields an experience not entirely dissimilar from that of some genuine "new fiction": a minimal and rather tedious plot, a very individual style, sparse characterization, and considerable ambiguity. It also yields a network of referents situated in some outside world where the action takes place; characters with their words, gestures, emotions, ideas; a sequence of events; and ultimately a meaning of the story which, as shall be seen, has a special status. In order to survey the referential process in each of these categories, I need to posit three types of referents, as follows:

1. Verbal referents

Even read as literature, *Godot* obviously privileges the type of referent which, in verbal discourse, may be expected to achieve the highest identity concordance for sender and receivers: *the quoted text*. Under normal circumstances,[18] the quoted text, dialogue or monologue, emerges as the fundamental referential constant of the literary reading. One reader, for example, may identify Lucky as strong, cynical, and distant; another as emaciated, sincere, and pathetic. Lucky's lines may then receive a different referential meaning; but the fact that he speaks these lines will not change and, especially, the lines themselves will remain the same and always available. The quoted text, as such, is thus almost "complete": ideally, it needs a minimum of additional properties to become its own referent. It is the stablest of the signs—in literary readings.[19]

2. Narrative referents

This category includes all the referents which make up the "story," on the basis of either didascalia or discrete signs contained within the quoted text. The reader progressively decodes them, that is, moves from signifier to signified, and then, in "the mind's eye," links the signified to a particular referent which has properties provided in the text but also other properties generated by associations that the concept triggers in the reader's memory, that is, in the network of his internal, individual representations. Thus first the location: the (incomplete) referent supplied by the text is an area along a road; but the process of visualization[20] may add properties which will diversify the individual referent of the receiver along such variables as: A path? A street? A highway? A turnpike? Straight, turning, or sinuous? Level or steep? Paved, concrete, or dirt surface? Grass or rocks or earth or rubbish around? Perhaps a stream or bushes or ditches? and so on. Some of these properties are less likely than others to be added, and not all categories will be covered by each reader. Some overly hasty or unimaginative may even not add any significant property, and thus visualize a referent very close to the concepts given by the signified. But variations will occur, contaminating other referents as well. Vladimir on a flowery bank near a country road will not be the same, *ceteris paribus*, as Vladimir on a concrete slab near an industrial highway. Yet all these variations will not affect the general agreement among readers about the identification of the locale and its function in the story. Besides, as reading progresses (and comes to an end), the initial visualization may be revised, enriched, or impoverished until, gradually becoming hazier, it fades in the memory and is absorbed into the general network of individual representations.

Let us now turn to the characters, to Vladimir, Pozzo, and Godot in particular. The minimal referent yielded by the complex sign Vladimir[21] is that of a "bum," wearing a hat, and moving around; he performs actions and makes statements which stress that he and Estragon are waiting for Godot. Clothing, gestures, voice, face, figure, etc., but also emotions, personality, ideas, are left to individual visualization. The latter may vary considerably, and yet a general identification of Vladimir's function in the story will not be dramatically affected: he will remain a "bum," and the source of the stable verbal referents that his lines generate. In the case of Pozzo, no clear status properties are displayed in the minimal referent, though it provides for physical deterioration (blindness) and a change of relationship with Lucky; on the other hand, his speeches and actions will suggest to most readers a number of psychological properties: vanity, cruelty, etc. Again, there is no real problem about his function in the story.

And Godot? Very few signs refer to Godot in the text; they amount to a name, the power to give messages, and the state of being expected. There is very little to trigger individual visualization, since even a human shape is uncertain, so that the specificity of the minimal referent in fact appears *insufficient* both for the purpose of identification and for a clear perception of Godot's function in the story. During the reading process, this insufficiency may serve, like a vacuum, to entice the reader hoping to find new signs which would generate new properties and permit a satisfactory visualization. The average reader, no doubt, gives up halfway, declaring the story to be nonsense. The sophisticated reader, already intrigued by possible divine connotations of the name, may persist to the point where, frustrated by the insufficiency of the minimal referent, he will feel the need for "a daring hypothesis" (about Godot's role in the story) and postulate a referent for Godot which does not rely on signs provided in the text. In other words, this reader will visualize or conceptualize a number of properties which, attributed to Godot, would make sense for the other referents in the story, by integrating them into a coherent "meaning." For many, this hypothetical referent of Godot will indeed be God, endowed in their "mind's eyes" with various God-like properties, and so perceived by anyone who accepts the hypothesis. Of course, all the other referents, such as Vladimir, Pozzo, and the locale, may then have to be appropriately adjusted, through a change of or additions to their properties. This entire process, however, calls for a different type of semiotic operation than in the case of verbal or narrative referents. The latter can be called *primary* referents in that they are given directly by the textual signs, whereas the process just discussed involves *secondary* referents, based on primary referents when they are treated as signs.

3. Secondary referents: meaning

In the literary reading of *Godot*, the insufficient minimal referent of Godot entailed recourse to the notion of "meaning" lest the story be declared nonsensical. In reading fiction (which does not present such problems) the determination of meaning depends on the individual choice of the reader, and may not take place. Nevertheless, since it is always possible, and involves *referential* processes, it should be further explored. The Godot case enables us to make the following observations:

(i) Before an "in-the-mind's-eye" referent can assume the function of a sign, a process of *reverse encoding* of properties added by the individual reader must first occur. The signifiers of these properties are encoded with the same signifieds as in the general cultural code. If Vladimir is visualized with a bum's clothes, emaciated body, clasped hands, and an inspired face, these material features will be viewed as signifiers associated with signifieds corresponding to the concepts of "bumming," asceticism, religiosity, holiness. Together, they will add to a *definition* of Vladimir in the reader's ideal dictionary: An inspired bum who, for example, is eagerly and trustfully waiting for Godot at the top of a mountain. The reader's Vladimir is thus reconstituted as a sign.

(ii) Such a sign, however, may be more or less complex or complete. In an extreme case, it will contain all properties visualized for Vladimir, with the result that its only possible referent will be Vladimir. Critics who carry anti-reductionism to this extreme in fact claim that this entire operation is therefore circular, and that, in general, only the totality of primary referents defines the meaning of fiction. Readers (and critics) who look for more manageable meanings are prepared to accept a *reduction* in the complexity (completeness) of the sign, scanning its signified properties with a view to retaining only those which will serve the original purpose of the operation: to supply a reduced (and hence distorted) concept of Vladimir which could be easily integrated with the other similarly derived concepts so as to form a coherent meaning. Such a reduction, depending how far it is carried, will yield a hierarchy of Vladimir concepts, from the one quoted above to, say, "an inspired person who, on some high place, is waiting for Godot," or "an inspired man who is waiting for Godot," or "a man who is waiting for Godot." The "best" level, of course, is determined by the ease with which it can combine with the other concepts to form a coherent unit.

(iii) A coherent unit of this kind entails a retroactive impact on most concepts in question. If Godot, for example, is reduced to God, then the Vladimir concept may be modified, at a convenient level of reduction, to that of "a man who is waiting for God," or "a pilgrim who is waiting for God," etc. Any of these individual variations modify the ideal individual dictionary of fiction, providing a different definition, or signified, for Vladimir and all other "in-the-mind's-eye" referents treated as signs.

(iv) At this juncture, the referential process enters its final state where the new signified is again translated into a particular manifestation. A semiotically trained reader will now state that Vladimir's referent is a particular man (or pilgrim) named Vladimir, waiting for God. Extended to the entire story, the (highly simplified) referent—or meaning—of *Godot* could be stated as follows: "The story of two men, Vladimir and Estragon, who are waiting for God, who does not show Himself, and of two other men, Pozzo and Lucky, who are involved in earthly matters, and deteriorate," or "The story of men who wait for God and of those who do not."[22] Such a meaning can now serve to clarify and adjust any discrete referent in the text.

(v) By their very individualized nature, secondary referents of sender and receivers may be expected to vary much more than primary referents, to the point where identification could be undermined. Most controversies about fiction turn indeed on differences in "meanings" (secondary referents). However, such differences rarely entail a failure in communication, a lack of identification. Secondary referents operate at such reductive levels that, when disagreements occur, they do not involve misunderstanding but rather the choice of meanings. When, for one reader, Vladimir is seen as a pilgrim awaiting God, and for another as a nihilist awaiting Death, neither reader has trouble identifying the other's referent when rejecting it. In other words, literary referents encourage rather than discourage discussion, critics, and scholarship.

(vi) As secondary referents reach the highest levels of reduction, the corresponding formulation of the meaning of a story comes increasingly close to the formulation of a concept. Thus, the referent draws closer to its signified, at least in form. For the sake of clarity, I have reserved the term "meaning" for the highly simplified, integrated sum of all secondary referents of a fictional creation; and I propose to use "message" to designate the equivalent integrated sum of the signifieds of that fiction. Like all signifieds, the message will be likely to occur as a universal cognitive or imperative statement. The message of *Godot*, corresponding to the particular meaning obtained above, could be formulated thus: "There are men who wait for God, and others who do not," or "One should believe in an uncertain God rather than in earthly life which is sure to end in death." The process whereby meaning yields a message is not at issue here, but one may speculate again that it involves a kind of reverse encoding whereby the reader, looking for a concept behind the referent, scans his memory of representations until he encounters an acceptable cliché (that he could find in an ideal dictionary of messages) or, if none fits, makes one up on the model of the others. Of course, any message may then in turn be embodied in various particular meanings, including the first, with additional properties determining the differences. Any further development of this process moves from the area of reading to that of writing.

IV. Theatrical referents: The "virtual performance" of *Godot*

Now that the basic referential processes have been identified, as well as the main problems in *Godot*, it is easier to understand what happens when the play is not read as fiction but as a step in the theatrical process, a performance-to-be. Such a reading will yield, "in the mind's eye," what shall be called a "virtual performance," an anticipation of, and substitution for, the elusive real performance. Obviously, this virtual performance must be first related to the script of the play, especially in ways which affect referential processes; but, as will be shown, its assumed potential manifestation as a real performance must also be taken into consideration.

1. The virtual performance as referent

When read as theatre, *Godot* no longer refers to an outside world but to an outside stage, real or imaginary, and its characters no longer refer to people but to actors playing the role of these people. In the virtual performance, which takes place in the "mind's eye," all referents of *Godot* thus become parts of that performance

which, in itself, becomes the referent of the text of the play. The question is: can
these theatrical referents be identified, communicated, and discussed with the same
success as the literary referents?

The first significant difference occurs in the process of visualization. Indeed, the
mimetic associations of concepts with the representation of reality are now made
to compete with associations derived from the experience of theatre, namely, representations of staging practice.[23] A road, for example, may be visualized on the
stage with additional properties drawn from the memory of roads seen (or imagined)
on some particular stage during some past (or imaginary) performance. It could be
an empty space, scaffolding, a wooden plank, a roof-like surface, or swinging
ropes, or even a "realistic" road. Similarly Vladimir and Pozzo may be visualized
(and probably *will* be by adepts of theatre) not in the context of lived experience,
and thus as unstable characters, but with features associated with specific and even
codified acting styles and stock characters. In other words, while a literary reading
basically moves from signs to referents which are intellectual realities, a theatrical
reading can move from signs to other signs before reaching the referents. It has
often been said that a cube on the stage may stand for a chair, a table, a car, a bed,
and so on, alternately. We know too that the referent chair, table, or bed in turn
functions as a sign referring to an outside (mental) reality; I shall return to this.
What interests me here, however, is that the awareness of stage codes increases
the variety of referents perceived by readers, since the use of coded signs as referents
on stage expands the pool of additional properties in the reader's memory. Just as
a road can be visualized as a wooden plank, so Vladimir or Pozzo can be visualized
as stock Commedia dell'Arte characters, or Pierrots, or men with sandwich-boards
appropriately inscribed, or masked figures in body-stockings, and so forth. For these
examples, I am drawing on my experience of theatre; it supplies me with a much
richer choice of referents than my experience of real roads or bums. Furthermore,
my theatrical experience is likely to be quite different from that of other readers of
Godot, and certainly quite distinct from our experience of reality. As a result, the
referents I visualize during a virtual performance are far more likely to differ from
other readers' referents, and more unpredictably than in the process of a literary
reading. But does that mean that the principle of identification is subverted, and
that no communication about the theatrical referents of *Godot* can occur? Not quite.
For a virtual performance places upon its referents the ultimate constraint of coherence and stability. Once visualized as a stage element, in whatever form, the
road will remain firmly anchored in the "mind's eye," directly and constantly
linked to the visualized movements of the actors. The latter, with their fixed physical
appearance and specific style of acting, will be constantly checked for the skill and
consistency of their performance. If, say, I visualize Vladimir as a slender, saintly-
looking man, with a face like Von Sydow, I shall not have him turn playful sum-
mersaults. And whereas I could visualize Pozzo as a truly protean character, moving
through a whole gamut of expressions, nonetheless, even in his case, I shall be
forced to eschew contradictions. In short, not only will my referents be relatively
fixed (in my version of the virtual performance), but also their interaction will have
to remain coherent, since they are viewed as elements of the dramatic space of a

specific stage. Thus, my theatrical reading of *Godot* will yield a much more controlled and better perceived network of referents than my literary reading. A much clearer overall meaning will emerge from this network. We have seen that there is no problem in identifying meanings, however they may vary; by the same token, the organized network of referents in the virtual performance may also be readily communicated.

But where and when does this unified meaning originate? During the literary reading, it was posited to supplement the insufficient referential properties of Godot. A theatrical reading, in theory, does not have to deal with Godot since Godot is not visualized on stage. The need for the meaning, however, generally appears to be more imperative for the virtual performance than for a literary reading. It does not derive from the (optional) wish for a better understanding of the play, but from the *necessity* of organizing the referents on stage. The problem then is how to locate that meaning. The referents in the virtual performance cannot function the way the primary referents in literary readings do, because rather than generating the meaning, they depend on it. The formulation of the meaning must precede the visualization of the performance. Where then does it originate? It would seem that only one answer fits: the meaning must be drawn from the literary reading. The virtual performance, when viewed as the referent of the text, thus always occurs after the play is read as literature, though the two readings may conceivably be simultaneous. All other things being equal, and despite a basic difference in referential processes, the problems of literary and theatrical referents could then be related without any risk of confusion. I shall stage Vladimir as a Von Sydow figure *because* I read him first as a pilgrim waiting for God.

2. The virtual performance as sign

However, all other things are *not* equal. When the written text of a play is viewed as a step in the theatrical process, its virtual performance must also be seen as leading to (or substituting for) an actual performance—a conglomeration of (verbal and stage) signs which in turn refer to some outside world. In other words, when I visualize a plank on a stage slanting from right to left, and at the top of it an actor looking like Von Sydow, hands clasped and eyes lifted in hope, I must not forget that these referents of the text are intended to function as signs for the fictional pilgrim Vladimir waiting for God at the top of an imaginary mountain; or that the actor playing Pozzo is supposed to generate, in the "mind's eye" of the audience, the image of a pathetic (or insufferable) ham. In many cases, this dual nature of the virtual performance (referent of the text and sign of an outside referent) is in no way problematic; the reader simply postulates that the ultimate outside referent is the same as the initial literary referent, at least insofar as the principal meaning is concerned. If his initial reading yielded God as referent of Godot, a pilgrim as the referent of Vladimir, an earthly, emotional, ambitious, pathetic character as the referent of Pozzo, a mountain road as their meeting place, and a story of believers and disbelievers as the meaning of the play, then his virtual performance will manipulate the verbal and stage signs so that the virtual audience will end up with a similar set of referents. (Such a practice is generally justified by a pretended loyalty to the author, and provides arguments for critics who claim to be able to discuss a future [virtual] performance of a play on the basis of the written text.) Yet an actual performance is not the translation of a text. It is a social act, and though it uses the text as its pretext, its motivation and intention cannot help being primarily social or psychological (profit, self-expression, the need to make an ideological statement, professional success, and so forth). Motivation and intention often play a crucial role in shaping the final referents of the performance, imposing a meaning different from the literary meaning. A specific ideological commitment (political or sexual), for example, can use the text of Godot in order to advance a particular cause such as political freedom or homosexual rights. Godot, in such cases, would be identified pessimistically as the embodiment of the ideal, or optimistically as the embodiment of the competing ideal. The rest belongs to imagination, and only Theatre knows its limits. I can only suggest, for the first instance, a prison court-yard setting, guards on a ramp above, Pozzo as an army officer, Vladimir in army fatigues; and, behind the massive Gate, through which Pozzo enters, a pastoral landscape, etc. For the second instance, one would probably rely on nudity, projected images, suggestive decorations, scrims, screams, and so forth. *Godot* does not lend itself particularly to such a performance, but it could be done. And if such happens to be the intention of a particular reader, his virtual performance of *Godot* will be oriented by his committed meaning, since it will contain an abundance of stage signs which no other reader could have foreseen, or imagined, and which certainly cannot be deduced from the written text of the play. One may add that these signs, as always in theatre, inevitably contaminate and transform other signs, especially verbal (that is, text) signs, so that one cannot speak of two meanings but of one.

For such virtual performances, where signs are dictated by externally defined referents, identification becomes arbitrary. Each reader's visualization contains too many individual properties and signs to insure effective communication. There is no discussion possible. By the same token, all referents become elusive for all but a single reader, dreams waiting for a future performance. In other words, one cannot find a referent for such virtual performances; one should not discuss it, and critical discourse ought to avoid it. Of course, there are other virtual performances which rely on the literary referents, and present no problem in identification and communication. And no doubt many mixed categories lie between the two extremes. But why look for their referents? The identification we have seen is all the more successful when the virtual performance keeps closer to the literary reading; so why not be satisfied with the literary referent, as the only one which can be safely grasped?

V. Conclusion

The preceding observations were intended to help clarify the function of referents in theatre. They entailed redefinition of a number of basic notions and scrutiny of referential processes at work in a specific play. This analytical operation, based on the hypothesis that plays should be read as a part of the theatrical process and not as a literary genre, brings me to a startling conclusion. The only safe way to deal with referents in theatre under present circumstances is to keep to the literary referents. No doubt, an extensive verbal transcription of a performance may supply the possibility of discussing theatrical referents; but such a transcription becomes itself a literary text, and the supposedly theatrical referent becomes largely literary. This does not mean, however, that plays should be read as literature. A theatrical reading, especially a semiotic reading, may indeed lead to a clarification of one related problem so far unexplored: the likelihood that a particular play will generate performances with referents close to or remote from the literary referents. Because the referents of performances, virtual or real, seem to elude present critical discourse (at least as a topic for scholarly discussion), it is all the more important to assess the practical influence literary referents (which *can* be studied) may have on future productions. One way of approaching this problem is to rely on the experience of theatre critics by examining their reviews of actual performances of particular plays; on this impressionistic basis, some plays appear to generate a whole range of referents while others generate only a limited number which a literary reading would yield as well. Such an approach, however, does not offer any basis for comparison between plays, since the range of referents observed on stage may simply correspond to the potential derived from the written texts; plays obviously differ in their degree of complexity, ambiguity, looseness, and so on, to the same extent as novels or poems. Furthermore, the reasons for repeated performances of a play depend on many factors, and likewise, the possibility of a comprehensive range of referents. Thus, I have identified elsewhere some of the properties of a written text which stimulate (or impede) the transformation of its verbal signs by stage signs, thus increasing the likelihood of productions. But plays with a higher "theatricality quotient" do not necessarily invite a change in, or departure from, the literary referent, although they make it likelier. *Godot* is a very theatrical play which has had many original productions, yet, so far as I am aware, even the most innovative have been derived directly from a literary reading of the text, without the interference of extraneous issues such as I suggested for my two improbable virtual performances. Perhaps, then, some plays, *Godot* included, privilege literary referents, despite, or rather because of, their inherent theatricality? Maybe the least theatrical plays are in fact the most likely to generate referents totally alien to the text? Or, finally, perhaps the answer lies not in any property of a given play, but in the encounter between some properties of the text and social concerns at a particular moment of history? Whatever the case, any further exploration of this problem obviously cannot rely on the evidence of the critical reaction to actual performances, but must focus instead on a careful reading of plays as plays, that is, as part of the whole theatrical process, in which the verbal signs already exist in a state of potential transformation by the stage signs. A successful analysis of the stability of literary referents of a play may then perhaps help solve another basic problem recently raised by Steen Jansen: the permissible limits of stage transformations of a text.[24] When does a production of *Godot* no longer qualify as a production of *Godot*? Can one determine a "field" of a dramatic work, within which all possible productions define the total potential of that work, and beyond which another work emerges? Is it conceivable that the literary referent, today's *parent pauvre* of theatre semiotics, holds the key to that problem?

NOTES

1. See J. Alter, "From Text to Performance," *Poetics Today* 2:3 (1981), 113–139.

2. One of the most successful accounts of this type, M. Corvin's description and analysis of D. Benoin's avant-garde production of *George Dandin*, while quite impressive in its wealth of detail and persuasive in its argument, nevertheless remains one man's experience, not necessarily shared by others. See M. Corvin, "Sémiologie et spectacle," *Organon 80* (Lyon: CERT, 1980), 93–152.

3. Cf. J. L. Austin, *How to Do Things with Words* (Oxford: Oxford University Press, 1962), especially pp. 93, 96, 135–136, 141–143; John R. Searle, *Speech Acts: An Essay in the Philosophy of Language* (Cambridge and London: Cambridge University Press, 1969), especially pp. 23, 26, 77–78, 89, 158–162, and p. 172 on the referring function of proper names; Willard Van Orman Quine, *Word and Object* (Cambridge, Mass.: The M.I.T. Press, 1960), especially pp. 112 and 119–121; P. F. Strawson, *Logico-Linguistic Papers* (London: Methuen, 1971), especially pp. 1–27.

4. Thus Searle, *Speech Acts*, p. 77, accepts as an axiom of reference that whatever is referred to *must exist*. See also Quine, p. 112. Most of the controversy concerns the notoriously bald king of France, statements shown to be false, neither true nor false, infelicitous, unsatisfactory, etc.

5. The seminal work in this field was no doubt J. Woods, *The Logic of Fiction* (The Hague: Mouton, 1974), but a good survey of recent work on referring in fiction is provided by the April 1979 issue of *Poetics* (Vol. 8, Nos. 1–2), where Jens Ihwe and Hannes Rieser's "Normative and Descriptive Theory of Fiction: Some Contemporary Issues" (pp. 63–84) and Robert Howell's "Fictional Objects: How They Are and How They Aren't" (pp. 129–179) offer an excellent overview of latest controversies and issues.

6. See Richard Routley "The Semantic Structure of Fictional Discourse," *Poetics* Vol. 8, Nos. 1–2 (1979), 9, and Ihwe and Rieser, p. 68; R. Howell, pp. 134–136.

7. Cf. Howell, pp. 172–173, who refers to an activity of the imagination, but does not limit it to strict "visualizations" since it may also involve conceptualizations.

8. Oswald Ducrot and Tzvetan Todorov, *Dictionnaire encyclopédique des sciences du langage* (Paris: Seuil, 1972), p. 133 (*Signe*).

9. Jacques Dubois *et al.*, *Dictionnaire de linguistique* (Paris: Larousse, 1973), p. 415: "On appelle référent ce à quoi renvoie un signe linguistique dans la réalité extra-linguistique."

10. Cf. Michael Issacharoff, "Labiche, la farce et la sémiotique," *Saggi e Ricerche di Letteratura Francese* XIX (1980), 209–221: "Il est indispensable, en utilisant ce concept de référent, de s'en tenir au sens linguistique propre; . . . pour que l'on puisse parler de *référent*, il faut qu'une *référence verbale* soit faite explicitement" (p. 211).

11. C. K. Ogden and I. A. Richards, *The Meaning of Meaning*, 8th ed. (New York: Harcourt, Brace, 1956), p. 5: "The word 'thing' is unsuitable for the analysis here undertaken, because in popular usage it is restricted to material substances. . . . It has seemed desirable, therefore, to introduce a technical term to stand for whatever we may be thinking of or referring to. . . . The word 'referent,' therefore, has been adopted." Elsewhere, Issacharoff (who has written several articles on theatrical reference) underwrites Strawson's definition: "We very commonly use expressions of certain kinds to mention or refer to some individual

person or single object or particular event or place or process; in the course of doing what we should normally describe as making a statement about that person, object, place, event, or process. I shall call this way of using expressions the 'uniquely referring use.' '' "Espaces mimétiques, espaces diégétiques," *Sartre et la mise en signe*, Issacharoff and Vilquin, eds. (Paris: Klincksieck, and Lexington: French Forum, 1982), p. 66.

12. Patrice Pavis, *Dictionnaire du Théâtre* (Paris: Éditions Sociales, 1980), pp. 368–370 (*Signe théâtral*).

13. Anne Ubersfeld, *Lire le théâtre* (Paris: Éditions Sociales, 1977), pp. 35–38.

14. In fact Ogden and Richards strongly opposed Saussure's scheme because, they claim, as a result "the process of interpretation is included by definition in the sign," and the scheme, "by neglecting entirely the things for which signs stand, was from the beginning cut off from any contact with scientific methods of verification" (pp. 5–6). As for Peirce, while acknowledging the interest of his extensive analysis of the sign, they criticize his cumbersome conceptual apparatus which discourages practical applications (pp. 279–290).

15. Thus Mukarovsky, studying an art object as a sign, distinguishes: 1. a signifier (to be perceived), 2. an *aesthetic* "signification" (coded in the collective consciousness), and 3. a relationship to a thing signified (in the total social, cultural, historical context). See Jan Mukarovsky, "Art as Semiotic Fact," *Semiotics of Art: Prague School Contributions*, L. Matejka and I. Titunik, eds. (Cambridge, Mass.: The M.I.T. Press, 1976), p. 9. His "signification" no doubt corresponds to the signified, but why must it be aesthetic? And why, again, reduce the referent (i.e., the "thing signified") to a historical reality, however mediated by cultural factors? Other Prague semioticians who specifically studied theatre, anticipating by several decades the current scholarship in that field, hardly used Mukarovsky's scheme, and in general focused their studies on relations between signs rather than on the referential problem. Cf. (in the same volume) the articles by Jindrich Honzl, Jiri Veltrusky, and Karel Brusak.

16. My use of the word "property" is borrowed from formal semantics, but does not imply commitment to that discipline. Terms such as "quality," "aspect," or "feature," for example, though synonymous, have confusing connotations.

17. Ogden and Richards speak in a similar vein of engrams, an unnecessary complication. It suffices to postulate that memory contains, in the form of representations, visualized or conceptualized experiences (personal or second-hand) which add up to a Representation of Reality, consisting of signs belonging to many systems. How a particular sign triggers the association with some of these representations is not pertinent here. It is more important to note that such associations, and the resulting additional attribution of properties to the referent, do not essentially vary with the real or fictional nature of the referent.

Thus, even a very concrete table perceived by sender and receiver at the same time is not necessarily identified by them with all the same properties. A table simultaneously referred to by the utterance "this table" and a pointing gesture may be seen differently by two persons and attributed different additional properties (rustic vs. elegant, small vs. big, etc.). *A fortiori*, real people, living or dead, though easily identifiable within a homogeneous social group, obviously cannot be expected to have similar properties attributed to them by the sender and various receivers, since everyone relies on a different network of representations. What was the color of Churchill's eyes? Was he flexible or rigid? Of course, one may object that most properties added in the "mind's eye" are somehow relevant to the topic of the discourse, and that such relevant properties can be expected to be generally shared. While this is largely correct, and, of course, insures easy identification of historical characters or personal acquaintances, the same observation can be made about fictional characters, say Anna Karenina who, for twentieth-century Americans who have read the novel, is probably perceived with additional properties similar to their representation of a Russian aristocrat of the nineteenth century. In both situations, however, there always remains the possibility of some variation, which in each case may cause a significant diversity of referents.

18. By 'normal circumstances,' I mean those in which there is no particular ambiguity as to the author of the quoted speech (as in some "new novels") or its mode of existence

(spoken, written, imaginary, etc.). Furthermore, and arbitrarily for the sake of a clear argument, I am assuming here as elsewhere that sender and receivers (author and all readers) not only share the same linguistic code, but have similar competence in that code—a totally implausible assumption which, however, underlies all critical discussion. Finally, I am also excluding from these considerations all problems related to the existential (social) circumstances under which the quoted speech may be sent and received. The entire notion of historical relativity and resulting variations is taken for granted, and as such, discounted.

19. In theatrical readings, of course, the quoted speech, placed on a stage and attributed to an actor, becomes totally unstable: one knows how voice, pitch, intonation, tempo, and accompanying gestures can alter any quoted speech! A literary reading generally eschews such speculations, and approaches the quoted speech as the most reliable element of a narrative, which may explain the prevalence of dialogues in so-called popular literature. That the quoted speech has its own referents, when it is referential, is not here at issue.

20. I shall be using the term "visualization" as an abbreviation for "in-the-mind's-eye representation," implying not only visual but also auditory, olfactory, tactile representation, where relevant, and even "conceptualization" when the representation deals with more abstract notions such as feelings, ideas, and so forth.

21. By a complex sign, I mean the totality of discrete signs, and their relations, which relate, or are related by a reader, to a single referent, in this case Vladimir. Whether the proper name *Vladimir* is itself a sign, or a "rigid indicator," is irrelevant in this respect. In practice, the proper name functions during the literary reading as a property, and in most cases as one of the essential properties composing the concept of Vladimir, coded in the ideal dictionary of fictional characters as a character in Beckett's *Waiting for Godot*. The referent of this sign (signifier and signified) is then the Vladimir that the sender or receiver perceives (with some additional properties) as having a particular existence in the world referred to by the play.

22. Three observations are essential here:

1. The meaning thus presented, at a very high level of reduction, must not be understood to be in any way privileged among many other meanings which could be suggested for *Godot*. In fact, it is probably one of the least original (though most popular) interpretations, which is why I have chosen it to illustrate the procedure. Among other meanings, similarly derived, one may even include the following "ambiguous" (though not meaningless) explanation, based on the "daring hypothesis" (suggested by the author) that Godot cannot be identified: "The story of men who are waiting for something which could be anything, and of those who are not waiting for anything." It should be observed that literary readings provide many meanings, and that a play read as literature remains largely an open work.

2. Obviously, the process of reduction, shown here in its end result, may follow various strategies, so long as it satisfies the requirement of integrating various referents into a coherent unit or story. The choice of strategies depends on the reader's (critic's) preferences, gifts, and internalized models of interpretative approaches (e.g., Souriau's system of functions, Greimas's actantial model). My own method, leading to a reductive account of Godot quite different from that which I am presenting here, is based on a theory of dramatic units whereby Godot is identified as "the meaning of life" (See J. Alter, "En codant Godot," *Sémiologie de la Représentation*, ed. André Helbo [Brussels: Éditions Complexe, 1975] pp. 42–62).

3. The "meaning" must not be confused with the notion of a "summary," though when very simplified, the two may appear similar. A detailed summary does not clarify the meaning, whereas a short summary, because it must select and simplify, often involves the elaboration of a meaning.

23. Similarly, cinematographic practices in styles of acting and types of characters such as a "bum" (Chaplin, for example), and so forth.

24. Cf. Steen Jansen's paper, "Texte dramatique et représentation scénique," read at the Congress of the British Comparative Literature Association in Canterbury, England, November 18, 1980.

V.

TOPOLOGICAL POETICS
ELUARD'S "LA VICTOIRE DE GUERNICA"

Jean-Jacques Thomas

> On April 26, 1937, the German air force, acting under the orders of General Franco, bombed and almost destroyed the defenseless city of Guernica on a crowded market day. This first example of modern mass bombing, during the Spanish Civil War, was a grim foretaste of what would happen on a larger scale in World War II.[1]

Of all the military atrocities perpetrated between the two world wars, the bombing of Guernica probably had the greatest impact upon the writers and artists of that era.[2] Fixed in time:

> *Le 26 avril 1937, jour de marché, dans les premières heures de l'après-midi, les avions allemands au service de Franco bombardèrent Guernica durant trois heures et demie par escadrilles se relevant tour à tour;*[3]

[In the early afternoon of April 26th (market day) Guernica was bombed for three and a half hours by relays of German Air Squadrons under General Franco's orders;]

and in space:

> *Guernica. C'est une petite ville de Biscaye, capitale traditionnelle du Pays basque. C'est là que s'élevait le chêne, symbole sacré des traditions et des libertés basques. Guernica n'a qu'une importance historique et sentimentale.*[4]

[Guernica: a small town and the traditional capital of the Basque country. It was here that grew the oak of Guernica, sacred symbol of Basque traditions and Basque freedom. Guernica's importance is purely historical and sentimental.]

the reality of this event was bound to attract the attention of the author of *Yeux fertiles* and *Donner à voir* who held that poetry should first and foremost reveal "le visage de la vérité"[5] [the face of truth]. The event obviously lent itself to journalistic writing and was reported in great detail.[6] Nonetheless it was to this same event (perhaps better suited to the epic form since it so magnified reality) that the poet turned for material he later exploited to symbolic effect. While depleting the events of their referential value, this symbolic effect progressively drains them of their reality, transposing them into a system founded on language universals and totally independent of the mimetic event which originally triggered production of the poem's verbal system.

The mere name *Guernica* binds the text to reality since, as Derrida points out, it acts on a "monumémoire"[7] or "monumemory" and constitutes a whole store of information related to this particular event.

Now, for there to be reference, the referent (the sign's third element and its only non-symbolic one—contingent on objective reality and thus "parasitic"), must figure explicitly in the text so that its textual presence can act as an extra-linguistic shifter, as something which speaks about reality while acting as a support for the other purely symbolic constituents of the verbal sign.

The name *Guernica* constitutes the poem's only historical emblem: it indicates the constraints and imperatives of time and space, imposed by history, and acts both as milestone and textual boundary. Against this background of reality the text constructs an autonomous sign system of its own. Thus from the title onwards, the exclusively referential value of the name *Guernica* is negated since, though primarily designating an atrocious massacre, the effect is counterbalanced by its link with "victoire"—"victory" being a term which contradicts what "we know" about events in Guernica as reported in the press.

This system of bipolar opposition provides a preliminary model for the entire text in that it is based on the principle of contradiction. Thus the referential presence underlined by *Guernica* exists for the sole purpose of allowing the opposite pole (signaled by *victoire*) to be developed. *Guernica*'s denotation and connotations have no value *per se*, since here Eluard is not concerned with pseudomimesis of the type found in the Annals of History.

Inevitably, though, one must recognize the proper name's particular function in this system. As Benveniste points out, the proper name's distinguishing linguistic feature is that, by its very nature, it incorporates its own actualization and self-determination, these being intrinsic components of any proper name. Whence the special referential status of a text engendered by a verbal component of this type. In an utterance such as *la victoire du génocide* [the victory of the genocide] one could recognize a contradiction similar to the one expressed in *la Victoire de Guernica*. There is, however, a fundamental difference between the two: "genocide" refers to an atopical and, alas, universal reality, while *Guernica* implies the reader's encyclopedic knowledge—knowledge which cannot possibly be anhistoric. The poem's contradiction, that is to say its *meaning*, is, of course, clear without referring to the event. But the event's importance (it justifies the text in relation to a particular system of meaning) in no way diminishes it as a referential anchor, one which functions as a *trigger* rather than a matrix. This is demonstrated by the fact that when Eluard wanted to commemorate the actual historic event, its site and meaning, he eliminated *victory* from the title (and consequently the principle of contradiction the word provided), keeping only "Guernica." This transformation in turn alters the way the text is treated: its meaning fades and what was elliptic, paratactic, and antithetical in the poem becomes direct, explanatory, and justificatory in the commemorative discourse:

> *On a tout lu dans les journaux en buvant son café; quelque part en Europe, une légion d'assassins écrase la fourmilière humaine. On se représente mal un enfant éventré, une femme décapitée, un homme vomissant tout son sang d'un seul coup.*[8]

> [People read all about it in the newspaper over coffee at breakfast: somewhere in Europe a legion of murderers had crushed a human anthill. It is hard to imagine a child disembowelled, a woman beheaded, or a man suddenly vomiting all his blood.]

Whereas the poem only exists by virtue of the tension created between deceptively vague reference on the one hand, and a system of symbols that refer to a highly specific context on the other, the commemorative discourse refers only to the specific event. If one compares the two versions, written fourteen years apart, the differences between the two modes of writing are quite obvious from the very first verse.

> Beau monde des masures
> De la mine et des champs
>
> [Beautiful world of hovels
> mines and fields]

becomes, in the second version,

> *Les gens de Guernica sont de petites gens. Ils vivent dans leur ville depuis bien longtemps. Leur vie est composée d'une goutte de richesse; et d'un flot de misère.*[9]

> [The people of Guernica are humble folk. They have been living in their town for a very long time. Their life is made up of a drop of wealth and a flood of poverty.]

Although in 1919 Eluard wrote in *Littérature* "Let us reduce, transform the displeasing language which satisfies mere talkers, language as dead as the crowns which sit upon our equally dead brows," and goes on to propose an aesthetics "aiming at an immediate rapport between the object and the person who sees it" *(Physique de la Poésie*[10] [Physics of Poetry]), when he speaks of the event itself, he cannot help developing an explanatory, metadiscursive level of discourse. Even when interpolating fragments of the original poem in the prose commentary, he feels it necessary to modify them so that the gap between the two not be too obvious. Thus:

Ils vous ont fait payer le pain
Le ciel la terre l'eau le sommeil
Et la misère
De votre vie

[They made you pay for the bread
the sky the earth the water the sleep
and the misery
of your life with your life]

becomes

Ils vous ont fait payer le pain
De votre vie
Ils vous ont fait payer le ciel la terre l'eau le sommeil
Et même la misère noire
De votre vie.[11]

[They made you pay for the bread
of your life with your life
they made you pay for the sky the earth the water the sleep
and even the black misery
of your life with your life.]

The repetition of *De votre vie* and the interpolation of *même* introduce a hierarchical distinction, whereas originally the mere juxtaposition and accumulation of words suggested equivalent, similar components, all equally essential to the life of the *beau monde*. "Bread" becomes something one acquires, the result of work; "sky," "earth," "water," and "sleep" are something given. *Même* is the author's intervention and a comment since the adverb hails both a reiteration and an amplification, so that *misère* becomes a sort of superlative in relation to the other terms, as is further underlined by the addition of *noire*. Or, if one were to use the terminology of traditional rhetoric, one might say that whereas a metabole suffices in "La Victoire de Guernica," "Guernica" is more explicit and takes the reader from one step to the next. And in case the reader or listener did not notice these distinctions, the prose commentary points them out quite unequivocally:

Leur vie est composée de tout petits bonheurs et d'un très grand souci: celui du lendemain. Demain il faut manger et demain il faut vivre. Aujourd'hui, l'on espère. Aujourd'hui, l'on travaille.[12]

[Their life is composed of small joys and one great worry: that of tomorrow. Tomorrow they must eat and tomorrow they must live. Today they hope. Today they work.]

This type of discourse is quite foreign to that of our poem, since, as Nicole Charbois notes, in the poem

"Eluard makes an utterance, then remains silent: no comment whatsoever. . . . Picasso conveyed the violence by the shrieking and convulsed colours and shapes he used, but Eluard chose silence to make us aware of this violence. He holds in his cry, masters his language—but he says all."[13]

There is no need for further demonstration since examples so far given abundantly prove the difference between the way the poem and the commemorative text treat the referential given. The didascalic inscription differs too: in the poem the symbolism generated by the referential trigger leads one to the meaning without there being any need for circumstantial reference. In the commemorative text, reference is the force which maintains the legitimate meaning, controlling and producing it by the discourse's underlying naturalism.

Thus a study of "La Victoire de Guernica" is also a study of a language system whose only postulate is to negate precise reference and endow it with a symbolic importance which transcends any *mimesis* of the specific, transposing it into a universal and anhistoric mode.

In our introduction, we pointed out the *antithetical* character of the title and, to that end, emphasized that the antithesis was not founded solely on the semantic qualities of *Guernica*, since this word, being a proper name, retains its essential designatory quality and implies, in the process of perception, the actualization of a set of extra-linguistic connotations that are indissociable from its denotative function. Indeed it is this aspect which creates the poem's special status, and leads me to place it in the category of *topological poetics*, since the fundamental trigger of the poem's system appears as a sign-signal. This process is distinct from the poetic practice of opposing two verbal signs in such a way that each is deprived of its complete sign status. For example, when Leiris writes *Étrusques aux frusques étriquées* [Etruscans in tight togs], *Étrusques* is only used so that it can appear as a reverse contraction (or porte-manteau word) of *frusques étriquées* and vice versa: *étr(iquées fr)usques*. Here language is only fighting itself: no extratextual reference is ever involved in this type of game which never goes beyond the simple sign's specific properties—that of the meeting of signifier and signified.

It would not be rash to claim that once the title's emblematic effect and its value as a referential trigger are established, the poem's significance and its role as a "universal and atemporal monument" are created in a language which brings into play an exclusively verbal system. Extratextual reference plays only a minor role in relation to the poem's main preoccupation, which is to show language pitted against itself. Thus in topological poetics, the status of reference is that of a pretext which legitimizes and justifies the creation of a complex sign whose referent is the excluded third component. Nonetheless its impact is felt marginally all along the symbolic chain, since, within the framework of the co-presence of an encyclopedic knowledge in each linguistic element's field, an allusion to the name *Guernica*—and, by the same token, to its referential context—can be attributed to each element.

This explains how, in the first stanza, *masures, mine,* and *champs* [hovels, mine, and fields] can be seen as offering a precise description of the lifestyle of Guernica's inhabitants; though one would have to be sufficiently well-informed to assess the accuracy of such a statement—a geographer's or sociologist's task rather than a literary commentator's. In fact, *masures, mine,* and *champs* all serve as general signs for a hard and laborious life; they are used in order to contrast with *beau monde,* a fixed expression which in French usually designates the idle, elegant world of the privileged. The sole purpose of this antithetical disjunction is to herald a theme which runs through the entire poem: namely, that the little these people possessed was a "treasure" compared to their plight after the disaster. This theme of life seen as a treasure as long as there is hope returns covertly in stanzas V, VIII, IX, XII and overtly in stanza XIII in a paradoxical formulation accentuated by the homophony of the two rhyming words:

> Hommes réels pour qui le désespoir
> Alimente le feu dévorant de l'espoir
>
> [Real men for whom despair
> feeds the devouring fire of hope.]

The importance given here to *espoir*—and it is of some intertextual comfort that Malraux was later to choose it as the title of his own account of the Spanish Civil War—brings to the text a set of variants such as: *feuilles vertes* [green leaves], green being associated with hope in French; *de printemps* [of spring], the season of germination; and *lait pur* [pure milk], *milk* is a metonym for motherhood, for promise, and *pure* contributes the image's meliorative value by connoting natural innocence and fragility.

The thematic pole opposing this *beau monde* is obviously *mort* [dead] and *vide* [empty], lines 6–7, which transform *feuilles vertes . . . dans les yeux* [green leaves in their eyes], line 20, into *roses rouges dans les yeux* [red roses in their eyes], lines 26–27. For here "red" is doubly overdetermined, first by *sang* [blood], line 28, which follows it, introducing violence into the field of utterance, and, second, by the fact that *rose rouge* is a metonym for extreme intensity and also the very end of a cycle.[14] A metaphoric extension of this opposition between foliage and flower is embodied in the formula which contains the poem's exhortation: *ouvrons ensemble le dernier bourgeon de l'avenir* [let us open the future's last leaf bud together]. *Bourgeon* [bud] refers directly to "leaf," to "green" and thus to "hope," whereas in the flower system the precise term for bud would be *bouton* rather than *bourgeon.*

The asyndetic construction of the third stanza and of its first line introduces a new cumulative series of notations which are presented as a figurative description not of a lifestyle, this time, but of the inhabitants themselves—though the description's "naturalist" flavor is again transformed into a negative value by an exclusively verbal semantic artifice. However, unlike the first stanza where the semantic opposition to the "beautiful world" was direct, disjunction now occurs within the syntactic framework implying the restitution of the fixed expression "bon à quelque chose" [good for something] and indicates a positive value, good for action or a particular state. Here *feu* [fire] and *froid* [cold] represent the entire paradigm of climatic conditions since they evoke its two extremes. *Bons au feu . . . bons au froid* [good for the fire good for the cold] is thus the interchangeable equivalent of "good for all weather" as far as meaning is concerned, but adds a certain concreteness to the utterance. The accumulation which follows it brings together a group of negative elements: *refus, injures, coups* [refusals, insults, blows] which, through analogical contamination, give *nuit* [night] (an *a priori* neutral element) a similar pejorative value that it retains from this first context when it recurs a second time in *la couleur monotone de notre nuit* [the monotonous color of our night]; "monotonous," usually laden with negative presuppositions, confirms this value. Thus the effect of semantic contrast relies upon the opposition between "good," considered as positive, and the negative value of the elements to which this term is structurally attached and which all indicate the natural or man-made atrocities these people suffered.

This type of syntactic dislocation of a fixed structure is used again in stanza V, since the syntagm *de votre vie* [of your life] can be linked equally well to both the preceding nouns (*le pain, le ciel . . . la misère de votre vie* [the bread, the sky . . . the misery of your life]), and to the verb if one allows for a stylistic inversion such as *Ils vous ont fait payer de votre vie le pain Le ciel . . .* [They made you pay with your life for the bread, the sky . . .]. In this case, the phrase would imply a simple *quid pro quo*, whereas the first structure would elaborate upon the idea of "treasure," by insinuating that "they" [*ils*] have so indulged in excess that they even put a price on the most complete destitution. This interpretation would concur with *ils exagèrent* [they exaggerate] in line 18. One should note, however, that any partial interpretation matters little here: for the dislocation of the syntactic structure creates ambiguity and, unlike what happens in the second stanza, where the ensuing disjunction concretizes the semantic opposition between the two poles (good/bad), in stanza five, dislocation reinforces meaning to the point of redundancy, since the co-presence of the two formulations serves to reinforce both of them and corroborate the notion of excess, being themselves a type of "overflow" of meaning.

In both cases, the use of syntactical possibilities forces language into a state of internal ambivalence and the resulting dichotomy removes any possibility of direct, unitary denoting: it produces a meaning which establishes either redundancy or opposition, as the case may be. It seems clear, then, that referential mimesis, always based on an utterance's direct meaning, is overshadowed by a symbolic process which introduces a certain number of exclusively verbal distinctions which then proceed to take over.

The asyntactic utterance in line 8, *La mort coeur renversé* [death heart overturned], derives its force from the encounter of verbal effects on different levels. The absence of an explicit grammatical or semantic link between the two parts is naturally perceived to be a case of symbolic disorder, the precise nature of their relation depending on how the reader construes it. Yet one cannot overlook the well-known expression *coeur renversé*, which adds to its physical meaning (upside down, upset, or even knocked over) a quite special psychological, figurative value making it the semantic equivalent of "emotionally upset" and "overwhelmed."

Such an interpretation would create a consecutive link between "death" and "upset heart": it is death that upsets. But *renversé* is also a synonym of "changed to the exact opposite," which is precisely what death has done in relation to the victims' former state. In this case *renversé* would simply appear as an expansion of "death," with a more limited meaning focusing on the result of the latter. Naturally one would still have to explain its association with "heart" since, given this meaning, "upset" and "heart" cannot constitute a fixed expression. But one can envisage that the sequence *coeur renversé* (taken in the sense of upside-down heart), instead of being a pseudo-mimetic representation of the victims' situation, plays an emblematic role in relation to "death" and that both terms could be joined to make a heraldic description. If a "beating heart" is a symbol of life, *coeur renversé* is its opposite: the blazon of death. The structure *La mort coeur renversé* would thus introduce the bearer (the enemy) and his sign, his "speaking arms." This brings us back, indirectly, to the original context, war; and also introduces the adversary, an undefined *Ils* [They] mentioned in the fifth stanza. Here again meaning results from symbolic densification (compression) and cannot, therefore, be reduced to singular, unequivocal reference.

Just as the hovels, mine, and fields could be seen as referring directly to the real world of Guernica's inhabitants, so the characterization in the sixth stanza could make us think that these are fragments of description referring metonymically to the chronicle's "nazi pilots." In fact the undefined "They" marks the moment at which the poem breaks loose from its specific frame of reference and introduces a generic dimension devoid of any specific actualization. What appear are thus generic qualities—hypocrisy, vanity, avarice. The opacity of *Ils saluaient les cadavres* [They saluted the corpses] hides a semantic short-cut which plays on the choice of a term indicative of finality instead of something in progress as expected.[15] "Corpses" can refer just as well to "dead heroes" as to victims of military atrocities—but that is beside the point. What the expression "They saluted the corpses" does indicate is a fetishistic and ritualized (salute) taste for death, the complete opposite of "life" (fifth stanza) and thus of the positive pole presented here as the only remaining goods of (future) victims. So it is that the overall effect of these connotations is to establish a semantic field based on the notion of excess. This is confirmed semantically in line 18 by *Ils persévèrent ils exagèrent ils ne sont pas de notre monde* [They persevere they exaggerate they are not of our world]. "They are not of our world" doubly defines the definition since, over and above the opposition life/death, the utterance also incorporates the opposition excess/destitution continued in the stanzas which follow. The "leaves," "spring," and "pure milk," in addition to their previously mentioned values, characterize women and children and so connote the victims' natural simplicity (these victims being "real men") in contrast, let us say, to *sou* in line 15; for a cent connotes a society which is organized, artificially based on monetary exchange (a society of conventions, just as the use of "salute" has already indicated).

The antithetical formulation of stanza XI

> La peur et le courage de vivre et de mourir
> La mort si difficile et si facile

[The fear of living and dying and the courage to do both
death so difficult and so easy]

could be put anywhere in the poem,[16] since it merely restates in an explicitly
paradoxical and abstract formulation what the various concrete expressions have
thus far sought to reveal: living out one's daily life is a continual and hard-won
victory, so precarious that at any moment it may be interrupted. Similarly, death,
always easy, within reach the moment one gives up, is nonetheless relentlessly
deferred by effort and work. As it stands, this statement applies not just to the
inhabitants of Guernica, but to many others, and this explains the way we interpret
"pariahs" (line 36) in the final stanza: as a term used to generalize, it destroys
once and for all the poem's specific meaning and gives it a collective dimension.

If it were still necessary to prove that stanzas VI, VII, XIII, and XIV lead us to
read the poem as a generalization, it would suffice to note that they are the only
ones which do not appear in "Guernica"; that is to say, the only ones excluded
from the substance of the chronicle, since, necessarily, the latter was restricted to
specific events in a particular place at a given time. But this demonstration provided
by "Guernica" is not essential, merely a confirmation, since a careful reading will
undoubtedly reveal that, through this *generalizing process*, the text frees itself of
referential implications. And indeed in each of the poem's sections one notices a
type of formulation which makes retroactive generalization a model of language
function, thereby allowing the text to expel the real and the specific and attain the
general and the universal. Thus each element of a paradigmatic series is picked up
by a term which both resumes and contains the whole series. This term, then, can
be regarded as a condensed version of the series and also appears, retrospectively,
as a particularizing and redundant anticipatory expansion of the series' closing
generic term. Thus *bons à tout* [good for everything], line 5, picks up *bon au feu,
au froid, au refus, à la misère, aux injures, aux coups* [good for the fire, the cold,
refusal, misery, swearing, blows]. *Ils vous ont fait payer . . . la misère* [They made
you pay for your misery] in line 11 picks up *ils vous ont fait payer le pain, le ciel,
la terre, l'eau, le sommeil* [they made you pay for the bread, sky, earth, water,
sleep] of lines 9 and 10; *les femmes les enfants ont le même trésor . . . de durée*
[women and children have the same treasure of lasting], lines 19 and 21, picks up
de feuilles vertes de printemps de lait pur [of green leaves of spring of pure milk]
of line 20; finally *la couleur monotone de notre nuit* [the monotonous color of our
night], line 38, picks up *la mort, la terre, la hideur de nos ennemis* [death, earth,
the hideousness of our enemies] of lines 36 and 37.

The repetition of the process, coupled with the practice of adding juxtaposed
terms, compounds, on a formal level, the semantic value of "monotonous" and
gives the poem a canonic structure typical of the plaintive ballad traditionally used
for the tragic poem. Here, however, instead of being based on a repeated refrain,
the repetition is maintained by the reappearance of the same asyndetic syntactic
structures and by the use of a general term to sum up the paradigmatic series. The
ensuing monotony is only broken by the final line *Nous en aurons raison* [We will
overcome them]: a collective appeal with which the poet associates himself—something already anticipated by *notre monde* [our world], line 18, *ouvrons ensemble*

[let us work together], line 35, and *nos ennemis* [our enemies], line 37, and which is another way of subverting Guernica's topical specificity "your life," "your death" (in lines 12 and 7) to give it a general and symbolic dimension. Moreover, one can hardly fail to notice that the exceptional quality of the last line conforms to the pattern of the *envoi* or *coda* which constitutes the traditional climactic ending of this type of poem.

Eluard concludes "Guernica" by extending the lesson of this particular agony to other grimly remembered landmarks: *"Guernica comme Oradour et comme Hiroshima sont les capitales de la paix vivante"* [Guernica like Oradour and like Hiroshima is the capital of living peace].[17]

The subject then broadens, and Guernica returns as one of several examples of a pattern of conflict which transcends all particular circumstances: *"Guernica! l'innocence aura raison du crime"* (Guernica! innocence will overcome crime).[18] From this standpoint the lessons of "La Victoire de Guernica" and "Guernica" are similar. But in "Guernica" Eluard is forced to abandon the chronicle form so that he can proclaim the event's universal and perennial quality. The referential model is brutally stripped of its specific value and becomes confused with other Guernicas, thus losing its particularity and all the spatio-temporal characteristics which make it a unique place and subject. In "La Victoire de Guernica" the process is more closely linked to intrinsically symbolic procedures and it is language which, by exclusively verbal operations (opposition, expansion, condensing, etc.), strips specific extra-linguistic reference of its naturalistic identity, thus transforming what is said into a victorious song of hope which is both plural and universal.

La Victoire de Guernica

I.	Beau monde des masures	
	De la mine et des champs	
II.	Visages bons au feu visages bons au froid	
	Aux refus à la nuit aux injures aux coups	
III.	Visages bons à tout	5
	Voici le vide qui vous fixe	
	Votre mort va servir d'exemple	
IV.	La mort coeur renversé	
V.	Ils vous ont fait payer le pain	
	Le ciel la terre l'eau le sommeil	10
	Et la misère	
	De votre vie	
VI.	Ils disaient désirer la bonne intelligence	
	Ils rationnaient les forts jugeaient les fous	
	Faisaient l'aumône partageaient un sou en deux	15
	Ils saluaient les cadavres	
	Ils s'accablaient de politesses	
VII.	Ils persévèrent ils exagèrent ils ne sont pas de notre monde	
VIII.	Les femmes les enfants ont le même trésor	
	De feuilles vertes de printemps et de lait pur	20
	Et de durée	
	Dans leurs yeux purs	

IX.   Les femmes les enfants ont le même trésor
             Dans les yeux
             Les hommes le défendent comme ils peuvent   25
X.   Les femmes les enfants ont les mêmes roses rouges
             Dans les yeux
             Chacun montre son sang
XI.   La peur et le courage de vivre et de mourir
             La mort si difficile et si facile   30
XII.   Hommes pour qui ce trésor fut chanté
             Hommes pour qui ce trésor fut gâché
XIII.   Hommes réels pour qui le désespoir
             Alimente le feu dévorant de l'espoir
             Ouvrons ensemble le dernier bourgeon de l'avenir   35
XIV.   Parias la mort la terre et la hideur
             De nos ennemis ont la couleur
             Monotone de notre nuit
             Nous en aurons raison.

Cours Naturel
Paul Eluard

The Victory of Guernica

I.   High life in hovels
             In mines and in fields
II.   Faces staunch in the fire staunch in the cold
             Against denials the night insults blows
III.   Faces always staunch   5
             Here is the void staring at you
             Your death shall be an example
IV.   Death heart overturned
V.   They made you pay for bread
             Sky earth water sleep   10
             And the poverty
             Of your life
VI.   They said they wanted agreement
             They checked the strong sentenced the mad
             Gave alms divided a farthing   15
             They greeted every corpse
             They overwhelmed each other with politeness
VII.   They insist they exaggerate they are not of our world
VIII.   The women the children have the same treasure
             Of green leaves of spring and of pure milk   20
             And of endurance
             In their pure eyes
IX.   The women the children have the same treasure
             In their eyes
             The men defend it as best they can   25

X.   The women the children have the same red roses
         In their eyes
         All show their blood
XI.   The fear and the courage of living and of dying
         Death so hard and so easy   30
XII.   Men for whom this treasure was extolled
         Men for whom this treasure was spoiled
XIII.   Real men for whom despair
         Feeds the devouring fire of hope
         Let us open together the last bud of the future   35
XIV.   Pariahs
         Death earth and the vileness of our enemies
         Have the monotonous colour of our night
         The day will be ours.

                                                     (Translated by Roland Penrose
                                                     and George Reavey)

NOTES

1. Anthony Blunt, *Picasso's Guernica* (New York and Toronto: Oxford University Press, 1969).

2. Cf. *Les écrivains et la guerre d'Espagne*, ed. Marc Hanrez (Paris: Panthéon Press, Les Dossiers H, 1975).

3. Paul Eluard wrote two texts on the subject of Guernica. "La Victoire de Guernica," the subject of our analysis, was composed in 1937, at the same time that Picasso was working on his famous painting *Guernica*, which was exhibited in the Spanish pavilion at the International Exhibition in Paris in 1937. The poem accompanied the painting. It was first published in *Cahiers d'art*, nos. 1–3, 36, in 1937. The English translation by Roland Penrose and George Reavey appeared in 1938, in the *London Bulletin*, no. 6, 7–8.

The full text of this poem and the translation appear at the end of this chapter. Any subsequent more literal translations are by Terese Lyons.

In 1949, Eluard wrote "Guernica," a text meant to accompany Alain Resnais's film on Picasso's painting. The text was published in *Europe*, nos. 47–48, Oct. 1948, 47–50. All italicized quotations in this chapter have been taken from this second text. The editions of these two poems on which the present study has been based can be found in Paul Eluard, *Oeuvres complètes*, ed. L. Sheler and M. Dumas (Paris: Gallimard, "Pléiade" 1968, 2 vols.). "La Victoire de Guernica" can be found in *Cours naturel*, vol. I, pp. 812–814, and "Guernica" in *Poèmes retrouvés*, vol. II. pp. 913–917.

4. "Guernica," p. 913.

5. "Baudelaire," in *Poèmes retrouvés*, p. 912.

6. Cf. this account of the event in *The Times* (April 1937):

Guernica, the most ancient town of the Basques and the centre of their cultural tradition, was completely destroyed yesterday afternoon by insurgent air raiders. The bombardment of the open town far behind the lines occupied precisely three hours and a quarter, during which a powerful fleet of aeroplanes consisting of three German types, Junkers and Heinkel bombers and Heinkel fighters, did not cease unloading on the town bombs and incendiary projectiles. The fighters, meanwhile, plunged low from above the centre of the town to machinegun those of the civil population who had taken refuge in the fields. The whole of Guernica was soon in flames, except the historic Casa de Juntas, with its rich archives of the Basque race, where the ancient Basque Parliament used to sit. The famous oak of Guernica, the dried old stump of 600 years and the new shoots of this century, was also untouched. Here the kings of Spain used to take the oath to respect the democratic rights [*fueros*] of Vizcaya and in return received a promise of allegiance as suzerains with the democratic title of *Senor*, not *Rey Vizcaya*.

7. A porte-manteau word, coined by Jacques Derrida in *Glas* to designate a *monument à la mémoire*, i.e., a monument in memory (of someone or something).

8. "Guernica," p. 914.

9. Ibid.

10. "Le langage déplaisant qui suffit aux bavards, langage aussi mort que les couronnes à nos fronts semblables, réduisons-le, transformons-le . . . il y aura recherche d'un rapport immédiat entre celui qui voit et ce qui est vu." Paul Eluard, "Les animaux et les hommes," *Littérature* 5, July 1919.

11. "Guernica," p. 913.

12. Ibid., p. 914.

13. Nicole Charbois, "Eluard et Picasso," in *Europe* 525, "Rencontres avec Paul Eluard," January 1973, 188–207.

14. Consider, for example, these famous lines of Malherbe in "Ode à Duperrier sur la mort de sa fille":

> *Et rose, elle a vécu ce que vivent les roses,*
> *L'espace d'un matin.*

15. Cf. in French, "cuire le pain," or in English, "to bake bread," said instead of "cuire la pâte," "to bake dough," the process whose result is the production of bread. Cf. also "percer un trou," "to drill a hole," *vs.* "percer un mur," "to drill (a hole in) a wall."

16. And indeed, in "Guernica," these lines come at the beginning of the poem.

17. "Guernica," p. 917.

18. Ibid.

VI.

RENAMING IN LITERATURE
FACES OF THE MOON

Françoise Meltzer

Frege's distinction between the *sense* (*Sinn*: connotation, meaning) of a sign and its *nominatum* (the object to which it refers) provides an indispensable complement to Saussure's concept of the signified. The *associated image* which Frege attaches to the configurations of reference is crucial in this respect:

> Both the nominatum and the sense of a sign must be distinguished from the associated image. If the nominatum of a sign is an object of sense perception, my image of the latter is an inner picture arisen from memories of sense impressions and activities of mine, internal or external.[1]

Literature poses an immediate problem, because the "nominata" evoked in the text are apparently designated objects, on the one hand, and on the other, are left for the reader to visualize, since they are not objects of sense perception. Moreover, the "associated images" which the literary object evokes in the reader must not interfere with its *customary sense*. The latter is problematic because one may say that an associated image gains strength when the object is described or named, but not physically or directly presented. This is the essence of literature. Indeed, Frege notes that in indirect discourse, what is referred to is not a designated object at all, but rather the customary sense of the sign.[2]

It would follow, then, that literature is an extended form of indirect discourse (narration), because what is referred to within the text is the sense of the sign and *not*, strictly speaking, a designated object. Since, as Frege says, "a sign expresses its sense and designates its nominatum," literature can be said to have no nominata at all, and to deal exclusively in sense and, it will be argued, in associated images. Frege's position is quite explicit:

> A sentence as a whole has perhaps only sense and no nominatum? It may in any case be expected that there are such sentences, just as there are constituents of sentences which do have sense but no nominatum. Certainly, sentences containing proper names without nominata must be of this type. The sentence "Odysseus deeply asleep was disembarked at Ithaca" obviously has a sense. But since it is doubtful as to whether the name "Odysseus" occurring in this sentence has a nominatum, so it is also doubtful

that the whole sentence has one. However, it is certain that whoever seriously regards the sentence either as true or false also attributes to the name "Odysseus" a nominatum, not only a sense; for it is obviously the nominatum of this name to which the predicate is either ascribed or denied. . . . But why do we wish that every proper name have not only a sense but also a nominatum? Why is the proposition alone not sufficient? We answer: because what matters to us is the truth-value. . . . In turning to the question of truth we disregard the artistic appreciation and pursue scientific considerations. (p. 90)

His view that fiction can have no assertoric force or reference is therefore logocentric, in that it assumes that language *outside* of fiction (sentences having both sense and nominata) has truth-value and signifies truth by referring "directly" to a nominatum. The person who regards the sentence about Odysseus as either true or false is attributing a nominatum to the name "Odysseus," but cannot, in Frege's view, ascertain truth-value. In other words, because fiction has no nominata, it is incapable of signifying truth. But the person reading the sentence about Odysseus clearly understands to whom the name "Odysseus" refers, creating what we may call a "cognitive nominatum." If we suspend the logocentric view that language may signify truth, then we may see in literature the mimesis of language's most cherished *fiction*: the notion that there is a logical, fixed connection between signifier and signified. If the language of fiction insists upon creating in the reader what I shall call "cognitive nominata," it does so because it mimics the fiction of language, which insists upon guaranteeing the connection between the signifier and the signified. It is precisely because literature has no "real" nominata that it becomes a fertile field for examining systems of naming. If for Frege literature can only be non-referential, then it becomes all the more intriguing that the reader provides the name "Odysseus" with a nominatum. Thus this essay will disregard "scientific considerations" with their assumptions of "truth value" and pursue "artistic" ones, with their assumptions of suspended belief.

Frege suggests, though does not develop, the implications of his position that literature is without nominata: "It would be desirable to have an expression for signs which have *sense only*. If we call them "icons," then the words of an actor on the stage would be icons; even the actor himself would be an icon" (p. 91). "Icon" is a strange choice of words (the original is *Bilder*), since it suggests an *object* of representation. But Frege seems rather to be emphasizing icon as representation in a more abstract mode: that which signals a sense.

It is to be noted that Frege omits the associated image in these kinds of signs, and yet the term *Bild* means, precisely, image or picture. And Frege is quick to link image to literature: "Surely, art would be impossible without some kinship among human imageries; but just how far the intentions of the poet are realized can never be exactly ascertained" (p. 89). One might say that it is this indefinable kinship among human imageries which allows for language in the first place and, in the second, for writing. The associated image can never be entirely personal and subjective because it is so largely derived from, and inextricably bound with, the sense. In discussing the sense and nominatum, and the subjectivity/kinship dialectic

of associated images, Frege uses a simile: a person viewing the moon through a
telescope. The moon is the nominatum. The "real image" projected by the lens is
the customary sense, and the retinal image in the eye of the observer is the associated
image. He comments:

> The real image inside the telescope, however, is relative; it depends upon the stand-
> point; yet, it is objective in that it can serve several observers. . . . One could elaborate
> the simile by assuming that the retinal image of A could be made visible to B; or A
> could see his own retinal image in a mirror. In this manner one could possibly show
> how a *presentation itself can be made into an object*; but even so, it would never be
> to the (outside) observer what it is to the one who possesses the image. However,
> these lines of thought lead too far afield. (p. 88; my emphasis)

What is to be noted from this passage is the following: the "real" image (customary
sense) in the lens is what permits the retinal image (associated image) in the viewer.
Thus the latter is made possible by the former, and we may add "associated image"
to Frege's "icon." Secondly, *icon* (or *Bild*) in rhetoric traditionally means simile,
or likeness, and it is precisely a simile which Frege uses to make his point.[3] In so
doing, Frege repeats the gesture of fiction vis à vis the assertory. The simile itself
necessitates a "cognitive nominatum" in order for the argument to be grasped. In
this way, then, *Bild* becomes redundant, repeating as both simile and signs-with-
sense-only the *likeness* of sentences with nominata.

But what happens in literature when there is a presentation of a "real" icon—
a portrait? Is this comparable to A seeing his own retinal image in a mirror? Of a
presentation itself being made into an object? If the portrait of a literary character
is presented, then (to continue Frege's simile) the "real image" of the telescope
lens reflects another image of the moon, but not a real moon. In other words, is
the evocation of a portrait in a literary text—a portrait with only textual "presence"—yet another addition to the system within the signifieds? Since the portrait
cannot have a nominatum, is its existence in the text any different from the other
"icons"?

Frege's article on sense and referring concerns itself with proper names only:
"From what has been said it is clear that I here understand by 'sign' or 'name' any
expression which functions as a proper name, whose nominatum accordingly is a
definite object (in the widest sense of this word)" (p. 86). It is at this point, then,
that we depart from Frege, for whom the discussion that follows would be futile,
centered as it is on fiction. Fregean terminology, however, will be retained as a
useful scaffolding, as will the assumptions it betrays.

The actual portrait of a character in a literary work is an icon (simile) for the
individual named in the text. In Madame de Lafayette's novel, *La Princesse de
Clèves*, the title itself is a proper name which refers to the character in the text so
named by the narrator. Here we already have what Frege calls an icon, one for
which the customary sense is not yet established, as yet conjuring up in the reader
only a limited sense and associated image. When the text refers to the portrait of
the princess, however (our sense and image of her have by this point been established

by our reading of the text), we have a double image, neither half of which has a "real" nominatum. The absence of nominata ("real," designated objects) which characterizes literature is thus further problematized by the presentation of a *textually* concretized object: the portrait. For the portrait is the iconization of the textual proper name.

In order to examine the function of the portrait in fiction, or at least part of its function, I have chosen portrait scenes from two French novels, *La Princesse de Clèves* and *Le Rouge et le noir*. While my choice of these two passages is somewhat arbitrary, my purpose is to explore Frege's sign system in the context of textual naming. More precisely, we will be applying Frege's system of references to the very area he discounts as non-referential: fiction.

Strawson noted that the sentence "the so and so is such and such" is neither true nor false if the "so and so" does not exist.[4] In this sense, the proper name in literature (the "so and so") is, as in Frege, a non-existent, since its presentation is limited to the world of the text and cannot be concretely identified. But we have said that what is at issue here is precisely not the true and false, but the relation between the proper name *per se* and its expression in the text. Within the bounds of the text, moreover, rhetorical systems are at play which have their own "proper names," and which mirror Frege's delineations. What I will attempt to show in my readings of the two texts is that within the given passages, the portrait functions as a predicate for the passage, and that the predicate concerns not the true or false, but a system of description which is at the heart of textual "naming."

Before examining the two (French) portrait scenes, however, let us consider a traditional portrait in Sir Walter Scott's *Waverly*. (The passage, describing a portrait of Waverly as Hero of the Highlands, comes from the end of the novel):

> There was one addition to this fine old apartment, however, which drew tears into the Baron's eyes. It was a large and spirited painting representing Fergus Mac-Ivor and Waverly in their Highland dress, the scene a wild, rocky, and mountainous pass, down which the clan were descending in the background. It was taken from a spirited sketch, drawn while they were in Edinburgh by a young man of high genius, and had been painted on a full-length scale by an eminent London artist. Raeburn himself, (whose Highland chiefs do all but walk out of the canvas) could not have done more justice to the subject; and the ardent, fiery, and impetuous character of the unfortunate Chief of Glennaquoich was finely contrasted with the contemplative, fanciful, and enthusiastic expression of his happier friend.[5]

This description, unlike the two we are going to consider, gives the reader a relatively vivid account of the canvas. We know, for example, what the surroundings are, what the background contains, how Waverly and Mac-Ivor are dressed, and the impression these two characters convey. We also know when and under what circumstances the portrait was painted, the size of the painting, and that it was done by an "eminent London artist" after having been sketched by a young man at the time the scene depicted took place. The irony of the portrait is that it shows Waverly as the "ardent, fiery, and impetuous" leader of the Highlanders—whereas the novel itself shows Waverly to be what his name implies: a waffling, confused, and gullible follower. Thus Scott's portrait shows us a Waverly who, rather than being a likeness of his "real" self, is rather an ironic opposite thereof. The portrait itself, however, is a clear rendering which the reader has no difficulty visualizing.

Such is not the case in the passage to be considered next. But like the *Waverly* passage, the following scene, taken from Mme. de Lafayette's *La Princesse de Clèves*, is iconic in two ways: it represents the princess, the figure whom the title names; and it is Frege's sign which has only sense and no nominatum.

> Il y avait longtemps que M. de Nemours souhaitait d'avoir le portrait de Mme. de Clèves. Lorsqui'il vit celui qui était à M. de Clèves, il ne put résister à l'envie de le dérober à un mari qu'il croyait tendrement aimé; et il pensa que, parmi tant de personnes qui étaient dans ce même lieu, il ne serait pas soupçonné plutôt qu'un autre.
>
> Mme. la Dauphine était assise sur le lit et parlait bas à Mme. de Clèves, qui était debout devant elle. Mme. de Clèves aperçut par un des rideaux qui n'était qu'à demi fermé, M. de Nemours, le dos contre la table, qui était au pied du lit, et elle vit que, sans tourner la tête, il prenait adroitement quelque chose sur cette table. Elle n'eut pas de peine à deviner que c'était son portrait, et elle en fut si troublée que Mme. la Dauphine remarqua qu'elle ne l'écoutait pas et lui demanda tout haut ce qu'elle regardait. M. de Nemours se tourna à ces paroles; il rencontra les yeux de Mme. de Clèves, qui étaient encore attachés sur lui, et il pensa qu'il n'était pas impossible qu'elle eût vu ce qu'il venait de faire.
>
> Mme. de Clèves n'était pas peu embarrassée. La raison voulait qu'elle demandât son portrait; mais, en le demandant publiquement, c'était apprendre à tout le monde les sentiments que ce prince avait pour elle, et, en le lui demandant en particulier, c'était quasi l'engager à lui parler de sa passion. Enfin elle jugea qu'il valait mieux le lui laisser, et elle fut bien aise de lui accorder une faveur qu'elle lui pouvait faire sans qu'il sût même qu'elle la lui faisait. M. de Nemours, qui remarqua son embarras, et qui en devinait quasi la cause, s'approcha d'elle et lui dit tout bas:
>
> —Si vous avez vu ce que j'ai osé faire, ayez la bonté, Madame, de me laisser croire que vous l'ignorez; je n'ose vous en demander davantage.[6]
>
> (La Princesse de Clèves)

[For a long time M. de Nemours had wanted to have the portrait of Mme. de Clèves. When he saw the one belonging to M. de Clèves, he could not resist the desire to steal it from a husband he believed to be tenderly loved. And he thought that, among so many people who were in the same place, he would not be suspected more than another.

Mme. la Dauphine was sitting on the bed and speaking softly to Mme. de Clèves who was standing in front of her. Through one of the curtains which was but half-closed, Mme. de Clèves caught sight of M. de Nemours, his back against the table which was at the foot of the bed, and she saw that, without turning his head, he was adroitly taking something on that table. She had no difficulty in guessing that it was her portrait, and she was so upset by this that Mme. la Dauphine noticed that she was not listening to her and asked her out loud at what she was looking. M. de Nemours turned at these words; he met the eyes of Mme. de Clèves which were still fixed on him, and he thought that it was not impossible that she had seen what he had just done.

Mme. de Clèves was not a little embarrassed. Reason wanted that she ask for her portrait. But to ask for it publicly was to inform everyone of the sentiments this prince had for her; and to ask for it privately was quasi to engage him to speak of his passion. Finally, she deemed it better to leave it to him, and she was quite pleased to grant him a favor which she could do without even his knowledge that she was doing it for him. M. de Nemours, who noticed her perplexity, and who quasi-guessed its cause, approached her and said in a very low voice,

—If you have seen what I have dared do, have the goodness, Madame, to let me believe that you are in ignorance of it. I dare not ask more of you.]

The first thing to be noted in this passage is that there is no description of the portrait. And yet description is unnecessary because the *effect* of the portrait centers on its presence and its theft, not on its specific artistic qualities. Moreover, the princess herself is never really described in the novel: we only know that she is the most beautiful, the most noble, the most virtuous personage at court—a series of superlatives which emphasize the absence of detail concerning her appearance. Thus the undescribed portrait remains as vague as its subject.

The question to be raised here, however, is how such a passage can be descriptive when there is no straightforward depiction of the art object. Part of the answer must be that, while the passage does not give us any overt description of the portrait, its presence in the text is effective because it evokes a chain of senses. The portrait represents the princess; the princess is represented by her name. The symbiotic relationship between naming and description thus begins to emerge: a name has no meaning without description. For Frege, such is certainly the case. Indeed, as one Frege scholar has put it, "the logical behavior of descriptions is, for Frege, indistinguishable from that of (denoting) proper names."[7] It follows then that the portrait in the passage works according to Frege's moon simile: the "lens image" is true to the "real object" it reflects, for since the princess is never physically described, the reader must remain equally ignorant of the physical characteristics of her portrait. Further, the proper names in this passage are as prominent as they are in the rest of the text, signaling the importance of rank and title (with all that these imply). This abstract but rigid social hierarchy is foregrounded by the very scarcity of individualized facial traits. The proper names here become to a large extent their own signifieds—the "phantom of duty" which the princess obeys is dictated by her rank, that is by her proper name. The situation is further complicated by the fact that the proper name in a text, as we have said, refers to sense and image only, and not to an existing person. We may then formulate the textual situation in this way: the customary sense of "la Princesse de Clèves" becomes a collection of abstract, moral convictions—the necessity of virtue in the dangerous world of a flighty and precious court; a commitment to speaking the truth despite the flowery and hyperbolic (therefore false) language of the society; the rigid ideals of conduct which must not be jeopardized in spite of emotions which are in conflict with those ideals (the princess's love for the duke), and the fact that the ideals are in direct contradiction with the superficial code of courtly love which her society has espoused. The appearance of the portrait in this passage, then, comes to *mean* the iconic rendering of the princess who, in turn, means a specific conflict of morals. The portrait, then, serves as an example of the power of description, for oblique as it has been, the name of the princess, and her portrait, ultimately designate a cognitive nominatum. Were this not the case, of course, the text would be nonsensical. The etymology of the word "description" reinforces this point: from the Latin *describere*, "to write down," description is in some measure any form of writing; conversely, any writing is a form of description. The mental proximity of name and description is then particularly evident in a text where a name is granted meaning without direct description, and where a portrait can be imagined by the reader as designating the figure it signifies.

The theft of the portrait in *La Princesse* is crucial: it is a purloining, the symbolic power of the duke over that moral code which is precisely emblematized by the princess's *good name*. When we say that in this novel the proper name begins to generate its own referent, we may say this of the portrait as well, for it is the simile (icon) of the princess's good, proper name. Wittgenstein's reminder is worth mentioning here: "don't confuse the meaning of a name with the bearer of a name."[8] The proper name of "La Princesse de Clèves," her title and that of the novel, provides us with a name which comes to mean itself, not the "bearer." Sense and image take on so much importance that the character designated by her name gradually loses vitality in its presence. It is her name, and not her emotions, which dictates her behavior, so that her name attains a life of its own, at her expense.[9] In this passage, she herself is silent, her interior monologue serving only to underscore her powerlessness. The portrait is referential in that it demonstrates the power of the name; but it is also referential in that its presence functions as a silent description designating that power.

Just as "real" nominata are absent from literature, allowing sense and image all the more emphasis, and creating a "cognitive nominatum" in the reader, so too the naming in this passage seems stripped of its normal function, becoming instead "description" at its most abstract, a figure of thought in its most literal sense. It is to be noted that the passage is filled with verbs of *sight*—surely a component of direct description. And yet what we are led to visualize is neither the portrait's qualities, since we are not given them, nor a vivid ocular image of the figures in the passage, since they are left essentially undepicted. Rather, it is the situation and the conflict of ideals (= names) and emotions which are vividly portrayed. Indeed, the function of the portrait is *reversed* in the same way as is the movement of the sign when the name in a text comes to designate itself: the figure of the princess in this text comes to represent her name, as does her portrait. Like the retinal image cast by the "real" lens image and generated by the real moon, the portrait of the princess represents her name, the sense of which is generated by the name itself. The portrait is the simile of the princess, though no two readers will "see" the portrait in exactly the same way.

For Russell, proper names are abbreviations for description.[10] But in this passage, the portrait is obliquely ecphrastic in the same way that the referential context (nominatum) is oblique ("cognitive"). The portrait, we have said, functions as clearly *as if* described, in the same way that we understand what the princess "means" as clearly as if she were designated. For Mill, a proper name's sole function is to denote the referent.[11] But in a text, there is no concrete referent, no "other," to be designated. It is only for Frege that, as Leonard Linsky puts it, "names contribute to the senses of the declarative sentences containing them by themselves expressing their senses."[12] It is ironic that while for Frege, literature must be non-assertoric, no formulation can better explain than does the one just cited the semantic weight the name assumes in literature, or explain its cognitive power. The Lafayette passage we have examined demonstrates this point: the names contribute to the senses of the text containing them by themselves expressing their senses. It is this process which makes what I am calling the "cognitive nominata" possible.

We have seen that for Frege, artistic appreciation (for example, a literary text) is at odds with scientific considerations and with "the truth-value." Scientific considerations have truth-value for Frege because they concern sentences which have both a nominatum and a sense. Indeed, it is Frege's constant wish that there be a Utopia of language which would *always* have an unchanging reference:

> A logically perfect language [*Begriffsschrift*] should satisfy the conditions, that every expression grammatically well constructed as a proper name out of signs already introduced shall in fact designate an object, and that no new sign shall be introduced without being secured a reference.[13]

Such a utopian language would, presumably, allow for a constant truth value, by virtue of fixed signs with fixed referents. Thus Frege's utopia of language not only grants power to a proper name, but also vests it with the truth. This view is the opposite of Socrates' position in the "Cratylus":

> Whether there is this eternal nature in things, or whether the truth is what Heraclitus and his followers and many others say, is a question hard to determine, and no man of sense will like to put himself or the education of his mind in the power of names. Neither will he so far trust names or the givers of names as to be confident in any knowledge which condemns himself and other existences to an unhealthy state of unreality.[14]

For Socrates, then, truth has little to do with the arbitrary process of naming. Indeed, language can only veil the truth by naming it. It is significant that Frege's search for truth-value is posited on an ideal ("logically perfect") language with unambiguous references. But these two views, apparently diametrically opposed to one another, are in fact essentially identical, in that they assume the presence of truth to begin with, and the ability of language to convey that truth (even if it is only to state the "truth" that language cannot name truth). It is further significant that this same view, expressed differently, necessitates the rejection of fiction as bearing truth-value. "But why do we wish that every proper name have not only a sense but also a nominatum?" Frege had asked, and answered: "because what matters to us is the truth-value." Literature, like the sentence about Odysseus, is thus discarded. So too, Socrates, after briefly considering returning Homer's poetry to the Republic, again rejects it as lacking in truth, "for we have come to see that we must not take such poetry seriously as a serious thing that lays hold on truth."[15]

In both views, the referent is a transcendental concept, designating Truth; in both views, literature (poetry) has no such referential potential and thus remains non-assertoric. But once again, if we suspend this insistence upon the Truth, we can see the systems of naming within literature as precisely indicative of, rather than in contrast to, the myth of pure reference. For the act of reading is mimetic of the power to reveal Truth which logocentrism vests in language: in literature, too, *nomen est omen*. The literary text is rejected by philosophers who insist upon purity of meaning and, therefore, on an inside/outside. Utopian language or "Republic": literature stands exiled. To grant identity (reference) to the literary would be to taint the purity which philosophy seeks to maintain, and undermine the concept of transcendental meaning, which is the fiction of language. Thus philosophy, by rejecting literature for not being "a serious thing," creates its own fiction of truth. Frege's *Begriffsschrift* is the "Republic" of Plato in print.

The problem is compounded when literature alludes to a historical figure—a figure known to us, precisely, by *description*. The next portrait scene to be examined, taken from Stendhal's *Le Rouge et le noir*, provides us with just such a figure. The protagonist, Julien Sorel, has become a priest because Napoleon has fallen; thus the military life no longer offers the possibility for an ambitious young man of modest circumstances to rise above his birth. A tutor in a rich man's house, M. de Rênal, Julien is also courting the virtuous Mme. de Rênal, and simultaneously playing the role of the pious clergyman. When Julien learns that the mattresses in the Rênal household are being restuffed, he realizes that his secret will be discovered: for Julien keeps a portrait of his hero, Napoleon, under his mattress. Julien asks Mme. de Rênal to steal the portrait back for him, and he begs her to do so without looking at it. She carries out both orders, convinced that the box containing the portrait encloses the likeness of another woman, a rival:

> Assise sur une chaise dans l'antichambre de cet appartement, madame de Rênal était en proie à toutes les horreurs de la jalousie. Son extrême ignorance lui fut encore utile en ce moment, l'étonnement tempérait la douleur. Julien parut, saisit la boîte, sans remercier, sans rien dire, et courut dans sa chambre où il fit du feu, et la brûla à l'instant. Il était pâle, anéanti, il s'exagérait le danger qu'il venait de courir.
>
> Le portrait de Napoléon, se disait-il en hochant la tête, trouvé caché chez un homme qui fait profession d'une telle haine pour l'usurpateur! trouvé par M. de Rênal, tellement ultra et tellement irrité! et pour comble d'imprudence, sur le carton blanc derrière le portrait, des lignes écrites de ma main! et qui ne peuvent laisser aucun doute sur l'excès de mon admiration! et chacun de ces transports d'amour est daté! il y en a d'avant hier.
>
> Toute ma réputation tombée, anéantie en un moment! se disait Julien, en voyant

brûler la boîte, et ma réputation est tout mon bien, je ne vis que par elle . . . et encore, quelle vie, Mon Dieu![16]

[Seated on a chair in the antechamber of the upstairs apartment, Mme. de Rênal fell prey to all the horrors of jealousy. Her remarkable ignorance was particularly useful to her at this point, since astonishment tempered her grief. Julien appeared, snatched the box without a word of thanks or a word of any sort, and ran to his room where he lit a fire and burned it on the spot. He was pale and haggard; he exaggerated the extent of the danger he had just run.

"The portrait of Napoleon," he said to himself, shaking his head; "and found on a man who professes such hatred for the usurper! Found by M. de Rênal, a black reactionary and in a bad humor! And as the height of all imprudence, on the cardboard mounting of the portrait, lines written in my own hand which leave no doubt of the depth of my admiration! Each one of these raptures of love is dated, too, and the last one just the day before yesterday!"

"My entire reputation fallen, destroyed in one moment!" said Julien as he watched the box burn, "And my reputation is my fortune, it's all I have to live for—and good God, what a life!"]

At first glance, this passage seems quite the opposite of the first: the language is different (over- rather than understated) and the lover, Mme. de Rênal, is actually *ordered* to steal the portrait. And yet what is at the heart of the Stendhal excerpt is also central to Mme. de Lafayette: the fear of shattering a reputation; a good name which is both a personal ideal and a willed identity. As in the Lafayette text, the portrait is never described. But because it is of a historical figure, it is easier to observe how it achieves its effect. The portrait (that is, its mere presence) owes its power to the scene in the novel: as in *La Princesse de Clèves*, possession is what counts. Like the princess, Julien lives for his reputation. Indeed, the words he chooses could just as well be uttered by the princess: "my reputation is my fortune, it's all I have to live for." For the reader, two things make the portrait "live": the historical description of Napoleon, which the text assumes is familiar to most readers; and the sense that that figure is given for Julien by the text and by the historical period of the novel's setting. For Julien, Napoleon "means" everything that he wishes to be: powerful, rich, and glorious, despite his humble origins. For nineteenth-century France, the name of Napoleon erases the determinist quality of the family name in the social hierarchy, for Napoleon's rise to power showed that title no longer need depend upon birthright. Thus the text plays upon several senses of the name "Napoleon": the nominatum of the historical figure, the specific sense that figure has for the protagonist, and the ironic fact that, in worrying about his own "good name," Julien hides the very figure whose name "means" the end of the tyranny of names within the class structure of nineteenth-century France.

The protagonist himself, however, is non-existent: that is, the name "Julien Sorel" has no nominatum, only sense. Here again, we have the same literary situation of an "icon" which depends upon sense and associated image alone. But within that iconic context is the portrait of a historical figure who even according to Frege does have a designated nominatum: Napoleon. In writing of Odysseus, Frege pointed out that a sentence can have sense and no nominatum. We have shown that in literature, however, the context of sense-only can ultimately designate a "cognitive" nominatum. In referring to historical figures, literature "deconcretizes" a direct referent by putting it in an "iconic" context. On this level, the name "Napoleon," when it is used in fiction, comes to be as void of "truth-value" as that of "Julien." Conversely, however, the nominatum of Napoleon, the historical figure, adds weight to Julien's "presence" in the mind of the reader. The very proximity of Julien to the figure of Napoleon in the text (his possession of the latter's portrait, his handwriting upon it, his identification with Bonaparte's life, etc.)—at once fictionalizes the "real" Napoleon, since we know the entire scene to be the invention of Stendhal; and simultaneously concretizes Julien, since he is placed in the same cognitive sphere as a figure whom we know by "real" description. If fiction neutralizes the reality quotient of a historical figure by placing it in a fictional context, it can also make us realize the extent to which the names "Julien" and "Napoleon" do, finally, have a nominatum of cognitive value, granted them by the text.

Unlike the vague princess, Julien is physically described in some detail by Stendhal. Nevertheless, both the names "Princesse de Clèves" and "Julien Sorel" mean something quite specific to the reader: they are particular figures who can, in fact, be mentally designated. Even if no "truth-value" may be attached to a predicate modifying literary proper names, the reader's comprehension relies upon the same cognitive mechanism: knowledge by description, rendering a cognitive nominatum for the name. It is not because we know that Julien is fictional that we cannot conceptualize him, any more than it is not because we have not met Napoleon that we cannot designate him. Our ability to identify Julien Sorel rests upon the same mental procedure as our capacity to do so with historical figures or even personal acquaintances on description. It is this mental knowledge which Plato sees as essential to understanding a designated object:

> For everything that exists there are three classes of objects through which knowledge about it must come; the knowledge itself is a fourth, and we must put as a fifth entity the actual object of knowledge which is the true reality. We have, then, first, a name, second, a description, third, an image, and fourth, a knowledge of the object. . . . In the fourth place there are knowledge and understanding and correct opinion concerning them, all of which we must set down as one thing more that is found not in sounds nor in shapes of bodies, but in minds, whereby it evidently differs in its nature . . . from the aforementioned three.[17]

It is this "true reality," however, which is, of course, the problem. In Plato's *Phaedrus*, writing and painting are compared, because the images of both are considered to be *less real* than those of existing beings. Here again is the problem of Frege's "icon"—and indeed, as Paul Ricoeur notes, the icon itself is the issue at stake in much of our thinking on mental optics:

The question here is whether the theory of the *eikon*, which is held to be a mere shadow of reality, is not the presupposition of every critique addressed to any mediation through exterior marks. . . .

Far from yielding less than the original, pictorial activity may be characterized in terms of an "iconic augmentation," where the strategy of painting, for example, is to reconstruct reality on the basis of a limited optic alphabet. This strategy of contraction and miniaturization yields more by handling less. In this way, the main effect of painting is to resist the entropic tendency of ordinary vision—the shadowy image of Plato—and to increase the meaning of the universe by capturing it in the network of its abbreviated signs.[18]

The present essay would seek to make the words "painting" and "pictorial activity" in the above citation interchangeable with "writing." Ricoeur notes, in fact, "If it could be shown that painting is not this shadowy reduplication of reality, then it would be possible to return to the problem of writing as a chapter in a general theory of iconicity."[19] Naming in texts is, in Frege's own terms, a form of "iconic augmentation." But Frege stops where Ricoeur would begin in the development of the problem of writing as a chapter in a general theory of iconicity. The irony is that the same philosophy of a transcendental Truth (Frege, Plato) rejects written fiction because of its "unhealthy state of unreality"—that is, because such referents are "shadowy images" without "real" nominata. The difference which philosophy insists upon maintaining between fictional and historical names is self-serving, because it gives "seriousness" to the latter by dint of trivializing the former. But since the systems of referring within the literary text necessarily resemble "real" reference, then the distinction between what is a "designated nominatum" versus an "iconicized" name becomes, at best, a privileging of speech, or of writing which conveys direct speech. If I speak the Truth, I am relating history, and may then write it down. If I tell stories, and then write them down, I am referring to nothing save, perhaps, my own text—this is the conclusion implied in the *Begriffsschrift* and the *Phaedrus*.

Rhetorical systems in general function to "clarify" the textual system of signs in much the same way that Frege's terms "explain" direct reference in naming: to designate a metaphor in a text, for example, by delineating its parts (vehicle and tenor) is the same act as disentangling the sense, image, and nominatum of a sign. Whether the two portrait scenes we have considered are labelled ecphrastic or iconically referential, the system in both cases is the same: naming. And in both cases, aspects of naming are renamed, like two telescopes projecting different faces of the same moon.

My point is not, of course, to argue that literature be viewed as the Truth; it is rather to insist that all writing be seen as referring to our mythologies on the Truth, to the names we choose to give to it, and to the assumptions we have concerning the power of the name. In this sense, literature indeed captures, through its abbreviated signs, the meaning we choose to agree upon. And the portrait in a literary text becomes the iconization of an *eikon*, yielding more by handling less. Fiction is then the best of "places" in which to look for the fictions of language.

NOTES

1. "On Sense and Nominatum," tr. Herbert Feigl, in *Readings in Philosophical Analysis*, H. Feigl and W. Sellars, eds. (New York: Appleton-Century-Croft, 1949), pp. 85–102. The citation is from page 87. The article was originally published as "Uber Sinn und Bedeutung" in *Zeitschrift für Philosophie und philosophische Kritik*, 100 (1892), pp. 25–50. The more standard translation is "On Sense and Reference" in *Translations from the Philosophical Writings of G. Frege*, P. Geach and M. Black, eds. (Oxford: Blackwell, 1952). I have chosen to use the Feigl translation because his terminology (based on that of R. Carnap in *Meaning and Necessity* [Chicago: University of Chicago Press, 1947]) is easier for my purposes. Feigl's use of "nominatum" rather than "reference," for example, allows a more subtle differentiation between all types of reference and the individual designated by a proper name. All future citations are from the Feigl translation and will hereafter be situated by page number only.

2. Feigl tr., p. 87: "In order to formulate this succinctly we shall say: words in indirect discourse are used *indirectly*, or have *indirect* nominata. Thus we distinguish the *customary* from the *indirect* nominatum of a word; and similarly, its *customary* sense from its *indirect* sense. The indirect nominatum of a word is therefore its customary sense."

3. The *OED* lists "simile" as one of the definitions of icon. And Lanham says, for example, "From Aristotle onward, *simile* is often the vehicle for *icon* or *image*." Richard A. Lanham, *A Handlist of Rhetorical Terms* (Berkeley: University of California Press, 1968), p. 93.

4. Strawson, P. F., *Introduction to Logical Theory* (London: Methuen, 1952). All of chapter six concerns itself with this idea.

5. (New York: Dutton, 1976), p. 473.

6. (Paris: Gallimard, 1958), pp. 106–107. Translation mine.

7. Leonard Linsky, *Names and Descriptions* (Chicago: University of Chicago Press, 1977), p. 7.

8. Cited by Linsky, p. 22. Wittgenstein, Linsky summarizes, was taking issue with Russell's idea that the meaning of a proper name is its denotation. In his notebooks of 1914–16, Wittgenstein also says, "In our language, names are *not things*; we don't know what they are: all we know is that they are of a different type from relations." *Notebooks 1914–16*, 2nd edition, tr. G. E. M. Anscombe, ed. Wright and Anscombe, (Chicago: University of Chicago Press, 1979), p. 111. And in another passage, Wittgenstein takes Russell and Frege to task, in a manner which (consciously or not) parodies Frege's telescope simile:

> The comparison of language and reality is like that of retinal image and visual image: to the blind spot nothing in the visual image seems to correspond, and thereby the boundaries of the blind spot determine the visual image—as true negations of atomic propositions determine reality. Logical inferences can, it is true, be made in accordance with Frege's or Russell's laws of deduction, but this cannot justify the inference; and therefore they are not primitive propositions of logic. (p. 100)

In the same notebooks, Wittgenstein adds another comment on naming and description: "One cannot achieve any more by using names in describing the world than by means of the general description of the world" (p. 53).

9. An extended, if differently focused, example of the loss of vitality in the face of an increasingly powerful "iconicizing" is to be found in Edgar Allen Poe's short story, "The Oval Portrait." In the story, a painter gradually saps his wife of life by putting, it would seem, all of her essence into the portrait he is painting of her. When the portrait is completed, she dies; the portrait, on the other hand, is life-like to the point of being terrifying. The

portrait scenes discussed in this article are shortened versions of readings of the same scenes, to a different end, in my *Salome and the Dance of Writing: Portraits of Mimesis in Literature* (Chicago: University of Chicago Press, 1987).

10. *The Principles of Mathematics*, 2nd edition (New York: W. W. Norton, 1938). Russell, however, creates a special group, the logically proper name, as distinct in logical function from description. See Linsky, p. 7, on this distinction.

11. John Stuart Mill, *A System of Logic* (London: Longmans, Green, 1900). See John R. Searle's attack on this view in *Speech Acts: An Essay in the Philosophy of Language* (Cambridge: Cambridge University Press, 1980), p. 93 ff.

12. Linsky, p. 9.

13. *Translations from the Philosophical Writings of G. Frege*, p. 56.

14. *Plato: the Collected Dialogues and Letters*, E. Hamilton and H. Cairns, eds. (Princeton: Princeton University Press, 1973), p. 474.

15. Ibid.

16. (Paris: Garnier, 1973), p. 56. My translation.

17. *Collected Dialogues*, Letter VII, pp. 1589–90.

18. Paul Ricoeur, *Interpretation Theory: Discourse and the Surplus of Meaning* (Fort Worth: Texas Christian University Press, 1976), pp. 40–41.

19. Ibid., p. 40.

I am grateful to my colleague at the University of Chicago, Professor Leonard Linsky, for his very helpful reading of this essay. I should add that for him this essay is not grounded consistently enough in Fregean logic. While this is a tactic which I have consciously chosen, Professor Linsky is in no way accountable for any ensuing complications.

VII.

HOW PLAYSCRIPTS REFER
SOME PRELIMINARY
CONSIDERATIONS

Michael Issacharoff

It is tempting to oversimplify the nature of fictional discourse by claiming that since it does not, supposedly, refer in precisely the same way as definite referring expressions in ordinary language do, it is a 'parasitic' form of discourse. Or so the argument usually runs in works on speech-act theory. Stanley Fish has convincingly argued that the simplistic 'serious' (or referential) language vs. fictional (or non-referential) language dichotomy is far from being as valid as some philosophers of language would have us believe.[1] It in fact may do a disservice both to speech-act theory and to literary theory.

The problem I propose to examine in what follows is the nature of referring in dramatic discourse. My inquiry will entail a preliminary consideration of the (referential) specificity of the dramatic *script*, that is, the features which distinguish it from other literary texts. It is my contention that the playscript *is* distinct and that its peculiar referential status enables us to establish its difference.

It is probably true to say that any literary text may be an amalgam of utterances referential and non-referential. Utterances closest to what philosophers of language such as Strawson, Linsky, and Donnellan call 'definite reference' (or 'definite descriptions')[2] in 'serious' discourse can be found in the form of references made by fictional characters or made by real authors to historical persons or places (that is, existents), for example. Thus, in *Travesties*, Tom Stoppard refers in the didascalia (and likewise his characters in the dialogue) to real people: James Joyce, Tristan Tzara, Lenin, among others. Stanley Fish is right in pointing out that the fictional vs. serious language debate has tended to oversimplify and thus cloud the issue. *Fictional discourse is not pure fiction, and 'serious' discourse utilizes techniques and games—pretending, lying, joking—more commonly associated with literature.* J. L. Austin's position on this problem, expressed rather (too) succinctly, has been distorted and did not, perhaps, help to clarify matters:

> A performative utterance will, for example, be *in a peculiar way* hollow or void if said by an actor on the stage, or if introduced in a poem, or spoken in soliloquy.

> This applies in a similar manner to any and every utterance—a sea-change in special circumstances. Language in such circumstances is in special ways—intelligibly— used not seriously, but in ways *parasitic* upon its normal use—ways which fall under the doctrine of *etiolations* of language. All this we are *excluding* from consideration. Our performative utterances, felicitous or not, are to be understood as issued in ordinary circumstances.[3]

Austin himself may be criticized for his confusing, if not question-begging, category, "ordinary circumstances." Serious discourse is not necessarily coextensive with "ordinary circumstances," and likewise, fictional discourse is not always merely 'parasitic' or simply an "etiolation of language." Searle has shown, by quoting a passage from a novel by Iris Murdoch, that "not all of the references in a work of fiction will be pretended acts of referring; some will be real references as in the passage from Miss Murdoch where she refers to Dublin."[4]

Whereas Searle recognizes that fictional discourse is not perhaps as simple as Austin would have us believe, neither he nor Fish (who quotes him) resolves another fundamental problem central to the referential process: *who* (in a literary text) is doing the referring? Searle, it will be remembered, insists that it is not *expressions* which refer, but *people* using them. This problem is particularly relevant to the *dramatic* text, given that contrary to other kinds of literary texts, the author *writes a script for performance by other speakers*. When we seek to identify the person referring in a play, all will hinge on whether we are considering the script *read* or the script *performed*. In the case of the read script, as we shall see, there is at least one level of discourse—the didascalia—which contains many of the attributes of serious discourse used in "normal circumstances," and is intended (by the author) to be taken seriously. The performed script, on the other hand, is, of course, the text minus the didascalia, but the actors can be considered as persons making references (in the technical sense), even though one can perhaps accept Austin's view that their utterances may be void of perlocutionary effect. The illocutionary force, however, may be perfectly valid.

While Austin excludes from consideration performatives in fictional discourse, Searle provides criteria for definite reference which, upon examination, are in fact at least partly relevant to the literary and, for our purposes here, the dramatic script. According to Searle, the criterion for definite reference is twofold:

> 1. There must exist one and only one object to which the speaker's utterance of the expression applies (a reformulation of the axiom of existence) *and*

> 2. The hearer must be given sufficient means to identify the object from the speaker's utterance of the expression (a reformulation of the axiom of identification.)[5]

Now dramatic discourse, despite Searle's comments about fictional discourse being "parasitic,"[6] *may* contain utterances true to the first criterion which requires the existence of a specific (that is, constant or fixed) object to which an utterance applies. The obvious instance is the mention of an existing place or person, existing, that is, either at the time of writing or prior to it. In such cases, mention may occur either in the didascalia or in the dialogue. Consequently, in drama just as in fiction, there is an obvious distinction to be drawn between, say, Balzac's Paris or Dickens's London and Butler's Erewhon. The former two places exist, the latter does not. Similarly, literary mention of Napoleon, De Gaulle, Churchill, Kennedy, and so on, should be regarded as referentially distinct from mention (in the dialogue or didascalia) of imaginary characters.

As Searle himself explains, the axiom of existence can be extended so that when *we* speak of a fictional character—Searle uses the example of Sherlock Holmes— we are able to make a valid reference, given that we are speaking of a character (or other entity) that exists in a particular fictional world. One could, though, go beyond the case Searle envisages and argue that *a character onstage can make valid references* (to other characters, places, or objects in the same play) since they, too, are referential acts which focus on *someone or something that exists in that particular fictional universe*. In the case of a script in performance, instances such as these in fact fulfill *both* Searle's criteria for definite reference: the axioms of existence and identification. In drama, then, it can be said that a character X refers to characters Y and Z who either appear in the same play or, failing that, hold some crucial part in the logic of the plot. The axiom of *identification* stipulates that "the *hearer* [my emphasis] must be given sufficient means to identify the object from the speaker's utterance."[7] Again, one can go further in applying this criterion than Searle undoubtedly intended, and maintain that the hearer in this case could be either another character onstage or, of course, the audience.

My remarks so far have been confined essentially to a commentary on Searle's and Austin's observations on fictional discourse and the various ways one can adapt Searle's axioms so as to find (unexpectedly, from Searle's point of view) cases of definite reference in fictional discourse. The preceding comments, however, are no more than a preliminary discussion pertinent to dramatic discourse, whose referential status is more complex than either of the two philosophers of language would lead us to believe. The axiom of existence may, as I have attempted to show, be fulfilled in at least two possible ways: through a mention in the dialogue (or in the didascalia) of a person, place, or thing that exists either in the real world or in a particular (coherent) fictional universe. References to imaginary persons, etc. may be termed, to borrow Strawson's phrase, "story-relative reference."[8]

Let us now attempt to examine the referential status peculiar to the dramatic script. While it is true to say that the author of a play (or a novel) provides a (contractual) label describing his mode of discourse—"A play in five acts," "Comédie," "Farce tragique," "A novel"—authorial intention in this respect is by no means a foolproof criterion for reference versus non-reference. Sartre, for example, on writing his *Les Séquestrés d'Altona [The Condemned of Altona]* had no intention of making a real (that is, definite) reference to Von Gerlach (a real person) whose name he used for a character in his play, imagining it to be fictional. Sartre realized his gaffe too late and added the following prefatory note in the printed edition of the play:

NOTE BY THE AUTHOR

I thought that I had invented the name Gerlach. I was mistaken. It was hidden in my memory. I regret my mistake even more because the name is that of one of the bravest and best-known opponents of National Socialism.

Hellmuth von Gerlach devoted his life to the struggle for *rapprochement* between France and Germany, and for peace. In 1933 his name was high up in the list of those proscribed by the Nazis. His property was seized, together with that of his family. He died in exile two years later, having devoted his last efforts to providing help for his refugee compatriots.

It is too late to change the names of my characters, but I beg his friends and relatives to accept this as an earnest expression of my apology and my regret.[9]

This means, of course, that someone who knew the real Gerlach in Germany during World War II would have some difficulty, despite Sartre's published apology, in reading the play non-fictively.

Furthermore, that referential intention is not a watertight guideline is clearly demonstrated, as Richard Gale points out, by the fact that authors of fictional texts have sometimes been found guilty of libel. "This is so," writes Gale,

even when the resemblance of his story to real life is purely coincidental. E.g. if in a fictional work there is a character named Frank Jones who lives at 547 Industrial Drive in Pittsburgh, is president of the United Steel Workers Union and embezzles union funds, and by coincidence there is a real-life Frank Jones who fits these descriptions with the exception of not being an embezzler, he could sue the author of this work and collect damages. This shows not only that a fictive use of a sentence can say something true (false) but also that a purely locutionary act of referring which is what a fictive reference is, can succeed in referring to some existent.[10]

In short, then, successful reference is by no means contingent on a speaker's or writer's intention; it may occur by accident or even by coincidence. In addition to instances such as these, of course, one need hardly mention the more felicitous cases where a play (or novel) acquires a new referential focus, unimagined by the writer, due to the impact of historical events. Thus in a work of satire, or in a play with political overtones, reference (to people) may be transformed, due to circumstances external to the text, from the indefinite or open-ended to the definite. A producer may decide, say, to make a Shakespeare play such as *Julius Caesar* or *Macbeth* 'refer' anachronistically to World War II. This may be achieved, without changing a word of the script, through the use of appropriate costumes and set. Reference in drama can therefore be *conveyed obliquely* through the visual channel.

The discrepancy between reference intended and reference inferred (a problem too often overlooked by speech-act theorists) is not confined to drama. It is common to all forms of literary (as well as to non-literary) discourse. What *is* peculiar to the (modern) drama script and distinguishes it *referentially* from other types of literary discourse is its two-layered structure consisting of dialogue plus didascalia.[11]

I say *modern* drama, since in many pre-nineteenth-century playscripts by such authors as Racine, Corneille, Shakespeare, and Molière, didascalia—especially information about the set and properties—tended to be inscribed in the dialogue, and not set apart in italics in accordance with modern convention. The upshot of this is a category of dramatic discourse distinct from ficuve discourse. It need hardly be pointed out that the didascalia in a playscript are the equivalent of an authorial voice, normally intended to be taken seriou:¹y, that is, non-fictively. Every play-script contains at least a minimal form of didascalic discourse, be it simply the dramatis personae on the first page and the names of the characters at the beginning of every speech. Stage directions are equivalent to a real speech act insofar as they amount to a set of instructions to the director and cast on how to (1) stage the dialogue, and (2) deliver the lines. It is this part of the text that frames the playscript. Didascalia are addressed by a *real person* (the author) to other *real people* (director and actors), and, save in cases where the dramatist is satirizing convention—the examples of Ring Lardner and Ionesco[12] immediately come to mind—are intended to be taken non-fictively. It should be remembered, though, that didascalia refer *not* to a speech event (that is, to what was said and how), but to a *future speech event*, namely to how something *should be said* and in what circumstances. Thus they are *not* merely a set of instructions akin to the directions for baking a cake, as Searle suggests,[13] but, usually, indications not only of *contents* (personages and objects present) but also information on the manner in which they *interact*. Didas-calia, then, are the element of the playscript providing cohesion for the purposes of the reader, director, and cast.

The fact that the didascalic portion of the script refers to a future speech event has important referential consequences. It means that didascalia fulfill one of Searle's criteria for definite reference. In a word, whereas the *axiom of existence* is not strictly adhered to (since didascalic utterances apply to objects and persons which change from one stage production of a given play to the next), the *axiom of iden-tification* is certainly complied with (since the hearer can identify the object men-tioned in the speaker's utterance). Finally, in this matter of didascalic discourse, it should be observed that the fact that didascalia may be in referential contradiction with the dialogue (as in Ionesco's *Les Chaises*) proves that (1) there must be a distinction between author's and characters' speech acts; and that (2) there is a hierarchy. Stage directions are normally cut-and-dried rather than tongue-in-cheek. Thus, even if the dialogue portion of a playscript is experimental or absurdist, as in Beckett's *Endgame*, Stoppard's *Dogg's Hamlet*, or Tardieu's *Un Mot pour un autre*, the didascalia tend to be quite conventional and 'serious.' If this were not the case, the production of such plays would be even more difficult than it is already. In technical terms, if the axiom of identification were not strictly adhered to in the didascalia, the reader as well as the producer would be totally confused.

The preceding comments on didascalia should enable us to achieve at least two objectives: (1) to note the referential specificity of the playscript in contrast to other kinds of literary texts, and (2) to make preliminary observations on the mechanics of reference in playscripts. It follows from all of this that the process of reference in the playscript as read is fundamentally distinct from the case of the playscript as performed. Clearly, when the playscript is staged, the explicitly authorial channel disappears from view.

We now need to turn to reference in dramatic dialogue. When considering the playscript *in toto*, it was apparent that we were dealing with what is usually a referential amalgam of (almost) genuine definite reference (the didascalia) and possibly non-referring discourse (the dialogue). But, in fact, what kind of beast *is* dramatic dialogue? Could it not also be considered an amalgam of referring and non-referring discourse? Obviously the answer must be sometimes in the affirmative. However, before reaching such a conclusion, it will be necessary to examine the identity of the utterers, since, if we follow Searle's criteria, it is not expressions that refer, but people using them. When an utterance is heard onstage, *who* is speaking? Clearly, it is not the author. There are exceptions, though. The obvious example is Molière, who chose to forego conventional authorial detachment by playing the lead or important parts in most of his plays—Arnolphe in *L'École des Femmes*, Orgon in *Tartuffe*, Sganarelle in *Dom Juan*, Alceste in *Le Misanthrope*, Argan in *Le Malade Imaginaire*, Jourdain in *Le Bourgeois Gentilhomme*, the title role in *Georges Dandin*, and so on.[14] One could argue, though, in cases such as these, that the playwright fictionalizes himself by becoming a player. For the contemporaries of the playwright, however, who saw the original productions, the referential ambiguity surely remained. Utterances would have had a different ring to them. Instances in which the ambiguity is greater, as the line between nonfictional speech event and theatrical speech act becomes more tenuous, are those in which an author gives his "fictional" character his own name as Molière does in *L'Impromptu de Versailles*, and likewise Ionesco in *L'Impromptu de l'Alma*. Molière even played the part of the character to whom he lent his name, and given that the character is Molière the theatre director, the degree of fictionalization becomes minimal.

These instances do not of course reflect standard practice in which the author *lends his voice* to his characters (and indirectly to his producer). If, then, the speaker in a dramatic dialogue is not normally the playwright-player or the fictionalized playwright, it is not the actor either. He is using borrowed utterances he has been instructed (or, rather, paid) to use. He does not have to believe what he is saying, although nothing precludes his so believing. (As for the characters—Macbeth, Lady Macbeth, Ophelia, Hamlet—they do not even exist!) It need hardly be emphasized that the lines spoken onstage are framed by the context of theatrical performance. To use Austin's terms, the locutionary force is normal, whereas the illocutionary and perlocutionary forces are weakened, if not eliminated entirely. Yet it would surely be wrong to consider that utterances spoken onstage are entirely cut loose from their regular illocutionary and perlocutionary anchors and are heard as so many innocent sounds floating freely in the air. An audience (just like a reader) is always at liberty to hear them non-fictively and transform them into fully engaged discourse. That this is so is clearly demonstrated by the fact that plays are sometimes censored or banned in totalitarian societies as well as in democracies, under certain circumstances when freedom of expression is temporarily curtailed. As we have noted already, a dramatist may also be charged and found guilty of libel. Presumably, in a court of law, a playwright could not disclaim responsibility for words spoken onstage on the pretext that he had not uttered them in person. Furthermore, the playscript does of course remain the writer's *literary property*, even if the apparent utterer of the text in performance is not the author. Thus, needless to say, an author can bring an action for plagiarism against anyone who tries to misappropriate his literary property.

Acts of definite reference, however, are not necessarily contingent on the hearer's knowing the identity of the utterer. Provided that an utterance in no way focuses on the speaker or on the hearer, its referential force is not in the least impaired. This means that all statements in a dramatic dialogue concerning real persons (living or dead) or places and so forth have virtually the same referential status as the same statements in a non-literary context. I say *virtually* since the only difference is the context of usage. Stoppard's *Travesties* provides us with an interesting illustration of this. His principal characters, James Joyce, Lenin, and Tristan Tzara, were all living people. In addition, nearly all of Lenin's lines (as Stoppard himself tells us) come from his own *Complete Works*. Many speeches, in fact, are taken verbatim from Lenin's published correspondence. Thus, for example, when we hear lines such as the following:

> LENIN: September 15, 1919, to A. M. Gorki, Dear Alexei Maximych . . . Even before receiving your letter we had decided in the Central Committee to appoint Kamenev and Bukharin to check on the arrests of bourgeois intellectuals of the near-Cadet type, and to release whoever possible. For it is clear to us too that there have been mistakes here.[15]

we are dealing with an unusual instance of discourse spoken by an actor playing the part of Lenin, using the Russian's exact words. Referentially, then, the only difference in the status of the lines as they were originally used in a letter written by Lenin and in the play is *the new context of usage*. In short, all the definite references occurring in the passage in its reincarnation still retain their illocutionary force. What is modified, however, is their perlocutionary force, since what has changed in the new context is Lenin's addressees. Lenin, of course, never met Tristan Tzara and James Joyce. Thus many of his lines, though still addressed directly to their original (though absent) addressees, are overheard by additional (indirect) addressees, not present at the time of the original speech event. In short, what has occurred is that an original speech event (a letter) has acquired a modified complementary referential status by virtue of its new discursive context. In fact this phenomenon is about the same as the referential status of a *quotation*, rejuvenated through reincarnation.

The Stoppard play eloquently exemplifies the problem of the referential status of dramatic dialogue. We are dealing with a multi-stranded mode of discourse which, at one extreme, can be the quotation of words actually spoken or written by a real person (living or dead). The definite referential force may still be valid, if at least some of the circumstances of the original speech event are retained. The minimum condition would be that speaker and hearer are unchanged. The Stoppard example, then, is about the closest that dramatic dialogue can come to definite reference in nonfictional speech events, although another technical possibility would be the use of a radio recording of an interview with a real person. (A device such as this would be comparable to the use of extracts from a newsreel in a feature film.)[16] Next to this are two other forms of definite reference, allusions to or mentions of real persons or places or things, and play-relative references. In Stoppard's *The Real Inspector Hound*, Moon's speech is an obvious example of definite reference: "Faced as we are with such ubiquitous obliquity, it is hard, it is hard indeed, and therefore I will not attempt, to refrain from evoking the names of Kafka, Sartre, Shakespeare, St Paul, Beckett, Birkett, Pinero, Pirandello, Dante and Dorothy L. Sayers."[17] An intentionally playful list of names, all of real people. Given, however, the purposely tenuous connexion between these names, their playfully alliterative linkage, together with the context of their mention in the play, they probably acquire some degree of unreality, if not fictionality. The same process occurs, of course, when a dramatist mixes definite reference to existents and story-relative referents.

Story-relative reference (or, to coin a term, play-relative reference) is the other mode of singular definite reference that is the norm in traditional dramatic dialogue. By this we mean that a character (or place or event, etc.) referred to by other characters in the same play remains constant and can thus be reliably identified. Strawson's definition: "The identification is within a certain story told by a certain speaker. It is identification within his story; but not identification within history."[18]—makes it clear that this form of definite reference does not imply or entail the axiom of existence. Almost any non-experimental play will furnish examples of this referential mode, ranging from, say, references to Molière's protagonist in *Tartuffe* (prior to his appearance onstage in act III, for instance) to comments about Macbeth made by other characters in Shakespeare's play. In all such cases we are dealing with an identifiable constant referent, a character whose existence is confined to a fictional universe. The reverse process is to be found in experimental drama where a title (such as *En attendant Godot*) names a character who *never* appears onstage and thus does not really 'exist' even in Beckett's fictional world. The other type of anti-reference is exemplified by the Bobby Watson anecdote in Ionesco's *La Cantatrice chauve* (The Bald Soprano). The name Bobby Watson, contrary to normal exclusive naming and identifying practice, 'refers' to several members of the same family (living and dead!) in the same sentence.

Two types of reference, both characteristic of dramatic dialogue, remain to be examined (though only in summary form here): referential mixing and referential subversion. By referential mixing, I mean that dramatic dialogue is normally an *amalgam* of referential modes and comprises concurrently at least two of the following: (1) definite singular extratextual reference (that is, reference to real persons, living or dead; places, events, etc.); (2) story-relative reference (that is, reference to entities existing solely within a given fictional universe); and (3) intertextual reference (that is, reference to other texts by the same writer or other writers or to literary conventions). A brief example from Stoppard's *Night and Day* will illustrate what I mean by mixed reference. Wagner, a reporter, comments: "I go to fires. Brighton or Kambawe—they're both out-of-town stories and I cover them the same way. I don't file prose. I file facts."[19] Brighton is a real place—a city on the southeast coast of England; Kambawe is a fictitious African country which provides a setting for Stoppard's play. This utterance, then, exemplifies mixed reference consisting of definite singular extratextual reference (Brighton) and story- or play-relative reference (Kambawe). A referential cocktail such as this is, of course, peculiar to literary discourse. The aesthetic result is double-edged and one of two things may occur. Either the reality (a sort of Barthesian *effet de réel*) of the definite reference may rub off onto the story-relative referent(s), or the fictionality of the latter may affect (and possibly undermine) the former.

Finally, referential subversion is a referring mode commonly present in dramatic dialogue and may occur on various channels, visual and auditory. It need hardly be pointed out that drama is the one literary medium in which the verbal may be enhanced, transformed, or even subverted through visual means, including costume, decor, and lighting. It would not be difficult to transform a play such as *Hamlet* or *Othello* into a farce by undermining it referentially with the aid of appropriate costumes and prosodic tampering. Hamlet's famous soliloquy could easily be dislodged from a tragic to a comic mode through a change in intonation and rhythm and, perhaps, with the addition of a few derisive sound-effects.

In the preceding discussion, my focus has been primarily on modes of extratextual reference that are peculiar either to the playscript or to the playscript-in-performance. Needless to say, there are probably other referential mechanisms at work, but I would contend that they are not characteristic of dramatic discourse *per se*. One such area that I have purposely left unexplored in this paper (and that I have examined elsewhere)[20] is the complex problem of *intertextual reference*. This phenomenon includes not only the obvious category of allusion to and parody of other literary (and non-literary) texts, but also reference to dramatic stereotypes and conventions. In research on this topic, I have discovered a general tendency (especially in the genre of dramatic parody) for the intertextual to expel and even obliterate the extratextual.

In this paper I have attempted to show that the position according to which fictional discourse is referentially quite distinct from non-literary discourse is untenable. The dramatic script contains various modes of definite reference ranging from the didascalia to story- (or play)-relative reference, and including virtually regular definite reference. In fact I have argued that, surprisingly perhaps, dramatic discourse often fulfills the criteria for definite reference as defined by Austin and later reformulated by Searle. To say, then, that dramatic discourse is somehow "parasitic" or an "etiolation of language" seems very far from the truth.

NOTES

1. Stanley Fish, *Is There a Text in This Class?* (Cambridge, Mass.: Harvard University Press, 1980); see especially pp. 97–111, "How Ordinary Is Ordinary Language?" and pp. 268–292, "Normal Circumstances . . ."

2. See P. F. Strawson, "On Referring," *Mind* LIX (1950), 320–344, reprinted in Strawson, *Logico-Linguistic Papers* (London: Methuen, 1971), pp. 1–27; Leonard Linsky, *Referring* (London: Routledge & K. Paul, 1967); Keith S. Donnellan, "Reference and Definite Descriptions," *The Philosophical Review* LXXV (July 1966), 281–304. See also J. Searle, *Speech Acts: An Essay in the Philosophy of Language* (London & New York: Cambridge University Press, 1969).

3. J. L. Austin, *How to Do Things with Words* (Cambridge, Mass.: Harvard University Press, 1962), p. 22.

4. J. Searle, "The Logical Status of Fictional Discourse," *New Literary History* VI (1975), p. 330; quoted by S. Fish, *Is There a Text in This Class?*, p. 235.

5. J. Searle, *Speech Acts*, p. 82.

6. Ibid., p. 78.

7. Ibid., p. 82.

8. P. F. Strawson, *Individuals: An Essay in Descriptive Metaphysics* (London: Methuen, 1959), p. 18.

9. J. P. Sartre, *Les Séquestrés d'Altona* (The Condemned of Altona), trans. S. & G. Leeson (New York: Alfred A. Knopf, 1961), p. 2.

10. Richard Gale, "The Fictive Use of Language," *Philosophy* XLVI (1971), 329–330.

11. I have attempted to examine the status of didascalia as a form of discourse central to the reading of drama in *Le Spectacle du discours*, (Paris: José Corti, 1985), pp. 25–40.

12. See especially Ring Lardner, *Taxidea Americana*, in *The Ring Lardner Reader*, ed. Maxwell Geismar (New York: Scribner's, 1963), pp. 621–623; *The Tridget of Greva*, in *Theatre Experiment: An Anthology of American Plays*, ed. Michael Benedikt (New York: Anchor Books, 1968), pp. 48–56; *Quadroon*, in *The Ring Lardner Reader*, pp. 603–608. See also Ionesco's parodic use of didascalia in *La Cantatrice chauve*, in *Théâtre* I (Paris: Gallimard, 1954); for example, pp. 19, 22, 29.

13. J. Searle, "The Logical Status of Fictional Discourse," *New Literary History* VI (1975), 319–332, reprinted in Searle, *Expression and Meaning* (Cambridge: Cambridge University Press, 1979), pp. 58–75.

14. See Georges Couton's notes to the individual plays in his edition of Molière, *Oeuvres Complètes* (Paris: Gallimard, 2t., 1971).

15. Tom Stoppard, *Travesties* (London: Faber & Faber, 1975), p. 88. In a note of acknowledgment at the beginning of the playscript, Stoppard tells us: "Nearly everything spoken by Lenin . . . herein comes from his Collected Writings" (p. 15). Verification in Lenin's *Collected Works* confirmed this. Passages used are indeed quoted verbatim, though in a slightly abridged form in some cases. The letter cited here appears in the *Collected Works*, Vol. 44 (Moscow: Foreign Publishing House, and London: Lawrence & Wishart, 1970), pp. 283–285. In the same way, letters used elsewhere in *Travesties* for Lenin's lines, for example on pp. 81 and 87, are taken from the *Collected Works*, Vol. 36 (p. 420) and Vol. 34 (pp. 385–386), respectively. Similarly, Lenin's famous lines on p. 85 of the play ("Today, literature must become party literature. Down with non-partisan literature!" etc.) come from a speech made in 1905 which appears in Vol. 10 (1962), pp. 44–49.

16. An interesting example was provided recently in Woody Allen's *Zelig*, in which three real people, Saul Bellow, Irving Howe, and Susan Sontag (played by Saul Bellow, Irving Howe, and Susan Sontag) are interviewed about the fictional protagonist Zelig! By their appearance in the movie, the three real persons are fictionalized. This example is, of course, distinct from that of a real interview that actually occurred and is later re-used in a fictional context.

17. Tom Stoppard, *The Real Inspector Hound* (London: Faber & Faber, 1968), p. 36.

18. P. F. Strawson, *Individuals*, p. 18.

19. Tom Stoppard, *Night and Day* (London: Faber & Faber, 1978), p. 38.

20. See, for example, "Labiche et l'intertextualité comique," *Cahiers de L'Association Internationale des Etudes Françaises* 35 (mai 1983), 169–182.

VIII.

ARE BAUDELAIRE'S "TABLEAUX PARISIENS" ABOUT PARIS?

Ross Chambers

"Poetic discourse is the equivalence established between a word and a text, or a text and another text."[1] This definition lies at the heart of the only currently prominent theory of poetic reference, that of Michael Riffaterre, who perceives poetic discourse as having "meaning" by virtue of its mimetic function but "significance" by virtue of purely textual and intertextual relationships, to which the reader's attention is directed by mimetic "ungrammaticality," that is "mimetic anomalies, interference with apparent referentiality."[2] Text, in this view, is "shaped like a doughnut,"[3] the hole being the absent and unexpressed verbal referent, or "hypogram."

Although it is true that mimetic representation "is founded upon the referentiality of language,"[4] the modes of linguistic referentiality are not exhausted by mimesis. All language (literary or otherwise) derives its meaningfulness from its use in context, and its reference is consequently best described as a relationship between the discourse and the total context in which it "makes sense." Such a context includes understandings about the nature of the "real world" in which the discourse is produced and received, and to which it is thought to refer (what is sometimes called the "encyclopedia of the text"); but it includes also understandings between speaker and receiver about the illocutionary relationship pertaining between them (that is, about such matters as the social purposes fulfilled by the communication and the constraints upon it, the rights and responsibilities which are distributed between the participants in the communicational act, the code employed, and so forth). In short, the illocutionary situation is as much a part of the reference—the situation in which discourse makes sense—as is the "referential" situation proper (in the "mimetic" sense); and indeed the latter is actually included in the former, if one understands the illocutionary situation to embrace *all* the relevant speaker-hearer understandings on which the communicational act depends.

In light of this, it seems very probable that such categories as the "literariness" of literature or the "poeticity" of poetry are most suitably described, not in terms of specific features of literary/poetic discourse, but in terms of the illocutionary understandings which prevail in given cultures and at specific historical moments as to which texts are literary or poetic, and what it *means* for a text to be so classified. In this respect, Riffaterre's most important contribution to literary theory lies perhaps in his long-term insistence on the fact that the literary phenomenon "resides in the relationship between text and reader, not between text and author, or text and reality."[5] However, the text-reader relationship is, unfortunately, not so much a simple given as a theoretical problem in its own right, and one of great magnitude. One reason for this is the inadequacy of the simple speaker-discourse-receiver model of communication to the literary situation, which in our modern Western culture defines literature in terms of its ongoing ability to produce meaning in situations of reception remote from the initial situation of production. Literature thus becomes one example among many of "deferred" communication, in which the notion of context is radically complicated not only by the fact that the context of reception is by definition distant from the context of production, but also by the fact that "meaning" is subject to continual drift, as it evolves from one changing context of reception to another. It is for this reason that literary referentiality appears so much more problematic than the referentiality of discourse situations in which production and reception co-occur (although many would argue that the more complex model is apposite, as well, to the apparently simpler situations of "everyday life").

But if interpretative indeterminacy is an actual criterion of literarity in the modern age, this fact perhaps accounts for a notable characteristic of texts which pretend to literary status. The paradox is that, in order to lay claim to a future history of indeterminacy, such texts must initially *determine* themselves as literature; their own literariness being subject to interpretative "drift" along with everything else, it becomes necessary for them to safeguard their own esthetic status from the outset. They do it by self-reference. I am not referring here to the well-known phenomenon of literary self-referentiality (poems about poetry, theatre in the theatre) as an autotelic device. Rather I am suggesting that this supposed autotelic device has a communicational function in establishing, or attempting to establish, for a future readership, the illocutionary situation which makes sense of the text, that is, those understandings about the purposes and means of the discourse which are necessary for an appropriate act of reading to take place. For this purpose, it is not enough, of course, for such texts to define themselves simply and generally as "literature," or as "poetry," "novel," etc., since such categories are subject to future drift; they must define themselves *specifically*, as a certain kind of poetry, or poetry in a certain sense, so as to determine future reading situations in such a way that they will be decoded in ways which speech-act theory might call "felicitous;"[6] and that is why a claim to a future of indeterminacy (as literature) must start by determining in a quite specific way the reading conditions of the text.

In my view, then (to summarize), so-called "self-referentiality" functions, in fact, as reference to an illocutionary situation, the contextual understandings posited by a text as necessary for it to make sense (to make sense as literature, that is, to *go on* making sense). Thus conceived, the illocutionary situation amounts to a set of instructions for decoding the text; and indeed, the distinction between "code" and "situation" is at best a heuristic one, since a felicitous illocutionary situation is a function of an agreed code, just as the existence of an agreed code implies a whole illocutionary situation. In texts, such illocutionary reference may be entirely implicit; or it may be directly expressed (by means of explicit textual self-comment); or—the most frequent case—it may be obliquely presented by means of figures of the text contained within the text. Such figures, like narrative "mise en abyme" as analyzed by Lucien Dällenbach (and "mise en abyme" is an example of the techniques in question), may reproduce the text as utterance (énoncé), as speech-act (énonciation), or as code;[7] but from the point of view of the illocutionary self-contextualizing of the text, it is the latter two types of figuration which are directly relevant. They "produce" within the text the text's own illocutionary situation, as it is conceivable or formulable in the circumstances of the text's production, and thus guarantee the survival of this illocutionary context as an essential component of all future contexts of reception. (Needless to say, if texts can produce their own contexts in this way, it becomes urgent, as a philosophical issue, to ask to what extent *all* the contexts, which in the ordinary way we regard as being distinct from discourse, are in fact products of discourse; but that is a line of thought I do not need to follow up here.)

"Tableaux Parisiens" [Parisian Pictures] is the title Baudelaire gave, in the 1861 edition of the *Fleurs du Mal* [Flowers of Evil], to a group of eighteen poems— some previously published in the 1857 edition, others not—which he placed between "Spleen et Idéal" and "Le Vin." Such a title appears to imply mimetic intent and to refer to descriptive poetry concerning visual aspects of the city of Paris. A superficial glance at the poems, however, quickly gives the lie to this inference and reveals an "ungrammaticality": relatively few of the poems are specifically set in Paris,[8] a number of the others might be more broadly described as "big city poems,"[9] but certain texts are not clearly or specifically related to city life at all.[10] One poem, "Rêve parisien" [Parisian Dream], although it incorporates Paris in its title, is mimetic not of the city of Paris but of an entirely imaginary spectacle.

This last title is instructive, however, because it offers an obvious coupling with the title of the section as a whole, "Tableaux Parisiens." For "Rêve parisien" does not necessarily mean a dream having Paris as its object; the sense could equally be a dream dreamt in Paris or a dream inspired by Paris, and this sense is supported by the narrative content of the poem, with its conclusion set in the "horreur de mon taudis" [horror of my hovel]. Similarly "Tableaux Parisiens" might be taken to imply "pictures inspired by Paris," "pictures done in Paris," or even (at a stretch) "pictures done by a Parisian." In these cases, the word "tableaux" would begin to suggest less the idea of mimetic *representation* and rather more that of artistic *production*, since a picture is, after all, as appropriately defined as a created product of art as it is in terms of the reproduction of its object. Thus, although the lines from "Les Petites Vieilles" ["Little Old Women"]:

> j'entrevois un fantôme débile
> Traversant de Paris le fourmillant tableau,

[I catch a glimpse of a flimsy ghost
Passing through the swarming Parisian landscape,][11]

might support the mimetic sense of the word; those from "Rêve parisien" ["Parisian
Dream"]:

peintre fier de mon génie
Je savourais dans mon tableau
L'enivrante monotonie
Du métal, du marbre et de l'eau,

[just like a painter
I enjoyed in my picture
The entrancing monotony
Of metal, marble, and water,]

quite clearly imply esthetic production—while in addition, the text as a whole
authorizes the equation "tableau" = mental representation, dream. The meaning
of "imaginary production" would apply without strain to *all* the non-city poems
in the section.

It seems, then, that the word "tableau" in the "Tableaux Parisiens" section may
mean either mimetic reproduction or mental representation, depending on the individual poem,[12] but that its primary or nuclear meaning lies in its suggesting the
creative involvement of a seeing subject, *producing* spectacles mimetically as "fourmillant tableau" [swarming picture] or imaginatively as "L'enivrante monotonie/
Du métal, du marbre et de l'eau"[The entrancing monotony of metal, marble, and
water]. A subject, then, whose function is to make sense of the visual object, be
it actually seen or a dream: "tout *pour moi* devient allégorie" [for me everything
becomes an allegory], comments the *ego* of "Le Cygne" [The Swan], while the
ego of "Rêve parisien" refers to:

ces prodiges
Qui brillaient d'un feu *personnel*!

[these marvels,
which shone with an intrinsic fire!]

(where "personnel" of course means "proper to the dream objects"; but also
inevitably suggests subjective involvement in the vision).[13]

This subject (as some of the above quotations illustrate) figures as an actor in
the poems, which dramatize his effort to produce meaningful representations. Thus,
on seeing a swan:

Andromaque, je pense à vous!

[Andromache, my thoughts are turned to you!]
                                                    ("Le Cygne")

or, a propos of the blind:

> Je dis: Que cherchent-ils au Ciel, tous ces
> aveugles?
>
> [I ask myself—What are they looking for
> in the sky, all those blind men?]
> ("Les Aveugles")

or again:

> Voilà le noir tableau qu'en un rêve nocturne
> Je vis se dérouler sous mon oeil clairvoyant
>
> [such is the sombre picture that in a dream,
> one night, I saw unfold before my seer's gaze]
> ("Le Jeu" [Gambling])

But also, this seeing subject *in* the poems becomes a speaking subject *through* the poems which produce him, and relate in verse the visual encounters and mental representations of which he is the subject. The *ego* who is the subject of the poetic utterance is the truly universal factor present in *all* of the poems of the "Tableaux Parisiens," all but one of which are couched in specifically first-person discourse, while the only third-person poem in the section, "Le crépuscule du matin" [Morning Twilight], dramatizes the speaking situation and the presence of "je" through a curious use of the imperfect tense as a deictic.[14] Consequently, one may conclude that the best sense attributable to the title is "Tableaux d'un Parisien" [A Parisian's Pictures], since it is the speaking *ego* who takes responsibility for the discourse through which the experiences of the seeing subject are conveyed. In this final interpretation of the title, the word "tableaux," in addition to its visual connotations, can be read as metaphoric of the poems themselves.

But in what sense is it accurate to say of the speaking *ego* that he is a Parisian? (I am taking it for granted that he is a "he.") I want to suggest that he is a Parisian in the sense that Paris is less the place he writes about than *the place out of which he speaks*, and hence the place *in which* the poems are supposed to be understood— the place, in short, which gives point to the poetic text as an utterance, and hence does so not as mimetic object but as illocutionary situation. But since the poems are presumably intended to be read wherever the French language and the conventions of its verse are known, and not just in the city of Paris, the "Paris" out of which the *ego* speaks and in which his voice must be heard cannot be too closely identified with the "real" Paris in which Charles Baudelaire produced his poems (to be fussy, some of the work was done at Honfleur). In other words, it is not so much the historical city which was the capital of France in the Second Empire as an imaginary Paris which figures as a cultural item in the encyclopedia of speakers of French, the "Paris" invented by Baudelaire and his contemporaries as a symbol of modern life, and which *we* continue to recognize, in Walter Benjamin's useful phrase, as capital of the nineteenth century. It is for *this* reason that the illocutionary situation in which "je" [I] produces his discourse functions to indicate the specifically modern status of that speech and to invite the reader to receive it in the same spirit. The "décor," in short, functions as code.

Within the poems themselves, the speech of "je" as a communicational act is frequently dramatized, and it is striking that the overall effect of these dramatizations is to convey a sense of his speech activity as lonely, and most often futile, verbal gesturing.[15] The interlocutors he takes and whom he addresses or questions are usually unable to hear him, let alone to reply: "Andromaque, je pense à vous!" [Andromaque, my thoughts are turned to you!]; "Telles vous cheminez" [Thus you pass on]; "O cité! . . ./ Vois! je me traîne aussi!" [O city . . . behold I also drag myself along!]; "Fugitive beauté . . . / Ne te verrai-je plus que dans l'éternité?" [O fleeting beauty . . . shall I never see you again except in eternity?]; "Dites, quelles moissons étranges/ Tirez-vous . . . ?" [Tell me, what strange harvests are you bringing in?]; "Quand je te vois passer" [When I see you pass by]; "*Je* n'ai pas oublié . . . / *Notre* blanche maison" [I have not forgotten . . . our white house]; "Endormeuses saisons! je vous aime et vous loue" [O drowsy seasons! I love you and praise you]. Consequently, the rhetorical question is one of the most characteristic speech patterns of "je": "Avez-vous observé que maints cercueils de vieilles . . .?" [Have you ever noticed that many old women's coffins . . .?]; "Viens-tu troubler, avec ta puissante grimace,/ la fête de la Vie?" [Do you come with your fearful grimace to disturb Life's festivities?]; "Es-tu le fruit d'automne . . . / Es-tu vase funèbre . . .?" [Are you Autumn's fruit? Are you a funeral urn?]; "Que pourrais-je répondre à cette âme pieuse . . .?" [What reply could I give this pious soul?]. So too is self-address: "Contemple-les, mon âme . . . / Je dis: Que cherchent-ils au Ciel . . .?" [Observe them, O my soul . . . I ask myself—What are they looking for in the sky?]; "Recueille-toi, mon âme, en ce grave moment" [O my soul, withdraw into yourself at this grave hour]. And finally, simple deixis: "Voici le soir charmant" [Here's the delightful evening]; "Voilà le noir tableau" [Such is the sombre picture]; "De ce terrible paysage/ . . . Ce matin encore l'image/ . . . me ravit" [The image of this terrible landscape entrances me again this morning]; "C'était l'heure où . . ." [It was the hour when . . .] functions to betray the presence of a speaker addressing—who knows whom?

The lack of contact thus dramatized is heightened by the hostility or indifference of the city environment in which "je" speaks. In one poem,[16] the city is too noisy for the poet's speech to be heard:

O cité!

Pendant qu'autour de nous tu chantes, ris et beugles,

. . . . .

Je dis: Que cherchent-ils au Ciel, tous ces aveugles?

[O city, while you sing, laugh and bellow

around us
I ask myself—What are they looking for in
the sky, all those blind men?]

In another, the street environment, "La rue assourdissante autour de moi hurlait" [The deafening street was howling round me], prevents communication between "je" and the woman passing by, the "passante." Finally, urban noise accounts for the movement of withdrawal by which the poet's speech comes to be completely inner-directed:

> Recueille-toi, mon âme, en ce grave moment,
> Et ferme ton oreille à ce rugissement
>
> [O my soul, withdraw into yourself at this
> grave hour, and stop your ears against this
> roaring din]

—and it is not accidental that this poem, "Le crépuscule du soir" [Evening Twilight], introduces the whole series of poems of mental representation (desire, nostalgia, the dream) which compose the nocturnal panel of the section. Urban noise, as the adversary of poetic speech, thus defines the illocutionary circumstances not only of the diurnal poems (the series of street-poems beginning with "Le Soleil" [The Sun], but also of the nocturnal poems (from which explicit indications of din are absent.)

Yet this speech, which is either drowned by the city's hubbub or else confined to a self-directed monologue, is one which we (the readers of Baudelaire) are permitted to hear, or to *overhear*, as it were. The speech which is dramatized in the poems as futile becomes available *through* poems which presuppose effective channels of communication. Thus, the lonely words in "Les Aveugles" [The Blind]:

> Je dis: Que cherchent-ils au Ciel, tous ces aveugles?
>
> [I ask myself—What are they looking for in the sky,
> all those blind men?]

are reported in a sonnet of deliberately jumpy prosody, perhaps, but one which is readable (and in which the jumpiness is *expressive*) to anyone familiar with the conventions of French verse. And the miscommunication in "A une Passante" [To a Woman Passing By], Car j'ignore où tu fuis, tu ne sais où je vais, / O toi que j'eusse aimée, ô toi qui le savais!" [For whither you flee I know not; nor do you know whither I am bound—O you whom I could have loved, O you who knew it!], is similarly related in a sonnet of essentially conventional structure. The reader, such poems assume, is one with whom acts of communication are possible because, on the one hand, he or she is culturally equipped and trained in the traditions of French poetry, and on the other, he or she is assumed to be familiar with the dilemmas of modernity, notably the experience of lack of contact which is the subject of the texts; and hence to be responsive to the poet's plight as it is dramatized in the poems.

What this means is that the dramatization of problematical circumstances of communication within the poems serves as a specific cultural *code* for readers who, in fact, have no technical difficulty in "reading" the texts: by such means, we are asked to read this relatively classical verse as the speech-act of a "modern" poetic subject. The poems' reference to Paris is, consequently, not so much representational and mimetic as it is metaphoric of an illocutionary situation outside of which the poems themselves would be meaningless (that is, could not be appropriately read). In this way, Baudelaire solves the difficult artistic problem of communicating a sense of the powerlessness to communicate, of writing meaningfully about the difficulty of being meaningful. The apparent contrast between the illocutionary situation presented in the poems and the illocutionary situation presupposed by them need not disturb us, then: the poems simply depend on a prior, conventional read-ability in order to indicate those non-conventional circumstances which can only be produced *in* the texts but which give them their "true" point. Of course, it happens also that this combination of the traditional and the modern meshes well with Baudelaire's doctrine of Beauty, as being formed of an absolute and continuing component, and a relative and changing one. It corresponds too to the actual sen-sation of Parisian experience developed in a poem like "Le Cygne" where continuity ("Andromaque, je pense à vous!" [Andromache, I am thinking of you!]) and change ("Paris change!" [Paris is changing]) are dramatized as the joint components of a specific tension:

> la forme d'une ville
> Change plus vite, hélas! que le coeur d'un mortel.

> [a city's pattern changes,
> alas, more swiftly than a human heart.]

But one final point emerges from the above considerations: if "Paris" as illo-cutionary context, or code, is metaphoric of the modern, the street, then the "deaf-ening" street is itself metonymic of Paris. As such, it comes to be a figure, within certain poems, of those poems themselves as modern discourse. It is not simply that in the diurnal series the events of the poems actually take place in the street, but that the street itself is projected as a model of modern poetic language (in short, here too the décor is the code). As I have shown elsewhere,[17] "Le Soleil" is strategically placed at the head of the diurnal series so as to establish the street not just as their locus but as the model of creative experience for the poetic *ego*:

> Le long du vieux faubourg, . . .
> Je vais m'exerçant à ma fantasque escrime,
> Flairant dans tous les coins les hasards de la rime,
> Trébuchant sur les mots comme sur les pavés,
> Heurtant parfois des vers depuis longtemps rêvés.

> [Through the old suburb . . .
> I go practising my fantastic fencing all alone,
> Scenting a chance rhyme in every corner, stumbling
> against words as against cobblestones, sometimes
> striking on verses I had long dreamt of.]

But here, poetry of the street is conceived in terms of a poetics of encounter (experiential encounters and linguistic serendipity). The poem on which I shall now focus at greater length also proposes the street as simultaneously locus and code, but it does so more specifically in terms of a poetics of modernity, conceived precisely as a fusion of the traditional and the urban. This is "Les sept vieillards" [The Seven Old Men], a poem which has been frequently read as allegorical, but which can most fruitfully be interpreted—like Mallarmé's "sonnet en -yx"—as a poem allegorical of itself.[18]

"Vous créez un frisson nouveau" [You create a new shiver, a new thrill]: Victor Hugo's comment on receipt of "Les sept vieillards" echoes the observation made by Baudelaire himself to Jean Morel: "it is the first number in a new series I am attempting and I fear that I've merely succeeded in going beyond the limits assigned to Poetry."[19] What defines this novelty, by which the limits of poetry are transcended? Much discussion has surrounded the question; I will content myself with citing Baudelaire's essay on Gautier, written the previous year:

> Besides, the nature of true poetry is to flow evenly like mighty rivers approaching the sea, which is their death and infinity; and to avoid sudden haste and jerkiness. Lyric poetry rushes, but its movement is always elastic and undulating. Poetry rejects anything abrupt or broken up, relegating it to drama or the social novel.[20]

This is the conception of poetry *against* which "Les sept vieillards" is written, the conception which is both assumed and transcended in the "new series" to which the poem belongs—assumed, that is, in order to be transcended. The new poetry has in common with the theatre and the social novel—those realist genres—a certain angularity and discontinuity in its movement, even while the image of the poem as a river approaching its infinite and its death in the sea is retained; for in the urban context it is streets, with their harsh angles and sudden encounters, which, as the "canaux étroits du colosse puissant" [the narrow veins of this mighty giant], replace streams.

The frequency of enjambment and irregular breaks in the versification of this poem (and other street poems such as "Les Aveugles" or "A une Passante") indicates, as Graham Chesters has pointed out,[21] an attempt to achieve in verse the condition of prose, with a view to matching the characteristics of the urban environment. But if one recalls the elastic and undulating movement which was said in the Gautier essay to be essential to the lyric, it is clear that the manner of a poem such as "Les sept vieillards" is more than a merely mimetic device; it is a means of rendering poetic discourse itself problematic, and of creating a new lyric code

suitable to modern life, at the risk of "going beyond the limits." This latter circumstance is in fact thematized in the poem itself, with its reference to an encounter
with absurdity and madness—that which lies beyond the limits of meaning, and
constitutes "its infinity and death." But I shall suggest that it is precisely this
transcending of the limits which constitutes the new poetic code, and that consequently the encounter related in the poem is synonymous with the adventure of
encountering the poem itself.

The narrative structure of the poem is that of a voyage to the sea. The river of
the outset:

> Les maisons . . .
> Simulaient les deux quais d'une rivière accrue,
>
> [The houses
> looked like the two banks of some swollen river,]

becomes the infinite sea of the final lines:

> Et mon âme dansait, dansait, vieille gabarre
> Sans mâts, sur une mer monstrueuse et sans bords!
>
> [And my spirit danced, danced, old barge
> With no masts, on a monstrous endless sea!]

But the river was a metaphoric river only, simulated by a street ("Le faubourg
secoué par les lourds tombereaux" [the suburb shaken by the heavy tumbrils]) in
which the vehicles of death (cf. the connotations of "tombereaux" [tumbrils] go
rumbling to their destination; *ego* is walking down that same street). The common
element of street and stream is a threatening liquidity: it is the fog which produces
the illusion of a river ("Les maisons, dont la brume allongeait la hauteur" [the
houses which the fog made taller]), and this same yellow mist invades the soul of
the poet just as it inundates space:

> décor semblable à l'âme de l'acteur,
> Un brouillard sale et jaune inondait tout l'espace.
>
> [decor resembling the actor's soul,
> A dirty yellow fog was inundating all space.]

But liquidity is the mark also of "mystery," of that which defies understanding
and challenges meaning:

> Les mystères partout coulent comme des sèves
> Dans les canaux étroits du colosse puissant,
>
> [Everywhere mysteries flow like sap

> In the mighty giant's narrow canals,]

the poem announces at the outset; whereas at the end the protagonist has been "Blessé par le mystère et par l'absurdité!" [Wounded by the mystery and the absurdity]. It follows, then, that not only is the "âme de l'acteur" invaded by the liquidity of mystery, but that that mystery is directly identified with the encounter which "wounds" him, that is, with the proliferating series of old men, even though these old men are characterized by their sharpness and angularity, and described with words like "roide," "cassé," "faisant . . . un parfait angle droit" [stiff, broken, making . . . a perfect right angle]. This sharpness explains their ability to wound; but it is not incompatible in the poem with the liquidity of mystery, since initially the first old man of the series is seen as a kind of emanation of the fog:

> un vieillard dont les guenilles jaunes
> Imitaient la couleur de ce ciel pluvieux.
>
> [an old man whose yellow rags
> Imitated the colour of that rain-filled sky]

Several observations are called for at this stage. First, all the components of the poem's action—the "actor," the "décor," the old men—bathe in a common element which is that of mystery. The soul is invaded, like a swamped boat (soon to become the "vieille gabarre/ Sans mâts" [the old wreck/ without masts]) by the yellow fog of which the old men are themselves an equivalent. The poem is thus subverting traditional distinctions such as those of self and other, the soul and the world, by making them all subject to the category of absurdity, meaninglessness. Secondly, the liquidity of mystery and the angularity of the street are here identified, both by the metaphor which makes rivers of streets and by the double quality of the old men. But, sharing its mysterious liquidity and its dangerous harshness, the old men are consequently equivalents of the street in its double aspect, a kind of emanation of it. Both street and old men thus recall Baudelaire's definition of the lyric as smooth flowing and of what opposes it as "anything abrupt or broken up," except that in this poem the two are uncannily combined in such a way that flow comes to represent "mystery" as the suggestion of elusive meaning—a last residue of traditional meaningfulness, perhaps—while the harsh and the angular represent the hostility of such "mystery" to traditional concepts such as the self, "mon âme déjà lasse" [my already weary soul]. Correspondingly, the poetic persona of *ego* reveals itself to be double also, and composed of an element already succumbing to the flow ("my soul") and a combative and heroic element more attuned to the realities of the world of the street:

> Je suivais, roidissant mes nerfs comme un héros
> Et discutant avec mon âme déjà lasse,
> Le faubourg secoué par les lourds tombereaux.

[I was making my way, steeling my nerves heroically
and nagging my already weary soul, through the
suburb shaken by heavy tumbrils.]

My final observation is this, that this world of equivalences (where soul, décor, and old men bathe in the common element of mystery and where liquidity and angularity, the stream and the street, are themselves identified) is a fictional or poetic world, a world of figuration and falsity. The street is a theatre, a "décor" in which the narrative *ego* is an "acteur"; similes underline the falsity of this world: "roidissant mes nerfs *comme* un héros" [steeling my nerves *like* a hero], and undermine the equivalences they produce: "décor *semblable* à l'âme de l'acteur" [a background comparable to the actor's soul], while two key verbs explicitly point to the false, and let us say hallucinatory, quality of this universe:

Les maisons, dont la brume allongeait la hauteur,
Simulaient les deux quais d'une rivière accrue,

[the houses seemed to be stretched upwards by
the mist and simulated the two banks of some
swollen river,]

Tout à coup, un vieillard dont les guenilles jaunes
Imitaient la couleur de ce ciel pluvieux, . . .
M'apparut

[Suddenly an old man whose yellow rags imitated
the colour of the rainy sky, . . . hove in sight]

What is real here is the street (the houses, the suburb) and the fog; the rest (the mystery, the river, the invaded soul, the old man) is a product of vision, of the vision which produces equivalences through the operation of metaphor. Thus, although the poem begins by presenting the city as a place "Où le spectre en plein jour accroche le passant!" [where the ghost accosts the passer-by in broad daylight], it hastens in the following stanzas to reverse this relationship by suggesting that the spectral quality of the city is a product of the metaphorizing vision of the "passant"—and on reflection that is the ultimate force of the run-on "M'apparut" [hove in sight] which concludes these introductory stanzas. Thus, the world of equivalences and mystery which is so threatening to the soul of the poet may itself be the product of that poet's vision: it is poetry as a factor of equivalence and indifferentiation, the poetry of the city as ant-bed—"fourmillante cité" [swarming city], *fourmi* means *ant*—which appears as the real source of the uncanny.

Certainly, if poetic equivalence is the key to the opening stanzas of the poem, a different aspect of poetic repetition is figured by the proliferating old men whose encounter forms the mediating event in the narrative structure of "Les sept vieillards." Poetry, as the type of discourse which constructs metaphoric equivalences, is also the type of discourse which, repeating itself stanza by stanza (just as the old men proliferate), approaches an infinity of resemblance and calls into question the distinctions from which meaning is derived. It is significant that the stanzas in which the appearance of the eight old men is related (seven effective appearances, plus one hypothesized) themselves number eight (from stanza 4, "Tout à coup" through stanza 11 "Mais je tournai le dos . . ."); the first apparition begins in the first stanza (although it spills over, by enjambment, into the second), and the eighth apparition is evoked in the eighth stanza. The poem does not, of course, proceed with a stanza-by-stanza identification of the verse structure and the old men; but it does suggest the resemblance between stanzaic repetition and that of the "vieillards" in a number of ways.

Thus, the early stanzas are concerned with the angular appearance and limping gait of the first of the men—a break and a syncopation which recur in the heavily run-on verse itself. The lines concerning

> la tournure et le pas maladroit
> D'un quadrupède infirme ou d'un juif à trois pattes

> [the ungainly shape and gait of some ailing
> quadruped or a three-legged Jew],

run on as they are from the *third* to the *fourth* stanzas of the description, clearly metaphorize the verse itself in its metric structure. The remaining four stanzas are concerned with the proliferation of old men; that is, their sameness and their re-petitiveness. Here the verses themselves exploit various forms of repetitiveness, summarizing the previous four stanzas by an enumeration: "barbe, oeil, dos, bâton, loques" [beard, eye, back, stick, rags]; repeating lexical items and syntactic struc-tures: "du même enfer venu,/ . . . Marchait d un même pas" [from the same hell . . . plodded at the same speed]; "A quel complot infâme . . . / Ou quel méchant hasard . . . ?" [What infamous conspiracy . . . or what evil chance?]; "de minute en minute" [minute by minute]; introducing phonetic patterns and parallels: "je comptai *sept fois* . . ./ Ce *s*inistre *v*ieillard"; "*s*aisi d'un *frisson f*raternel"; "saisi . . . Sosie" [I counted that sinister old man seven times; seized with a brotherly chill; seized . . . an identical double]; metaphorizing in various ways the notion of similarity and repetition: "jumeau centenaire"; "vieillard qui se multipliait"; "So-sie"; "Phénix"; "fils et père de lui-même" [centenarian twin; multiple old man; a double; phoenix; his own son and his own father].

In this way, then, the "cortège infernal" [hellish procession] figures the language of the poem itself, a language in which the *poetic function*—exactly Jakobson's projection of the principle of resemblance onto the syntagmatic axis—no longer reproduces the majestic flow, the smooth flow of the poem as stream, but embodies the absurdity and lapse into meaninglessness inherent in modern discourse, in the poem as street. The flow has not disappeared: it is still present in the slippage of one old man into the next, a slippage reproduced by the stanzaic enjambment in the text; but discontinuity and repetition now predominate (as the jerkiness of the enjambments also records) and now constitute a sense of meaninglessness, the meaninglessness of signs which have undergone a loss of differentiation, so that they flow dangerously into each other and frighteningly repeat each other in endless absurdity: "Ces sept monstres hideux avaient l'air éternel" [These seven hideous freaks had a look of eternity about them]. The problem of meaning in a world of signs which has lost its transcendental guarantee, the consequent "drift" of signifiers which cannot be anchored to a single, stable signified, thus constitute the major problematics of the diurnal poems of the "Tableaux Parisiens" (that of the nocturnal poems being the closely related problematics of desire); but it is only in "Les sept vieillards" that this sense of meaninglessness is carried to its extreme in the intuition that ultimately all signs, despite their apparent diversity, are one sign and simply repeat each other indefinitely.

This is not the place to enlarge on the philosophical import of indifferentiation in "Les sept vieillards"—a topic which would require, in any case, a joint reading with the other poems of the diurnal series. What is interesting, in terms of my present inquiry, is the fact that, in the abstract, it is obviously not *necessary* to read lines of French verse structured like those of the central stanzas of "Les sept vieillards" (by enjambment and repetition) as expressive of a poetics of the modern—of angularity and indifferentiation, an (urban) poetics of the street as opposed to, or superimposed upon, a (natural) poetics of the stream. The difference, at the technical level of versification, between such lines and (say) Baudelaire's own earlier practice is perhaps not so striking as to justify *in itself* such a reading of them. If I do read into the poem in this way, it is because the poem *asks me to*—and it does so by projecting its *apparent* mimetic referent (Paris as "décor") as an *actual* indicator of poetic code, an illocutionary context: Paris as the site of a modern experience of threatening indifferentiation, that is, Paris as a "décor semblable à l'âme de l'acteur" [decor resembling the actor's soul]. "Décor semblable": a manifestation of the problematics of indifferentiation; but "décor semblable à l'âme de l'acteur," a *constructed* site ("décor"), emblematic of the "place" ("l'âme") out of which the poet speaks—and, perhaps, constitutive of that place.

Michael Riffaterre would point out, justly, that my reading of the poem was triggered by a "mimetic" anomaly (the *invraisemblance* inherent in the poem's fantastic mode); and that I have read the poem like a doughnut surrounding an absent textual matrix—the word "indifferentiation," perhaps, or the text from the essay on Gautier cited at the outset. My point is not to dispute his theory but to add to it the observation that the referential apparatus characteristic of poetry is that which makes us read it as poetry (or as a specific kind of poetry), that is, the illocutionary context assumed by the text and communicated, by various means, to the reader as a guide to his/her reading. The literary phenomenon is indeed best described in terms of the text-reader relationship; but that relationship is inscribed (implicitly, obliquely, or directly) within the text.

This is perhaps clearest in the opening lines of "Les sept vieillards," which summarize the narrative and thematic content of the poem, but simultaneously dramatize its illocutionary status:

Fourmillante cité, cité pleine de rêves,
Où le spectre en plein jour accroche le passant!

[O swarming city, city full of dreams,
where the ghost accosts the passer-by
in broad daylight!]

Who is this passer-by? In narrative terms, he is the protagonist of the poem, the *ego* who is to encounter the spectral old men; in thematic terms, he personifies mortality and points to the narrative encounter as a meeting with death in the guise of the city's proliferation, its undifferentiated *fourmillement*. But in illocutionary terms, he figures the reader of the poem, whose function is to be accosted by the spectre *as a figure of the poem*; and to be involved in his or her dangerous encounter with the text in just the way that the *ego* of the poem is caught up in, and wounded by, *his* encounter with the phantoms. Here, then, is a final identification which completes the set of equivalences installed by the opening stanzas: the reader, like "je," is invited to experience the adventure of a soul encountering that—the street-river, the text-spectre—which puts its existence in jeopardy. The whole poem, as narrative, thus figures the process of reading it; it serves as its own illocutionary code.

What more striking way could be imagined of illustrating the function of poetic reference as a self-reference which figures its own illocutionary context? By establishing the code common to the text and to its readership, it seeks to make of the reader the *only* subject such a text—as literary discourse, set adrift from its original context—can hope to have.

NOTES

1. M. Riffaterre, *Semiotics of Poetry* (Bloomington and London: Indiana University Press, 1978), p. 19.
2. "Les anomalies de la mimésis, les troubles de la référentialité apparente." M. Riffaterre, *La production du texte* (Paris: Ed. du Seuil, 1979), p. 77.
3. *Semiotics of Poetry*, p. 13.
4. Ibid., p. 2.
5. ". . . se situe dans les rapports du texte et du lecteur, non du texte et de l'auteur, ou du texte et de la réalité." *La production du texte*, p. 27.
6. I am using "felicitous" to describe a speech-act in which the illocutionary understandings of speaker and receiver coincide. But the "felicitousness" of an interpretation depends not only on the relationship between interpreter and text, but also on that between interpreter and audience. See R. Chambers, *Meaning and Meaningfulness* (Lexington, Ky: French Forum, 1979), pp. 172–180.
7. *Le récit spéculaire* (Paris: Ed. du Seuil, 1977).
8. Cf. "À une mendiante rousse" ("Au seuil de quelque Véfour/ De carrefour"); "Le Cygne" ("Comme je traversais le nouveau Carrousel/ . . . Paris change!"); "Les Petites Vieilles" ("Traversant de Paris le fourmillant tableau"); "Le squelette laboureur" (" . . .

sur ces quais poudreux/ Où maint livre cadavéreux/ Dort . . .''); "Le crépuscule du matin"
("Et le sombre Paris, en se frottant les yeux,/ Empoignait ses outils . . .''). Cf. in translation:
"To a Red-Haired Beggar-Girl" (At the door of some shabby cornerhouse); "The Swan"
(As I was crossing the new Carrousel bridge . . . Paris is changing!); "The Little Old
Women" (Passing through the swarming Parisian landscape); "The Digging Skeleton" (In
the book-boxes on the dusty quays where many a corpse-like book sleeps); "Morning Twi-
light" (And gloomy Paris, rubbing his eyes, laid hold of his tools).

9. "Paysage"; "Le Soleil"; "Les sept vieillards"; "Les Aveugles"; "A une passante";
"Le crépuscule du soir"; "Le Jeu." In translation: "Landscape"; "The Sun"; "The Seven
Old Men"; "To a Woman Passing By"; "Evening Twilight"; "Gambling."

10. "Danse macabre"; "L'amour du mensonge"; "Je n'ai pas oublié . . .''; "La servante
au grand coeur . . .''; "Brumes et Pluies."

11. Where possible the translation is taken from F. Scarfe, *Baudelaire* (Harmondsworth,
Baltimore, and Victoria: Penguin Books Ltd., 1961).

12. In fact the "mimetic" poems and the poems of mental representation form two sets
of serially arranged poems, which structure the section as a whole in terms of "diurnal" vs.
"nocturnal" experience. Cf. R. Chambers, " 'Je' dans les 'Tableaux Parisiens,' "*Nineteenth
Century French Studies*, XI, 1–2 (Fall-Winter, 1980–81), 59–68.

13. My italics in the quotations. From a different perspective, Karlheinz Stierle has also
concluded that the focal point of the "Tableaux Parisiens" lies in the figure of the observer
and his lyrical transformation of the scene. See K. Stierle, "Baudelaires *Tableaux Parisiens*
und die Tradition des *Tableaux de Paris*," *Poetica* (Juli 1974), 285–322; and cf. my " 'Je'
dans les 'Tableaux Parisiens.' "

14. The poem is built on a series of verbs in the imperfect tense ("La diane chantait,"
etc.). These appear to be setting the scene for the eventual introduction of a narrative event,
which however never occurs. The only possible point can therefore be to dramatize the
speaking situation itself, as a present opposed to the past being described.

15. See Klaus Dirscherl, *Zur Typologie der poetischen Sprechweisen bei Baudelaire*
(München: Fink, 1975).

16. See R. Chambers, "Saying and Seeing in Baudelaire's 'Les Aveugles,' " in R. Mitchell,
ed., *Pre-Text/Text/Context* (Columbus: Ohio State University Press, 1980), pp. 147–156.

17. "Baudelaire et l'espace poétique; à propos du 'Soleil,' " in *Le lieu et la formule:
Hommage à Marc Eigeldinger* (Neuchâtel: La Baconnière, 1978), pp. 111–120.

18. On allegory in Baudelaire, see especially Nathaniel Wing, "The Danaïdes' Vessel:
On Reading Baudelaire's Allegories," in *Pre-Text/Text/Context*, pp. 135–144. N. Wing
shows that in "Les sept vieillards" the poem deconstructs its own allegorical structure by
"figuring the reiteration of an allegorical figure as a repetition cut from any link to its
signified." By reading the poem as an allegory of itself (of its own failure to produce
meaning), one incorporates this deconstruction as a component of the poem's own code (of
its illocutionary axioms).

19. C. Baudelaire, *Correspondence I: 1832–1860* (Paris: Bibl. de la Pléiade, 1973), p.
583. Translation by Anna Whiteside.

20. C. Baudelaire, "Théophile Gautier," in *Oeuvres complètes II* (Paris: Bibl. de la
Pléiade, 1976) p. 126. Translation by Anna Whiteside.

21. "Baudelaire and the Limits of Poetry," *French Studies* XXXII, 4 (October 1978),
420–434.

REFERENTIAL INTERTEXTUALITY
PRE-CODE, CODE, AND POST-CODE

Bruce Morrissette

Referential polyterminology proliferates in current literary criticism to such an extent that the term "reference" becomes an element in that other quasi-universal terminological mix of our times, generative structure. No doubt reaction will set in, so that eventually the dozens of words and phrases, many of them neologisms and figurative usages, that have revolutionized critical vocabularies will diminish or disappear; but for the moment their heady brew intoxicates us, and we feel we are making critical discoveries of real importance as we add to the Saussurian innovations of *sign, signified, langue*, and *parole* such spin-offs as (poly)semantics, (poly)semiotics, destructuration, metaphoric displacement, metonymic condensation, syntagmatic and paradigmatic, metalanguage, diegesis, narrativity, and generative chains based on the concept of the code. It was while reading certain remarks by Roland Barthes on code and pre-code that it struck me that the coding process in literature also involved an essential further step, the post-code, in order to avoid creative stagnancy and to allow an endless creative spiral: this article is an effort to justify such an assumption.

The term code is, of course, so widely applied that it transcends literature and cinema. It originated outside these artistic domains, making literary and cinematic codes in a strict sense metaphoric or metonymic transfers. Indeed, there seems to be no form—written, auditory, visual, sociological, political, intellectual, or instinctive—that does not correspond in one way or another to some *code*. Man's mental content appears to be as codified as the very structure of his brain. And as cerebral codes demonstrably evolve, vary, and change forms in the course of mental activities, one is easily persuaded to see analogies between this procedure and the evolution of codes within the creative structures of literature and the arts.

In the life or progress of a code, we may search out its origin (often as a development of other pre-existent codes), its use in one or another art form (narrative literature, for example), its "infraction" (in a moment of rupture engendered by an intrusion of one or more contradictory codes), and finally its state of "pre-code," in which the code of an art work of advanced structure seems to disappear, before becoming in its turn—either in the same work, or in a later intertextual work—a "post-code," appearing in the chain of forms as a new coded point of departure.

The works of Alain Robbe-Grillet offer, both theoretically and at the level of *écriture*, perhaps the most highly developed and successful example of generated and generative chains of codes. The procedure can be seen in retrospect as already present in his first novels and films, with their radical manipulations of the traditional narrative modes of chronology, point of view, and scene linkages. Moreover, in his early works, extensive use is made of thematic sub-codes, such as the Oedipus myth-complex, parodied semi-seriously in *Les Gommes* [*The Erasers*], Steckelian sado-eroticism in *Le Voyeur* [The Voyeur], textbook schizophrenic paranoia in *La Jalousie* [*Jealousy*], and even, in the same work, conventional socio-political codes observed first by Jean-Paul Sartre and then treated in book length by Jacques Leenhardt.[1] Without here attempting a complete re-examination of code structures in these early works (something that remains to be done), we will use as a take-off point the theoretical and practical code processes described and illustrated by the preface, the text, and the film *Glissements progressifs du plaisir* [Progressive Slippages of Pleasure],[2] moving on then to the even more complicated stages of intercodes found in Robbe-Grillet's most recent works, *Topologie d'une cité fantôme* [*Topology of a Phantom City*][3] and *Souvenirs du triangle d'or* [*Recollections of the Golden Triangle*].[4]

The system expressed and developed in *Glissements progressifs du plaisir* and subsequent works is based on the passage from pre-code, code, and infraction of code to a re-coding through what Robbe-Grillet terms "un mouvement de rétrogradation du sens à mesure que l'oeuvre s'accomplit" [retrogradation of meaning as the work develops; *Glissements*, p. 13]. The "degraded" elements are thematic and structural materials drawn from literary and cultural conventions: folklore, detective stories, horror films, horror legends (for example, Bluebeard), pornographic paperbacks—what Robbe-Grillet calls a "panoply" of popular sources, reminiscent of Rimbaud's taste for "low class" literature and art as he describes them in the "alchimie du verbe" section of *Une Saison en enfer* [*A Season in Hell*] and of the Fantômas predilections of Breton and the surrealists. These codes create in the reader of the novel or the viewer of the film certain established expectations of situational development, of character, or of plot, based on familiar assumptions of interpretable themes. These assumptions Robbe-Grillet calls *sens*, or meaning, and it is the goal of his new code structure to destroy them, downgrade them, contradict them, make them impossible of logical understanding (as done almost unobtrusively with the time patterns of *La Jalousie*). As the new code progresses, the retrogradation of meaning creates what Robbe-Grillet terms "the irreplaceable Saussurian opposition between *langue* and *parole*." This structuralist analogy implies for the idea of the Saussurian *parole* a division between language or *pré-parole* and *parole* itself not unlike the distinction proposed here between pre-code and code. The borrowed, popular elements of Robbe-Grillet's system make up the *parole* of our culture, created by man and his groups out of the elements of *langage* found in the "dictionary" of our cultural life, the source of our popular Saussurian artistic-cultural *langue*. But, the author points out in his preface to *Glissements*, the cultural *parole* becomes merely the source or *langue* from which the writer-cinéaste takes the elements of his own *parole*: or, in our terms, the code (the source materials, already structured) becomes pre-code for the artist's new codes and forms. Thus, "les scènes de comédie, le goût du sang, les belles esclaves, la morsure des vampires, etc., ne représentent pas la parole de ce film, mais seulement sa langue" [the comedy scenes, taste for blood, enslaved beauties, vampire bites, etc., only represent this film's *langue* and not its *parole*): popular *parole* becomes *langue*, the source of a new *parole*. Robbe-Grillet adds, "C'est la parole d'une société qui a été découpée en morceaux afin de la faire rétrograder à l'état de langue." [It's the *parole* of a society which has been cut up into little pieces to make it regress to a state of *langue*.] This new *parole* formed by the structure of the created work, is "une structure non réconciliée . . . ma propre parole" [an unreconciled structure . . . my own *parole*]. The base elements (*langue* or pre-code used by popular writers and artists) are first structured in a cultural *parole* (code), which in turn becomes *langue* or pre-code for a passage into creative *parole* or post-code.

Adopting the three terms of pre-code, code, and post-code avoids a certain ambiguity in Robbe-Grillet's use of the same word, *parole*, to identify first his material sources (popular speech), and then my own speech or his own restructured encoding, or post-code. It should be noted that Robbe-Grillet's re-use of objects, themes, narrative situations, and the like from pre-existing coded materials creates a new *parole* or post-code in a sense different from that of Raymond Queneau, for example, in his famous *Exercices de style* [*Exercises in style*], in which the re-coding introduced by the author imitates so wittily stylistic elements from various domains of popular rhetorical codes. Robbe-Grillet's "infractions" and "degradations" function quite otherwise, passing by a sort of entropic process to a topological reconstruction leading to a degradation (rather than to a heightening, as with Queneau) of pre-existing codes and new structures at a level of heightened contradictions, in which the creative energy does not enhance (even satirically) the source code (as in *Exercices de style*), but surpasses and replaces it.

To name an object, said Mallarmé in an often quoted text, is to eliminate most of the enjoyment of a poem, which consists in gradual discovery; to suggest is the ideal.[5] Similarly, to point out or emphasize the transition from pre-code to code, or from code to post-code, runs the risk of making too obvious a reconstruction of the original and subsequent coding processes. Robbe-Grillet recognizes this danger: the various explanatory passages in the printed text of *Glissements*, which are numerous, alter or partially nullify the code infraction or the degradation of meaning intended by the writer: "rupture ceases to be abrupt, subversive, scandalous," he writes, "at the moment that I call it a rupture, and thereby integrate it into the structural continuity that it was supposed to destroy" (p. 12). This threat to the system's code inversions makes necessary a new movement towards deconstruction, described by Robbe-Grillet as a suite "de fragments, de ponctuations, de plans isolés (comme situés entre parenthèses), de répétitions ou de dédoublements" [of fragments, interruptions, isolated (and seemingly bracketed) shots, repetitions, or doublings] which appear to block the formation of a new code, meaning, or coherent discourse.

At the same time, another danger arises: if the fragmenting or deconstructive procedure applied to a given code involves the length or duration of narrative elements, if this time span is insufficient to allow, in the reader-spectator, the recognition or esthetic sensation of the presence of the original, point-of-departure code, the resulting incoherence leads not to a new *parole* or post-code but to a total absence of code, and a failure to establish a *parole*. The attack against coded meaning cannot therefore be absolute, since there must exist, at every moment of text or image, "un sens précaire, glissant, toujours prêt à s'effondrer" (p. 13), [a precarious, slippery meaning, constantly on the brink of collapse]. The "glissements progressifs" of Robbe-Grillet's title are metaphoric then not only of the slipping movements of erotic pleasure, but also of the slippages between elements of successive manipulated codes.

At this point, critical scrutiny reveals an apparent contradiction in the system described thus far: namely, the presence and identification of a new *sens* or coded meaning in the author's "proper parole" that in principle proposes only a progressive degradation of meaning. *Glissements progressifs du plaisir* illustrates this problem, and its preface and inner commentaries show Robbe-Grillet's awareness of it. In principle, as stated, the massive decoding of basic thematic elements (violence, falsehood, tortures, blood, death, and the like) aims at the annihilation of all meanings, and yet the metaphoric and metonymic interplay of images and dialogues in the film, the constant interaction of digital/linear and analogous/non-linear structures creates an immense figurative code of meanings surrounding the central code of sexuality that engulfs the smallest elements (for example, the shoe fetish), as well as scenes and décors of widely varied magnitude (dismembered mannequins, girls tied to wheels, secret torture caves, and many others), all leading to more complicated sequences that become the subject (in the printed text) of authorial commentaries that constitute baroque extravaganzas of analytic terminology: "rapport réaliste direct . . . rapport métaphorique . . . liaison métonymique . . . (où) chaque type de liaison peut subir des glissements vers les autres catégories . . ." (p.126), [a direct, realistic connection . . . a metaphorical connection . . . a metonymic link . . . (in which) every type of linkage can merge with the other categories . . .], commentaries which establish the idea of the title phrase, *glissements progressifs du plaisir*, as the central metaphoric meaning of the work, the multiform image junction between artistic creation and prolonged coitus. In a sense, the post-code of image slippages or *glissements* among the structural elements reverts to the pre-code of point of departure: for, as in traditional Freudian doctrine, the eroticism of the basic elements (popular sado-masochistic materials) all arise from the Freudian pleasure principle.

Thus, parodied, retrograded, inverted popular erotic images, supposedly annihilated in their transformation into the personal *parole* of the author, emerge reconstructed at a higher creative level in which Freudian desire reappears (as in the paintings of Magritte, who constantly uses the term *desire*) and assumes supremacy in the esthetic constructs of man, if not domination over his basic libido. If this interpretation is valid, it must be admitted that Robbe-Grillet does not totally destroy meaning: his deconstruction or de-coding is followed by a subtly coherent new and personal reconstruction or post-code, with its own identifiable meaning.

The creative artist, such as Robbe-Grillet, has recourse to yet another coding/re-coding technique analagous to the procedure thus far discussed. Again, the basic elements have already passed through one or more textual codings, in the form either of a published text by another writer (or a visual image by another artist), or of a pre-existing text, already printed or not, by the author himself. For this procedure I have used the term intertextual assemblage, a technique or procedure which at the present time forms the principal generator or encoding process in the newest fiction of Robbe-Grillet.

The intertextual technique of generative assemblage recalls procedures dating far back not only among writers who re-use portions of their previous works, with or without textual changes, but also among painters and, especially, composers; Bach's *B-minor Mass* is an assemblage of seven cantatas composed by Bach over two preceding decades. The music critic Andrew Porter, in an important article on Pierre Boulez,[6] describes Handel's *riscritura* of his own works, the self-quotations of Prokofiev, and other examples. Boulez's work uses as a structural base the fact that Mallarmé towards the end of his career wished to incorporate all of his texts into a single Work. Boulez, similarly, makes a final assemblage of his own Mallarméan compositions, some of which date back to 1958. The Italian critic Renato Barilli has studied the *riscritura* of such devotees of assemblage as Calvino, and everyone knows that the central idea of Balzac's *Comédie humaine* involved a total re-framing of his life work.

Such re-coded assemblages from the distant and recent past are, however, ex-ceeded by what Robbe-Grillet has proposed and accomplished in his latest works in a number of ways. Most of the re-integrated texts have their origins in composite compositions already involving more or less intercalated elements of a visual nature (pictures, photographs, lithographs, etchings) by artists whose works played or still play a self-reflexive role in the author's structural processes. The novel *Topologie d'une cité fantôme* (1976) contains texts taken from two early illustrated books with photos by David Hamilton (1971–72), a work with eleven etchings by Paul Delvaux (1975), a text accompanied by some twenty-one lithographs by Robert Rauschenberg (ca. 1976), the text of a Japanese advertisement for Suntory liquors (ca. 1974), and one large portion of a composite work using seventy-six reproductions of drawings and lithography by René Magritte. *Topologie* has been followed by *Souvenirs du triangle d'or* (1978), an assemblage containing the rest of the text related to Magritte pictures, the verbal text of a composite work using eighty-three black-and-white or sepia photographs by Irina Ionesco (1977), and the written portion of the catalogue prepared by Robbe-Grillet for the Jasper Johns exhibit held in June 1978 at the Georges Pompidou Centre National d'Art et de Culture. Titles, cuttings, transpo-sitions, and other details of these sometimes complicated splicings are given in my book *Intertextual Assemblage in Robbe-Grillet from Topology to the Golden Tri-angle.*[7] In the case of the living artists involved (Hamilton, Rauschenberg, Delvaux, for example) a kind of pseudo-collaboration has occurred; in the case of an already dead artist, Magritte, it is Robbe-Grillet who creates the illusion of collaboration, as he does with a living artist when he merely appropriates and uses existing works by Jasper Johns or integrates the photographs of Irina Ionesco into the developing text of a novel in progress.

Since the only creative hand involved in the Robbe-Grillet/Magritte work *La Belle Captive*[8] is Robbe-Grillet himself, it is instructive to examine the coding, re-coding, and other structuring processes used to produce the work, and to which the production of the "collaborative" books (for example, with Rauschenberg and Delvaux), may be compared and contrasted. On the back of *La Belle Captive*, Robbe-Grillet pays homage to Magritte as "un peintre qu'il aime entre tous" [one of his favorite painters]; elsewhere he has identified his susceptibility to the force of Magritte's neo-surrealist objects, such as the bowler hat, crescent moon, the famous *quille* (bilboquet, ninepin, chessman, baluster, spindle), drinking glasses, eggs, pipes, birds, *grelots* or harness bells, keys, candles, musical objects, doors, stones, and so on: a list which imperceptibly melds with "Robbe-Grilletian" objects already established in the author's *chosiste* dictionary, as they are joined by bicycles, shoes, eyes, valises, masks, phonographs, bottles, pistols. . . . All these become generators of diegesis for Robbe-Grillet, but they generate more than diegetic story line or narrative plot, for the Magrittian objects, along with the titles of the pictures in which they figure, undergo a chronological rearrangement and a titular evolution which impose on Magritte's works a narrative organization which at once engenders and reinforces a wholly new fictional form. This derived yet invented diegesis is sometimes quite close to the subject matter or title of an accompanying illustration, sometimes so far from the picture that the visual element seems denied, contradicted, decomposed. An example of close *rapport* between picture and plot is Magritte's painting "L'Assassin menacé" [The Threatened Assassin] and its development as the criminal on his own traces which underlines the story of *La Belle Captive* [The Beautiful Captive] as well as that of the other intercalated plots in both *Topologie* and *Souvenirs du triangle d'or*. Astonishingly coincidental, in the manner of the surrealist *hasard objectif*, Magritte's picture (admittedly discovered fairly late in Robbe-Grillet's career) seems already to "illustrate" pre-existing scenes from the author's early novels, films, or short texts. The killer pursued, watched, threatened: Mathias in *Le Voyeur*, Johnson in *La Maison de rendez-vous* [*The House of Assignation*], the interchangeable murderers in *Projet pour une révolution à New York* [*Project for a Revolution in New York*], Elias in the film *Trans-Europ-Express*, Alice in *Glissements progressifs du plaisir*, the Magrittian hooded killer of *La Chambre secrète* [The Secret Room], which was dedicated to another painter of similar scenes, Gustave Moreau. The fact that Magritte's picture derives from a scene in Feuillade's 1912 movie *Fantômas* further extends the chain of intertextual assemblage. Such is Robbe-Grillet's insistence on deconstruction that even where he accepts a wide general similarity in decor and plot, as in "L'Assassin menacé," he introduces alterations both large and small. In Magritte's picture, it is the two massive figures armed with cudgels and nets, watching from the sides of the door, who wear bowler hats; in the text, it is the murderer standing beside his victim. The phonograph in the painting is the old-fashioned mechanical type of the "His

Master's Voice'' era; and in the text, an even older one using a wax cylinder. The murdered girl on the divan in Magritte's painting becomes a mere "mannequin assassiné" in the text, diluting the diegetic realism. This constant interaction between text and image becomes a game for the reader-spectator: parallelism and deviation accompany the interplay of visual and verbal codes.

Of equal interest is the presence or absence in Robbe-Grillet's text of actual titles of Magritte pictures. A very few are used in quotation marks, referring directly to an illustration; most, if they are found at all, are worked into sentences and diegetic phrases. Not all of these, in turn, appear in the text proper of *La Belle Captive*: for example, the page of *Topologie* which precedes the beginning quoted passage from the Magritte/Robbe-Grillet work contains a "message" on a crumpled piece of paper reading: "Après les vendanges, l'assassin menacé prendra garde aux oeufs de l'oiseau qui brûle," an amalgam of (forthcoming) titles (after the grape harvest, the threatened assassin) and visual images (eggs, bird on fire) from Magritte. A number of persistent themes used by Magritte prefigure and reappear with an air of inevitability in Robbe-Grillet's narrative: such is the theme of the double. I have discussed elsewhere the many doubles in his early novels and films, relating them to the doubles of such literary predecessors as Poe and Dostoevsky. Magritte himself intercalates and quotes Poe extensively, and in the Poesque painting of the man looking into a mirror at the back of his own head ("La Reproduction interdite"[The Forbidden View]), the allusions to Poe there and elsewhere are reinforced by the presence of a book lying on the mantlepiece before the mirror, "Adventures d'Arthur Gordon Pym.'' It is especially the double of Poe's *William Wilson* that links paintings of Magritte to many passages in Robbe-Grillet's *Topologie* and *Souvenirs* in which the central narrator pursues one or another double of himself, "le criminel déjà sur mes [sic] propres traces" [the criminal already following me [sic]]. Intertextual assemblage becomes itself a series of mirror images and doublings; again, creative method, textual coding, becomes metaphoric of itself, of its own diegesis.

A final example of the complexities of coding or re-coding to be found in *La Belle Captive*, along with that of the enigmatic valise of the title page (the valise of the criminal-narrator, which does not appear in the picture of that title, but in other paintings of Magritte reproduced in the book), is the initial visual image, "Le Château des Pyrénées," minutely described in the novel's first pages. Research reveals that this picture of an aerolithic falling rock, with a château on its top, contains interrelated references to an early essay by Robbe-Grillet on Raymond Roussel, Breton's edition of Mathurin's *Melmoth* and his preface to that Gothic novel, Gautier's *Les Jeunes-France*, and an 1803 novel erroneously attributed (by Magritte as well as others) to Ann Radcliffe, author of the much admired *Mysteries of Udolpho*. Just as Magritte himself, in later paintings, removed the château and joined the large rock (now fallen) to the image of a woman with a rose, so Robbe-Grillet omits any reference to the château which he had formerly used in his Roussel analysis, and makes an important diegetic linkage with his rose/woman construct. We find in all this a kind of code-within-code operation which could be termed a spiraling *mise en abyme*.

Turning to Robbe-Grillet's fiction involving visual materials from living collaborators, such as Delvaux and Rauschenberg, we move towards a new dynamics of coding, decoding, and re-coding. Robbe-Grillet has described, in interviews and lectures, how the Delvaux section of *Topologie* (which appears with the Delvaux etchings in *Construction d'un temple en ruines à la Déesse Vanadé* [Construction of a Ruined Temple for the Goddess Vanadé], 1975) was produced: each of the 10 "chapters" was first written by the novelist, then sent to the artist, who made his etching and returned it to the writer, who then "transformed" the pseudo-illustration, creating in principle the same kind of interplay of similarities and differences, of reinforcements and contradictions, that the author had established alone in his work with the Magritte paintings. A picture-by-picture, text-by-text, study of *Construction* reveals that Delvaux's etchings do not constitute the kind of "transformation" of Robbe-Grillet's "chapters" that the author had in mind; it is possible to find almost everything that appears in Delvaux's pictures in the texts that precede them, so that the deconstructive generation sought by Robbe-Grillet becomes entirely a matter of his own re-codings, alterations, and departures. Instead of leading Robbe-Grillet towards new elements, Delvaux's etchings cause him rather to abandon specific visual correspondences. Nevertheless, a certain Delvaux atmosphere, doubtless due to the author's familiarity with Delvaux's style and the fact that, after all, the work was to be a kind of collaboration, persists in *Construction* and may be felt in reading the unillustrated corresponding pages of *Topologie*: neo-Roman architecture, reclining nudes, tramway lines, columns, wharfs, beaches, and the like. Just as Magritte's paintings seem like already existing illustrations of Robbe-Grillet, so does a certain neo-baroque, neo-romantic stylistic imagery already present in Robbe-Grillet seem to correspond almost naturally to Delvaux's subject matter and style.

Although stylistic similarities between the works of Rauschenberg and Robbe-Grillet are less evident, they too may be discerned as early non-"intentional" relationships in the case of Robbe-Grillet's use of objects already employed by Rauschenberg. As early as 1963, Marceline Pleynet in *Tel Quel*[9] pointed out possible relations between the Pop Art *chosisme* of the everyday objects of Rauschenberg's "combine" paintings (Coke bottles, chairs, neckties, ladders, and the like) and the minute object-descriptions of Robbe-Grillet's early novels. At the same time, the anti-war collages of bomb-blasted cities, urban blight, and other strongly socially-oriented pictures of Rauschenberg bore, at the time, little if any resemblance to the concerns of Robbe-Grillet. It was, and is, the formal materials used by Rauschenberg that attracted Robbe-Grillet, and a study of the over two dozen lithographs made by Rauschenberg for the joint work *Traces suspectes en surface* [Traces Suspect on their Surfaces] (1972–78), whose written text has been inserted into *Topologie*, reveals borrowings and transformations by the novelist and a lesser number of images created by the artist from materials of a purely verbal nature. A key work used by Rauschenberg in one lithograph, "Construction," is developed by Robbe-Grillet into a central metaphor for the fictionalization of his phantom city; Rauschenberg's familiar objects (wrecked cars, corridors, ruined buildings) are worked into Robbe-Grillet's diegesis. An enormous black bull, with dilated nostrils and bloodstained eyes, emerges from a lithograph and enters the text. Even the three eggs already excerpted from a Magritte picture for *La Belle Captive* occur coincidentally, and not suggested by any text sent to Rauschenberg, in one of his lithographs. Now and then, a written text furnishes material for a lithograph: thus the smoking volcano on page 20. But in general, the interchange between the writer and the artist involves constant transformations and re-codings, corresponding more closely to the compositional method used with less "success" in the case of Delvaux.

Much remains to be done to study *Traces suspectes en surface*, a task made difficult by the non-availability of the expensive book of lithographs and zinc plate written texts. The critic Tony Towle has described the physical and some of the structural aspects of the joint work in a valuable article which reveals how, even at the level of printing and coloration, various codings are involved:

> Rauschenberg's images were created for the book as he has created lithographs before, by transferring materials torn or cut from magazines to lithographic stones. He may alter images, or combine them before transferral. . . . There is an occasional image that exactly coincides with the text—for example, that of an egg, or a bull— but that is not usual.
>
> The crayon and brushwork with which Rauschenberg often enhances his images are themselves master strokes of abstraction. . . . There are three main color themes: red, in the variations of cardinal, lake, and fire; gray, in the form of silver gray, graphite, and blue graphite; of off-white and ocher. . . . There is also some orange, an occasional accent of green, an occasional light blue. A touch of color on one page often foreshadows its more extensive appearance on the next; there are rhythms of contrast and similarity from page to page.[10]

By far the most complicated fictionalization of visual inserts into narrative text thus attempted by Robbe-Grillet is found in a twenty-page section of *Souvenirs du triangle d'or* (pp. 130–150): a tour-de-force in which a dazzling array of image objects taken from the works of Jasper Johns is not only worked into diegetic situations and actions, but is reformed into interlocking relationships between hitherto discrete pictures. Robbe-Grillet supplied his text, as indicated earlier, to serve as a "Catalogue" for a large Jasper Johns exhibit in Paris, and published the text accompanied by reproductions of Johns's works from Michael Crichton's *Jasper Johns*, (Abrams, 1977); readers of *Souvenirs* can use Crichton's book as a readily available visual adjunct to the text. Robbe-Grillet's catalogue bore the title "La Cible" [the target], one of the central sources of images used repeatedly by Johns, and a natural diegetic source for the related fictional episode by Robbe-Grillet. The basic re-coding procedure used by Robbe-Grillet issues from the fact that whereas Johns subjects his image materials to almost unlimited formal variations (numbers overlapping or in separate units, in black, gray, and almost all other colors and arrangements; targets with and without faces and other objects, in many colors), he never interlocks different elements to create structural or metaphoric relationships. Between the twisted coat hanger of one picture and the bent spoon of another, Johns makes no specific connections. Robbe-Grillet, conversely, in diegetizing such elements, animates them in a narrative that brings together, in astonishing connections, almost all of Johns's materials; as the narrator in the *Souvenirs* text says, "tous les éléments . . . sont forcément reliés entre eux" (all elements are necessarily linked with each other). Johns's various number sequences generate narrative circles in which each number takes on coded meanings involving items from other Johns pictures: ale cans, broken mirrors, hand prints, light bulbs, strings ("bout de corde avachi, dit 'du voyeur' dans le rapport" [a length of old string, supposedly belonging to 'the voyeur' in the report]), shoe with mirror on the toe, flashlight, ruler, and other objects become the essential features of the diegesis, as the narrator pursues his complicated description of and escape from the "generative cell" in which he is imprisoned. So persuasive are the intercalations and reinterpretations of Johns's forms that one has the feeling that the painter himself *should have* foreseen all these possibilities. It would be difficult to find a clearer example of the intertextual progress from pre-code (the "real" pop objects, such as light bulbs and coat hangers), code (Johns's paintings and lithographs of Ballantine ale cans and the like), and post-code (Robbe-Grillet's narrative structures incorporating and extending these objects: a sort of "tels qu'en eux-mêmes Robbe-Grillet les change").

Auto-citation, *contaminatio*, *riscritura*, allusions and references to other authors, fictionalization of visual objects, rearrangements and redefinitions, in short all the techniques of generative intertextuality produce in *Topologie* and *Souvenirs du triangle d'or* a veritable *stretto* of coded forms in which appear such "combine materials" as the eggs of Rauchenberg and Magritte, the umbrella of Magritte and Lautréamont's *Maldoror*, the phonograph of *Projet pour une révolution à New York* and of Magritte's "L'Assassin menacé," the circles of Johns's numbers and the time-cell architectures of the narrator's prison in *Souvenirs*, and a vast panoply of old and new Robbe-Grilletian codes involving, in other "generative cells," chains, broken glass, keys, iron beds, bound girls, painter's easels with *mise en abyme* repetitions of narrative sequences, nudes descending iron stairs, fractured doubles, and so on and on. The post-code thereby becomes the state often referred to as post-modernism, with its doctrines and techniques of the anti-referential, the deconstructive: rupture of previous codes, annihilation of meaning, destruction of existing forms. But these negative creative operations lead, as we have seen, to a massive new coding in which meanings reappear and proliferate, since they are transformed into the new constructions themselves. The analytic process thus carries the critic into a new quasi-symbolic forest of intermixed images and texts, among new correspondences of metaphoric and metonymic condensations and displacements, in a domain of new codes of contemporary fiction which look out at the reader/spectator "avec des regards familiers."

NOTES

1. Leenhardt, J. *Lecture politique du roman: "La Jalousie" d'Alain Robbe-Grillet* (Paris: Minuit, 1973).

2. *Glissements progressifs du plaisir* (Paris: Minuit, 1974) has not yet been translated into English. My translations of passages cited.

3. *Topologie d'une cité fantôme* (Paris: Minuit, 1975); tr. J. A. Underwood, *Topology of a Phantom City* (New York: Grove, 1977).

4. *Souvenirs du triangle d'or* (Paris: Minuit, 1978), *Recollections of The Golden Triangle*, tr. J. A. Underwood, (London: Calder, 1984).

5. "Nommer un objet, c'est supprimer les trois-quarts de la jouissance du poème qui est faite du bonheur de deviner peu à peu: Le suggérer, voilà le rêve." Mallarmé, "Réponse à une Enquête" (1891).

6. "Alphabet of the Stars, à propos of Boulez' *Pli contre pli: Portrait de Mallarmé,*" *New Yorker*, March 20, 1978, 130–138.

7. (Fredericton, N. B.: York Press, 1979); cf. "Constructional Appendix," pp. 79–80.

8. *La Belle Captive* (Lausanne and Paris: La Bibliothèque des Arts, 1975).

9. No. 13 (Printemps 1963), 68–69.

10. Tony Towle, "Rauschenberg: Two Collaborations—Robbe-Grillet and Voznesensky," *The Print Collector's News Letter*, Vol. X, No. 2 (May-June 1979), 37–41.

X.

PRODUCTION, RECEPTION, AND THE SOCIAL CONTEXT

Patrice Pavis

Sign production: some theoretical problems

That theatre begins with a script which culminates in stage presentation is self-evident. Yet some scholarship in the semiotics of drama has taken as its premise the unity of the sign and the final product (performance) as a collection of signs. This approach does not reflect the development of signs and sign series, which starts with the writing of the text and ends with its vocal and visual emission by the actor. To forget that production stems from diverse sources and rhythms (including, for example, isolated signs such as lighting or costume, or complex signs with several levels such as plot or character), is to oversimplify signifying systems, and to fail to account for performance as a hierarchically structured entity. Moreover, the attention given to particular signs taken out of context fragments the performance and often leads to the naïve realist illusion that these signs are given in the theatre with their referent actualized on the stage and that it suffices, therefore, to examine them in isolation without relating them once more to the whole signifying structure from which they have been extracted. This "referential illusion" (that we see the *referent* of the sign, when, in fact, what we have before us is only its *signifier*) is the basis for the spectator's pleasure (seeing the real world represented before him). But this same referential illusion is the root cause of the theoretician's dissatisfaction (seeing the sign confused with reality). This misunderstanding results from a confusion of several levels of reality. Ingarden,[1] for example, suggests the following three categories:

1) Objects discursively referred to. Those not shown on stage, except "negatively," by their absence, and by the emotive impact they may have on what is made visible (actors, decor, etc.). Such "objects," then, are never made tangible; their function is to convey signifieds and their significance is the link between them and the visible action of the play.

2) Objects shown directly (actors, props)—not discursively referred to. To a large extent it is they that trigger the referential illusion, for the playgoer, like the theoretician, is convinced that such objects are the referents of the theatrical sign, or are both referents and signs.[2]

Now, from a semiological point of view, this kind of object is not the referent of a sign, but the signifier (tangible element) enabling one to reconstruct signified object X or character Y. We shall see, on examining the relationship between the sign and the world, that the *referent* is very closely linked to the signifier through the signified. But it is not the referent that we actually have before us on stage.

3) Objects discursively referred to and shown on stage. Here again, we get the impression of *being in the presence of* a stage referent which actualizes the referent of the linguistic sign. A common error is to assume that stage production, or *mise-en-scène* (literally, 'putting-on-stage,' namely, putting-on-view) consists solely in showing the referent of the text. This is where illusion reaches its peak, for it may seem that the stage is the exact referential translation of the referent spoken about in the text. In fact, in both categories of objects (shown and evoked), we have a sign whose signifier is present. The object/table that is seen and spoken about interests the spectator only insofar as he "semiotizes" it, by transforming it into a sign. What is perceived on stage, be it a "real" object or discourse about such an object, is not a referent but a signifier, the illusion of a referent. In the theatre *everything* is real *except* reality. Everything, including stage machinery, colours, forms, actors; *except reality*, since reality is transformed into signs as soon as it appears on stage.[3]

The spectator is thus the victim of a *referential illusion* when he thinks he sees Hamlet, his crown, his madness, whereas he perceives merely an actor, a stage prop, and the simulation of madness. In this kind of communication by ostension, therefore, it is not the referent of an object which is shown, but simply "an element of the class of objects to which it belongs."[4] As Evelyne Ertel rightly points out: "whether the stage object (a term which includes everything—human beings, stage sets, movements—produced on stage) is frankly a sign or pretends to be real, its fundamental status as a sign is not modified, only its ideological and aesthetic function varies."[5] Thus the referent is not actualized; it is fiction that we take to be real. Theatre (in the Western mimetic tradition) could be defined as a reality that the audience continually transforms into signs. One could invert Anne Ubersfeld's happy turn of phrase used to define theatre semiologically: "un réferent (un *réel*) qui fait signe"[6] [a referent (a *reality*) which makes a sign], and say that theatre is also *un signe qui fait réel* [a sign which seems real].

Does this mean that everything becomes a sign on stage? This is Evelyne Ertel's position in the wake of Saussure, whose thinking had a profound impact on the Prague Circle (especially Mukařovský, Honzl, and Veltruský). For Anne Ubersfeld, however, the stage should not be regarded as a total "mise-en-signe" [putting-into-signs]. Referential elements are still left (stage objects, and so forth) which are signs of nothing more than themselves, with the result, as Ubersfeld puts it, that "the concrete theatrical sign is both sign and referent."[7]

As I have tried to show, what is seen on stage, then, is not an actualized referent, but the *illusion of a referent*. Furthermore, the stage is perceived in two distinct modes which constantly overlap:

1) *Fiction*: character, plot, illusion, and consequently a semiotic system formed by coherent groups of signs.

2) *The real world*: the awareness of an actress's body, real stage, stage lighting, a space we share with the actors, and so on. Here the spectator refuses to cooperate by exchanging his real world for the fictional world that the actors offer him. He sees only real objects which have not been semiotized and translated into signs. This naïve mode of reception is obviously not "prohibited"—it is the prerogative of children and distracted persons, and it is conceivably one of the pleasurable sensations experienced by the spectator.

The fiction/real world dichotomy has nothing to do with the sign/referent distinction. What we are dealing with is the contrast between 1) the *possible fictional world* of an illusion created by systems of signs, *versus* 2) the *real world* in which we, the members of the audience, with our particular desires and powers of perception, exist.

The complexity of the semiotics of drama (just like the pleasure of the spectator) stems from the interplay between these two worlds. In fiction we always find, strung together, bits and pieces of our own reality and of our psychological and social universe. Identification with a character or with an ideological situation is thus possible only on the basis of lived experience. Curiously enough, it is ideology— through the phenomena of recognition and eroticism (the combined effects of familiar reality and the actor's body)—which attracts us and draws us into the spectacle. Hence ideology and the social context superimpose, on the fabric of a work of art, a living trace of the *spectator's* reality. In the ideology given form by the artistic sign, just as in the body lent by the actor to his character, there is always a "physical residue" which cannot be semiotized and which Anne Ubersfeld calls "L'être-là de l'acteur" [the actor's physical presence]. It is first and foremost this body and the living and unpredictable person that we have before us. The "physical residue" could, for example, be the pretty legs of the actress which have an erotic effect on me; it will also be, on an ideological plane, what I recognize in the fiction that corresponds to my own ideological situation. Thus it becomes necessary, in order to understand the fiction offered, to compare the *possible world* of the dramatic universe with the *real world* of an audience, at any given moment of reception. It would thus seem that in considering the production of the sign and determining its meaning, attention needs to be refocused on the problem of reception and on a comparison between the sign and the ideological universe of the receiver. The sign cannot therefore be taken as a self-contained entity; it is necessarily to be interpreted as a unit forming part of a discursive and ideological whole.

It follows that the theatrical sign does not refer to a visible and isolated referent. Its meaning is contingent on a discursive construct. Discourse has become a major preoccupation of linguistics, for it was soon realized that Saussure's distinction between language and speech did not hold when the meaning and usage of words in the linguistic system had to be defined, and that the meaning of a word depended on a concrete speech (discourse) situation: "It is in discourse," remarks Émile

Benveniste, "that language is formed and takes shape. That is where all language begins. As the classical saying has it: *nihil est in linguo quod non prius fuerit in oratione.*"[8]

This semiological principle of an exchange between a system (language) and speech (discourse) is fundamental for the semiology of art, in which every element of the message derives its meaning from its context in the whole in which it appears. This is true of every sign produced in a text or in a performance. The sign is subordinate to the social and historical situation of its use. Benveniste called this relation between the sign and the exterior world *semantics* (as opposed to *semiotics*, the interrelationship of signs): "With semantics we enter into a specific world of meaning which is engendered by discourse. . . . The semantic order is identified with the world of enunciation and the universe of discourse."[9] This entails decoding *theatrical* signs not only structurally, in their internal relationships with other systems of the text and performance, but also *semantically*, that is, from the perspective of their discursive and ideological context. Mukarovsky's semiological model will help illustrate how meaning (the *signified*) is produced, beginning with the *signifier* and passing through the "total context of social phenomena" (the discursive referent). His model (fig. 1) will enable us to synthesize modes of production and reception in the light of some major existing theories.

I shall be concentrating here on two aspects of production and reception: concretization, and ideology and text theory. Is the exclusion of the element that connects text and stage, the production of textual and stage signs and their reception by the audience? (Needless to say, this is a vast problem in itself, which would require an appropriate theory of fiction to account for the ambiguities and multiple possible readings of the same text, as well as the staging of spatial, temporal, and actantial aspects of a playscript.)

The diagram, which divides artistic communication into production and reception, should first be read vertically, starting with the four main columns which include the main theories of production and reception: (1) formalism, (2) sociology of contents, (3) aesthetics of reception, (4) the theory of speech acts. The distinction between (1), (2) and (3), (4) is determined by the function of the sign. *Production* will entail examining the sign with special emphasis on its signifier, by establishing syntactic oppositions (formalism), or by focusing on its signified and its reference to reality as expressed through the work of art. For *reception*, the determining factor is the relation between the sign and its user; in other words, the pragmatic dimension. The aesthetics of reception is concerned with the way the reader (or spectator) receives signs. The theory of speech acts (which will not be discussed here) examines the ways an utterer produces meaning by analyzing utterances in the context of their use.

1A) Emphasis on the signifier and the syntactic dimension led to a *formalist method* concerned exclusively with the functioning of signs within a closed system. A distinction should be made between two kinds of formalism: the first, stemming from the Russian Formalists, with a focus on literary forms and their evolution, and the attempt to determine the specific properties of the literary text (literariness)

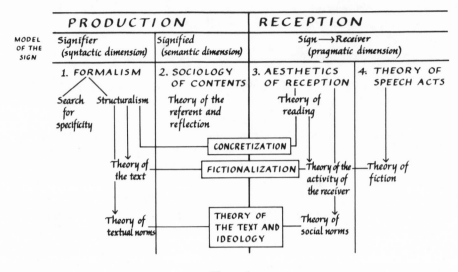

Figure 1

or the dramatic text (theatricality), by comparison with so-called ordinary language. Its failure was to be foreseen, given that no account was taken of the pragmatic criteria of the circumstances of usage of a text.

1B) The second mode of formalism, *structuralism*, has been far more fertile, for it has (sometimes) succeeded in opening the text to history. The semiological variant of structuralism (the Prague Circle, for instance), has even managed to produce a model integrating, with a certain degree of flexibility, the reader or the spectator.

2) These two modes of formalism developed as a reaction against a sociology of contents centred on *the signified*. This sociological approach, informed by the social and psychological circumstances of literary production, nevertheless always lacked a theory of the text (which stems from structuralism), leading thus to a dead end, all the more regrettable for having blocked a Marxist theory of literature, which might have been more exacting than a simple doctrine about the way reality is reflected in a work, or about ideology as an inextricable jumble or false consciousness.

3) With regard to *reception* and the pragmatic dimension of the sign, methodologies which normally reject production theories have evolved recently, privileging phenomenology (Ingarden), hermeneutics (Gadamer) and especially "Rezeptionsästhetik" (the Konstanz School—Jauss and Iser in particular).[10] This reversal, although necessary in view of the stagnation of traditional aesthetics, has tended sometimes to adopt too unilateral an approach by confining itself, for example, to the effect produced on the audience to the exclusion of the techniques that triggered a particular reception. Nevertheless, reception studies have provided useful theories regarding the different levels of reading and the history of effects produced (*Wirkungsgeschichte*), reader response, as well as social and literary accounts of literary history.

In what follows, my purpose will be to build bridges among the four production and reception theories briefly outlined by utilizing in each case elements common to all four. Three links will be emphasized (see fig. 1): 1) *Concretization*—structuralism, in its very opposition to the theory of the work as reflection, can be taken as a theory of reading and therefore as a structuring of dramatic and stage material by the spectator. 2) *Fictionalization*—the theory of fiction, stemming from studies on convention, possible worlds, and rules of fictional discourse, can be confronted with the structuring activity of the reader, who himself organizes narrative material according to a theory of the text, structuralist in origin. (This problem will not be dealt with here.) 3) *The Theory of the Text and Ideology*—brings together a theory of the text (as devised by various semiologists) and a theory (which has not yet been fully articulated) of the relationship between the text and discursive and ideological structures.

Reception and Concretization

We have so far observed the inadequacies of two theories. In the one, the sign is inward-looking and autonomous; in the other, on the contrary, the sign surreptitiously becomes the referent. Ideally, both pitfalls should be avoided. To achieve this, a semiological model is needed which transcends Saussure's binary system and offers a mediation between the sign and the social reality in which it is produced and received. Mukarovsky's concept of "art as a semiological fact" provides an excellent starting point. Mukarovsky distinguishes between the artifact (the signifier), the aesthetic object (the signified), and the "relation to the thing signified" in these terms:

> "Every work of art is an autonomous sign composed of: 1. an *'oeuvre-chose'* (a work of art as a thing) which functions as a tangible symbol; 2. an 'aesthetic object,' lodged in the collective consciousness and which functions as meaning or 'signification'; 3. a relation to the thing signified; this relation aims not at a separate existence—since it concerns an autonomous sign—but at the total context of social phenomena (science, philosophy, religion, politics, economy, etc.) of a given milieu."[11]

Mukarovsky's semiology, going beyond Saussureanism, is concerned with the production and reception of a work of art (literary, or if theatrical, a dramatic text, a performance or specialized aspects of theatrical form such as the stage, dialogue, stage signs, and so forth). Production and reception occur as follows: a) perception of the artifact, namely the signifying substance and structure of the work: whether it be the text heard, a lighting effect, or a gesture, the *"oeuvre-chose"* is first perceived as a tangible symbol; b) in order to be assimilated (endowed with a signification "lodged in the collective consciousness") in its capacity as signified, the signifier must first be located by the receiver (reader or spectator) in the "total context of social phenomena" (hereafter designated as the *Social Context*). The sign therefore acquires its signified (its meaning) only after contact with the social context of the work and its receiver (interpreter). The aesthetic object (the meaning of the work of art) thus comes into being only after the sign (whose signified is so far only approximately determined) is linked to Social Context. At the end of this process, as we shall see, the *"oeuvre-signe"* (the work of art as a sign) becomes a specific aesthetic object or concretization.[12] The latter is a particular reading of the work more or less clearly objectified (in a commentary or series of reactions). To be explicit, the concretization itself must be reconstituted. In the theatre, the director concretizes his reading of a play through his production (a "concretization of a concretization"), while the spectator engages in a "concretization of a concretization of a concretization." In order to *read* the text produced, the spectator experiences a dramaturgical reading, then the director's stage reading (or, if the latter does not yet explicitly exist, the production). In practice it is not possible for the spectator to differentiate between the reading of the text by the director (its first concretization) and the latter's work of stage transposition (its second concretization). This is not important, though. What counts is the result—the work as produced on stage. Reading a production, reading theatre [*Lire le théâtre*], to borrow Anne Ubersfeld's expression, means reading a visual performance as well as reading a theatre director's reading of a playscript.

The most complex phase of signification and concretization is the linkage with the Social Context. Suffice it to say here that this includes: 1) the content of the work (as well as elements referred to therein in various ways), and 2) the social and ideological link with the receiver performing the concretization. This link determines and elucidates the content of the work. Linkage with the Social Context enables the receiver to construct the imaginary referent of a work and its fictional world; this, in other words, is the process of fictionalization.

It follows that a work is neither a single 'correct,' signifying structure, nor an infinite number of amorphous possibilities; rather, it assumes meanings which are historically differentiated according to changes in the Social Context. Consequently, the structuring of a work results not from formalist games, but from the awareness of a change in the Social Context of reception.

Thus for the first time, perhaps, it is possible to assert with Mukarovsky the structural and therefore the formal significance of social and ideological awareness. Structuralism and ideological content are therefore not incompatible, but may be linked dialectically, thereby shedding light on the whole of the production/reception dimension of a work. This is close to the position of Adorno, who placed even greater emphasis on the dialectical tension between a work and society: "The immanence of society in the work is the essential social relationship of art, not the immanence of art in society. Because the social content of art is not established externally in its *principium individuationis*, but is inherent in individuation, itself a social element, the social essence in art is hidden, and can only be grasped by interpretation."[13]

Let us return briefly to the fundamental difference between the artistic sign and the linguistic sign as devised by Saussure (fig. 2). In the Saussurean model, the linguistic sign is defined only as the unbreakable bond between a signifier (the sound) and signified (the concept); the referent is not taken into account at all,

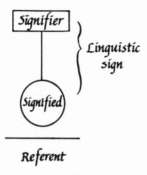

Figure 2

except insofar as it is seen as identical to the signified. The referent is detached, and so created and named, by the linguistic division, and follows in "the wake of the signified." Saussure claims that the relationship between signifier and signified is arbitrary. Benveniste corrects this assertion by showing that "what is arbitrary is that one particular sign rather than another is applied to a given entity rather than to another."[14] The break which takes place is therefore between the sign and the referent; there is no relationship of motivation (necessity or iconicity) between the world and the sign. Benveniste posits two types of sign relationship. The connection between signs within a system he calls *semiotic*, and that between the sign and its referent, *semantic*. Saussure's theory does not require a third term for the sign, the referent, since the latter is constructed by the division of the sign. Whether it is "real" or discursive, the referent is never more than an extension of the signified. Furthermore, the referent is constructed and stabilized by the practice of language. Its existential dimension can be verified by the concrete relationship between us and the world.

The artistic sign, and consequently the semiology of art, cannot be based simply on the linguistic model. In fact, the artistic sign (be it literary, theatrical, cinematic, architectural, etc.) is not initially given as a recurrent unit already detached from the continuum of the work and clearly divided up into signifier and signified. For a work to become meaningful, the artistic sign can only be defined by a receiver external to the work and thus belonging to (Mukařovský's) Social Context, in fact, to the referent. The latter is created by fiction; it has no existential value. Hamlet's court or a scene represented in a painting do not exist as such, as an autonomous external world. They are no more than a referential illusion. Nonetheless, it does have close links with the reality of the Social Context (our real world). This is why the artistic sign always has a motivated rather than a "mimetic" link with the referent of the Social Context (even in the case of abstract art, music, or concrete poetry). The motivated link, however tenuous, is never broken. A cow, whether it is represented by a photograph, a drawing by Picasso, or even the gestures of mime, always has something to do with the cows we come across daily—quite simply because we can identify the cow in the photo, picture, or gesture on the basis of our experience or knowledge. From his vantage point in the Social Context, the receiver perceives in the signifier forms, colours, sounds, material elements to which he can give meaning.

Unlike the linguistic sign (which is already isolated and determined by a code and an accepted convention, grammar), the artistic sign must be identified and extracted from a work of art by the receiver. Obviously this cannot be achieved without reference to the work of art itself, which contains signifiers linked to the Social Context, and specifically, to ideology. The latter is thus not the content "above" or outside the work, but a semiotization or codification of the referent in the form of discursive practices. Ideology is therefore "textualized," absorbed into the work in the form of a discursive referent. A reciprocal process then occurs from the Social Context (the referent) to the signified. Thus defined, the sign becomes the concretization of the work, with the result that a specific signified (or concretization) corresponding to a given response on the part of the reader/spectator can now be associated with the signifier.

Figure 3 illustrates the process.

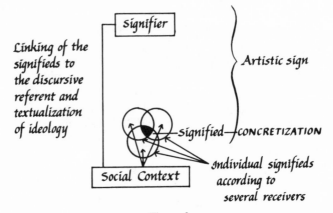

Figure 3

Textualization of Ideology

I now come to the central problem to be examined here: the infiltration of ideology into a literary work and its textualization. The fictionalization that occurs in reading any text provides the links between the text and Social Context. In order to construct the possible world of a text, we must refer to our own real universe. Any theory of ideology or of the ideological must necessarily examine the make-up of the Social Context. By "ideological" I do not mean a closed system of (distorted) ideas about the world, but rather a characteristic of the text on a par with the autotextual and the intertextual. The ideological is not limited and locatable like a theme at a specific point in a literary text, but present at all levels, especially in a text's structure, form, and materiality. The ideological is a mediating force between production and reception, between the text and social context, as well as between literary *form* and social *content*.

It is, of course, very difficult indeed to determine the precise nature of the relationship between ideology and the artistic text. Rather than oversimplify a complex problem, my remarks will be confined to a textual and semiotic analysis of ideology, the latter thus being firmly anchored in dramaturgical and stage materiality. Any reflection on ideology must begin with Marxism and the *camera obscura* in which ideology is glimpsed as false consciousness and a mystification of social relationships: "Consciousness can never be anything but the conscious Being and the Being of men is their process of real life. And if, in the whole of ideology, men and their relationships appear in an upside-down position as in a *camera obscura*, this phenomenon results from historical being, in exactly the same way as the reversal of objects on the retina results from physical being."[15] This inverted image, linked, according to Marx, to the ideological domination of the middle class, has become the unique and universal characteristic of ideology seen as "false consciousness" (Lukacs) or even, significantly, as the hallmark of all literature, since the literary text is defined (by Étienne Balibar, for example) without any concern for nuance, as "the *operator* of a reproduction of ideology in its entirety."[16] A typical Marxist standpoint. Thus it seems that Marxist aesthetics often limits the role of ideology to that of gamekeeper in the economic domain of the middle class. Even France Vernier, whose work represents a notable advance in Marxist literary theory, restricts dominant ideology to the role "of helping to maintain the power of the dominant class as part of the complex and contradictory processes whereby capitalism strives to reproduce the production relationships necessary to it."[17] The purpose of ideology, the enslavement of others for the benefit of one class, has been taken for granted for a long time; it still remains to be seen whether this is its sole function and above all why it is so effective and so difficult to eradicate from man's consciousness and from the literary text. The conceptual figures of the traditional theory of ideology (the distorted reflection, the inverted image, darkness and obscurantism, and so forth) do not use visual metaphors innocently. This is the confusion that a modern theory of ideology can avoid with the help of a semiological system whose focus could be the signifying structure of text or stage. It is thus possible to eschew the nebulous vision of the text as a slavish reflection of the social element or of a specific ideological allegiance. Ideology is, on the contrary, absorbed into the very fabric and structure of the literary text.

The coupling of text to referent is not done directly. It is contingent on a theory of the referent and referentialization that links the text to an ideological frame; it is, of course, the task of the reader or spectator. The theory of reception is therefore particularly well suited to studying the manner in which a literary work acquires meaning by being linked to an ideological discourse extraneous to it. To conclude from this, as does Bernard Valette, that "if there is an ideology, it can scarcely be anyone's but the reader's,"[18] is a step we must be careful not to take, for this would privilege the reception mode to an excessive degree, entrusting it with full responsibility for the construction of meaning. Clearly, though, as we have seen, the work foregrounds the signifier in ways that linkage with the Social Context cannot entirely eliminate.

The coupling of text to discursive referent brings us back to the link between discourse and the world (words and things), and implicitly to the distinction between signifier, signified, and referent. The referent, in my view, not to be conceived of as a real object, is the mediator between words and things.[19] Things do not exist autonomously, but are constructed by discourse. Of course, this does not mean that the external world does not exist and that there is only a maze of words, but that the world is contingent on discourse, needs to be named. Thus, for example, we can identify the object to which the expression *the little blue table near the radiator* refers in the real world; but *a coffee table* only refers if the situation in which this kind of table is used is reconstructed. The referent "coffee table" only means in a specific context of usage; the same applies *a fortiori* to literature. If I read that Orgon hides under the table, I must, in order to understand this utterance, construct in my imagination a fictional world (a story told by Molière) in which Orgon and his table assume meaning. This is true even in the theatre. Orgon's table may be in front of me on stage, yet it is no more real for all that; the table on stage is not the actualized referent, but a re-presentation of what it could be in Molière's fictional universe. (My position is thus diametrically opposed to the frequent argument that theatre, unlike the other arts, represents its referent).

The linking of the text to an ideology extraneous to it is not merely a process of recognition (of the signified); it is, rather, a semiotic mechanism, connecting text to a field of discourse (that is, a discursive referent). As Baudrillard rightly points out, Marxism nearly always has a "mythical" conception of ideology, for it defines it as an extraneous thought content: "The [Marxist] 'criticism' of ideology rests on a magical notion of it. It does not decipher ideology as form, but as content, as a given transcendent value, a sort of *mana* which might attach itself to a few great representations, magically imbuing floating and mystified subjectivities called 'consciousnesses.' "[20]

To understand a text, then, is not to visualize or imagine the realities of which it speaks (a virtually impossible task in many cases), but to link it to the discursive practices in which it is rooted. This is particularly essential when a text mentions things (a palace, a prince, a counsellor) that I cannot comprehend from my solitary standpoint and knowledge of relevant history alone, without referring them to discursive and political practices peculiar, say, to the eighteenth century. But is it enough to refer the reader/spectator to a discursive structure that can be reconstructed from contrastive forms of discourse? Can one, like Foucault, hover between words and things, by confining oneself to a discursive structure to which words refer, without determining their referent?

From an analysis like the present one, *words* are as deliberately absent as *things* themselves; there are no more descriptions of vocabulary than there is recourse to the living plenitude of experience. One cannot return to the nether side of discourse— where nothing has yet been said and where things can barely be discerned in the grey

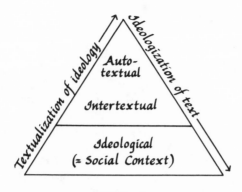

Figure 4

light; one cannot transcend discourse to rediscover forms it has deposited and left behind; one remains, one endeavours to remain, on the level of discourse itself.[21]

"To endeavour to remain on the level of discourse": is this not tantamount to admitting a very precarious balance between two extremes: a closed syntax of discursive mechanics described "from the inside" (constraining the critic and the historian by forcing them to describe the rules of a game whose implications escape them), and a materialist theory of discursive structures (be they economic, political, or infrastructural)? Thus, after taking the one step forward that Foucault hesitates to take (despite the encouragement of his Marxist critics) there is this new pitfall: a materialist and historical theory of ideological relationships.[22]

In the light of the preceding discussion of concretization, fictionalization, and discursive and ideological structure, I propose to delineate some guidelines for the study of ideology in a literary text and beyond it. Between a text and its discursive anchor, several constraints govern the manner in which ideology is textualized and the reader/spectator locates ideology in textual, dramaturgical, and stage forms. Both two-way processes occur simultaneously. 1) *Textualization of the Ideological*: A discursive referent and a given ideology culminate in a specific text, concretized in a signifying structure. This process occurs on two levels, autotextual and intertextual. 2) *Ideologization of the Text*: The linking of text to ideology occurs first on the autotextual, then on the intertextual level, and thus entails a filtering process, culminating in the text in its final concretized form. In figure 4,[23] three levels (ideological, intertextual, autotextual) are apparent; each represents a modalization of the previous one, and thus a semiotic structuring of a given discourse or ideological perception of reality.

1) *The ideological* was examined in detail earlier in the discussion on the discursive referent. This is the first phase of the structuring process. The main object is to link snatches of discourse on the basis of common social practice. The constructed text continues to refer to this as a "they say" level which guarantees textual content.

2) *The intertextual* comprises the various subtexts (verbal as well as visual and

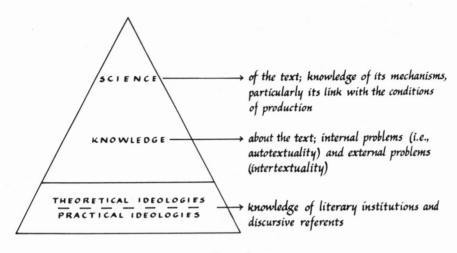

Figure 5

artistic) with which a literary work is (or can be) associated thematically, structurally, or stylistically. The intertextual is both what the text is made up of and
what it is written against. Though invisible at first glance, the intertextual is an
integral part of a literary text.

3) *The autotextual* is the self-contained, self-referential level whereby a text claims
autonomy and adopts the perfectly rounded form of a monad, thus fending off
outside influence, intertextual or ideological. This type of self-referentiality, though
common especially in modern literature, is to be found in any text which calls
attention to the processes it employs. In the theatre, where it takes the form of
theatricality, it is the crux of the illusion/disillusion dichotomy, hovering between
the "real" and the "theatrical."

There is a dialectical tension between the autotextual and the intertextual (and
hence between unity and multiplicity); the artistic text aims either at originality or
at the imitation of earlier models. A second, deep-seated tension is to be observed
between the autotextual, purportedly autonomous, and the ideological, supposedly
universal and pervasive.[24] Thus, surface text itself is no more than the tip of the
iceberg: it is made up of the same "ice" as its self-referential parts and its subtexts,
the whole being linked to ideological roots. It is up to the reader, though, to
"concretize" it. We could superimpose on figure 4 a new diagram (see figure 5),
drawing on theories of Althusser, Foucault, and Lecourt, linking ideology, science,
and knowledge. Some reservations are in order, by way of caution and clarification:
1) The concretized text is comparable to a science for the reader who masters the
mechanisms that control it. 2) Knowledge about the text concerns the autotextual
and intertextual dimensions, which are contingent on the relationship between signifiers and intertext. The "science of the text" stems from this knowledge, which
denotes the activity of the reader in the semiotic process of textualization. 3) Ide-

ology is divided into practice and theory, practical ideologies determining the form and limits of theoretical ideologies.[25] For literature and theatre, institutions (type of theatre, control and circulation of books, etc.) constitute practical ideology and form part of the Social Context and social status of the writer and text.

Figures 4 and 5 illustrate in broad terms the impact of ideology on concretized text; detailed analyses would help ascertain the permeability of the various levels. Ideology infuses a text gradually, but the process only rarely (and usually unreliably) permits identification of an ideological theme. It is located more subtly in the formal properties—in the signifying structure and in passages where autotextuality invites reflection on the means it employs to conceal its ideological origin. In the theatre, the process is exemplified by phenomena such as the Brechtian alienation effect, characters' conflicting points of view, the so-called objectivity of theatrical communication, or theatrical foregrounding (or sign effects).

Ideology thus encourages focus on the *form* of a work of art. This has the immediate effect of enabling the receiver to escape from the autonomous work and to link the text to the discursive referent outside it. Ideology is not located on the "direct" level of content, nor on the level of pure forms, which are meaningless until linked to the Social Context.

Ideology plays the role assigned by Barthes to connotation, which expels from the text secondary signifieds, only meaningful in the context of the referent and ideology: "These signifieds are closely linked to culture, knowledge, history; one could say that through them the world penetrates the system; in short, *ideology* is the *form* (in the Hjelmslevian sense of the term) of the connotation signifieds, while *rhetoric* is the form of the connotators."[26] Thus literary form alerts the reader to what ideology instills into him subconsciously. But ideology is neutralized by literary form as soon as it enters the work of art. For Adorno, this is art's only merit, for it allows ideology to speak through it: "Works of art are great only insofar as they reveal what ideology hides."[27]

Thus the debate between form and content, temporarily rejected, though not eliminated, by structuralism, is reopened. It raises many complex issues, difficult to pursue methodically. If ideology is indeed *the other* in the text (which the text seems to deny) and if as Baudrillard had it, "it is a ruse of form to be continually veiled in the conspicuousness of content,"[28] it is a waste of time to look for forms which conceal other forms. It is, however, the task of unveiling forms behind forms (or, to use Brecht's words, "processes *behind* processes") that we must now pursue in two directions: the textualization of ideology and the ideologization of the text.

NOTES

1. R. Ingarden, "Les fonctions du langage au théâtre," *Poétique* 8 (1971).
2. A. Ubersfeld, "Sur le signe théâtral et son référent," *Travail théâtral* 31 (1978), p. 123.
3. To illustrate the ideological linking of the sign, a simple example will suffice: the

sign /prince/ in a play by Marivaux. For the linguistic sign, like the visual sign (the actor who portrays the prince), there is no direct referent; to understand this term one has to look for its meaning not in the thing, but in the word, or rather, in discursive practice in the eighteenth century and today. It is the discursive referent and the possible context of usage which enable us to determine its meaning. See C. Buzan, "Dictionnaire, langue, discours, idéologie," *Langue Française* 43 (1979), p. 41.

4. U. Eco, *A Theory of Semiotics* (Bloomington: Indiana University Press, 1976).

5. E. Ertel, "Eléments pour une sémiologie du théâtre," *Travail théâtral* 28–29 (1977), p. 147.

6. "Sur le signe théâtral et son référent."t p. 121.

7. Ibid., p. 123.

8. *Problèmes de linguistique générale I* (Paris: Gallimard, 1966), p. 131.

9. E. Benveniste, *Problèmes de linguistique générale II* (Paris: Gallimard, 1974), p. 64.

10. R. Ingarden, *Das literarische Kunstwerk* (Tübingen: Niemeyer, 1931); *Von Erkennen des literarischen* (Tübingen: Niemeyer, 1968). H. G. Gadamer, *Wahrheit und Methode-Grundzüge einer philosophischen Hermeneutik* (Tübingen, 1972, 3rd ed.).

On the "Konstanz School" see R. Varning, *Rezeptions-ästhetik* (München: Fink, 1975); *Poétique* 39 (September 1979), "Théorie de la réception en Allemagne." For an approach to reception in the theatre, see A. Ubersfeld, "Notes sur la dénégation théâtrale," *La relation théâtrale*, R. Durand, ed. (Lille: Presses Universitaires, 1980); P. Pavis, "Pour une esthétique de la réception théâtrale," ibid.

11. Jan Mukarovsky, "L'art comme fait sémiologique," *Poétique* 3 (1970); originally published in *Actes du huitième congrès international de philosophie* (Prague, 2–7 septembre 1934), Prague, 1936, pp. 1065–1072.

12. This theory on concretization, borrowed from Mukarovsky (*The Word and Verbal Art*, tr. John Burbank and Peter Steiner; New Haven & London: Yale University Press, 1977), is developed by F. Vodička who uses Ingarden's term, concretization. The latter is a convenient label for several theatrical concepts including individual readings, dramaturgical analysis, and stage presentation.

13. Th. W. Adorno, *Asthetische Theorie* (Frankfurt: Suhrkamp, 1970), p. 345 (my translation).

14. E. Benveniste, *Problèmes de linguistique générale I*, p. 52.

15. K. Marx, F. Engels, *L'idéologie allemande* (Paris: Editions Sociales, 1968), p. 50.

16. E. Balibar, P. Macherey, "Sur la littérature comme forme idéologique: Quelques hypothèses marxistes," *Littérature* 13 (février 1974), p. 46.

17. France Vernier, *L'Écriture et les textes: Essai sur le phénomène littéraire* (Paris: Editions Sociales, 1974), p. 53.

18. B. Valette, "*Cendrillon* et autres contes: lecture et idéologie," in C. Duchet, ed., *Socio-critique* (Paris: Nathan, 1979).

19. M. Pêcheux, on rereading Althusser, makes this point very clearly: "everything said here about 'words' concerns in fact the entire area of discursive processes, and is *ipso facto* applicable to the most general of expressions, formulations, etc., which happen to represent, in circumstances of varying historical importance, politico-ideological *stakes* . . . (by expressions like 'the oil crisis', 'the dictatorship of the proletariate', 'the purpose of history' . . . or utterances such as 'man makes history', 'class struggle is the mainspring of history')." *Les Vérites de la Palice* (Paris: Maspero, 1975), p. 195.

20. J. Baudrillard, *Pour une critique de l'économie politique du signe* (Paris: Gallimard, 1972), p. 174 (my translation).

21. Michel Foucault, *L'Archéologie du savoir* (Paris: Gallimard, 1972).

22. Althusser seems to warn him of this danger in a long comment in *Positions* (Paris: Editions Sociales, 1976), pp. 124–125. Similarly, D. Lecourt, in his review of *L'Archéologie du savoir*, advises Foucault to quit his intermediary stance "between words and things" and to draw the materialistic conclusions from his descriptions of discursive regularities. See also Lecourt's *Pour une critique de l'epistémologie* (Paris: Maspero, 1974).

23. Figure 4 owes much to Wladimir Krysinski's excellent diagram and analysis of modalization in fiction in his *Carrefours du signe* (Paris & The Hague: Mouton, 1981), pp. 1–75.

24. Cf. Adorno, *Théorie Esthétique* (Paris: Klincksieck, 1974), p. 14.

25. Dominique Delcourt, *Pour une critique de l'epistémologie: Bachelard, Canguilhem, Foucault* (Paris: Maspero, 1974), p. 130.

26. R. Barthes, *Eléments de sémiologie: Le degré zéro de l'écriture* (Paris: Gonthier, 1971), p. 165.

27. Th. W. Adorno, *Noten zur Literatur I* (Frankfurt: Suhrkamp, 1958), p. 77. Adorno arrives at a negative dialectic which opposes art (form) to the social element (content).

28. J. Baudrillard, *Pour une critique de l'économie politique du signe* (Paris: Gallimard, 1972), p. 175.

XI.

POLAND OF NOWHERE, THE BREASTS OF TIRESIAS, AND OTHER INCONGRUITIES, OR REFERENTIAL MANIPULATION IN MODERN DRAMA

Wladimir Krysinski

I.

In the *Poetics*, Aristotle interprets the relationship between the dramatic text and reality as one of dependency. Occurring on several levels, this dependency primarily affects the realization of the dramatic fable (the plot) which in various ways imitates "human actions." One can contend that *logos* (the dialogue) or *lexis* (the expression) supports the dramatic fable (*muthos*) solely to the extent that what is said by a character confirms the logical and referential presuppositions of the dramatic fable (*muthos*). These refer to a given "reality" composed of actions, human agents, and events. Imitation (*mimesis*) is a verbal, structural, and specular linkage between reality and the tragic text. When Aristotle says: "Thus tragedy is the imitation of an action, and of the agents mainly with a view to the action,"[1] or "Tragedy is an imitation of an action that is complete, and whole, and of a certain magnitude," or "Tragedy is an imitation not only of a complete action, but of events inspiring fear or pity,"[2] he emphasizes the need for textual restraint in relation to a world wherein there are actors, completed actions, and past events. Their relation is referential insofar as the action (*praxis*, which supports the *muthos*) occurs as the necessary or probable outcome of what has already taken place.[3]

We may describe the referent in tragedy as a reality represented by the *muthos* and transcribed textually in diction, song, and spectacle. Such transcription is possible, however, solely because there are objects to represent: that is, the dramatic fable (plot), characters, and thought, all related to what has already taken place. In Greek tragedy, the dramatic fable reflects the logical and referential presuppositions of a mythic or real world. Their verification by the spectator is possible insofar as the logical and referential presuppositions are given him by the tragedy in its role as transcriber of representable objects. These objects exist in a mythical and ideological world which the spectator recognizes as transformed; yet, at the same time, as sufficiently referential for the structure of tragedy to be recognizably imitative. Every sign and referent in tragedy partakes of this referentiality. Tragedy necessarily reflects a reality whose referents are already given to the spectator as the relations between the gods and men, and as action and thought.

This referentiality implies a referential solidarity between the characters' thoughts and actions. Antigone cannot say "God does not exist; it is a myth." Likewise, no character in Greek tragedy can say, like a character in Mrozek's *Tango*: "Give me God and I'll make an experimental theater."

II.

In the light of these preliminary (Aristotelian) considerations, the following characteristics of the referent in drama can be delineated:

1. The dramatic fable is doubly constrained. As *muthos*, it must already exist in reality; as *praxis*, it must be textually and structurally transcribed in order to be represented.
2. A referential solidarity exists among the *logos*, *lexis*, and plot, as well as between the actions and systems of referents (mythological, ideological, real).
3. The concept of the referent (as proposed by Frege and applied by Russell, Strawson, Quine, and, in semiotics, by Greimas, for example) allows, within the limits of the drama, a logical and semantical formulation of verbal communication, plot-structure, and function of the characters.
4. The referent has thus a primarily heuristic function, situating the text and its interpretation according to presuppositions implied by referents common to the dramatist and the spectator.

III.

The transition from Aristotelian to non-Aristotelian drama is one of the semiotic programs of the modern theater. Where can the process first be observed? In Victor Hugo or, even earlier, in Shakespeare? Certainly "referential restriction" and "referential solidarity" in modern theater assume specific forms and manifest a range of referential manipulations similar to those of tragedy or Aristotelian drama. In modern drama from Strindberg to Beckett, references to logical and referential presuppositions will be of a different order. They will be subverted by a specifically modern manipulation of the text. The Aristotelian *vs.* non-Aristotelian drama dichotomy is generally equivalent to mimetic and referential drama as opposed to autonomous drama. However, even in the case of a clearly formulated program as in Brecht, dramatic autonomy cannot dispense entirely with reference to reality. In fact, this is especially so in Brecht's case. We refer to him, however, since he introduced the distinction between his own non-Aristotelian drama and traditional Aristotelian drama.[4] Brecht's semiotic activity is autonomous, that is, further removed from the real, as the distancing seems to imply. The epic plot is distanced by the stage manipulation of the message and even of the act of communication, dialectically reflected in the prism of the Distancing-effect (*Verfremdungseffekt*). Between the fictitious plot and the audience, an interpretive space is created which is at once open and restricted. This space is implicitly posed above and beyond catharsis. Here, "verifiable reality" corresponds to a system of values established by the stage's play on distance. In Brecht's theatrical system (semi-realistic compared to that of Ionesco or Marinetti), the referent retains its heuristic function. The spectator must recreate distance, but always in terms of the systems of logical and referential presuppositions of a second-degree reality, rendered dialectical by its ideological and historical prerogatives.

In recent avant-garde (non-Aristotelian) playscripts, the referential mechanism is multiple. Though the real is not altogether dismissed, it is treated allusively and manipulated to serve as one of the subversive components of a theatrical process which will claim its own autonomy.

IV.

In modern drama, the disruption of mimesis occurs through a series of referential strategies that transform the referent into a tool, object and sign of theatrical autonomy.

However, the stage manipulation of the referent is not our main consideration here. Rather, given the complexity and polyvalence of theatrical signs, we will consider a certain number of examples of early avant-garde theater. Plays by Jarry, Apollinaire, Pirandello, the Italian Futurists, and Witkiewicz constitute a sort of semiotic laboratory where theatrical autonomy is developed. Various procedures are used, some more coherent and systematic than others, but each relating the text to the referent.

The concept of referent and of referentialization[5] thus acquires a specific meaning in the theater, in that each text or theatrical system is subject to specific constraints. Thus, our purpose will be to examine the modalities of referential manipulation in the modern theatrical text even before the advent of the so-called "Theater of the Absurd," where referential manipulation becomes a systematic procedure. The latter is probably best exemplified by *The Bald Soprano* in which the relation between sign and referent constantly changes. Ionesco thereby establishes a deceptive model of communication in which signs are deprived of possible referents. Ionesco's purpose is to show how the audience can be semiotically manipulated. The title "The Bald Soprano" has no denotation; the number of times that the text requires the chiming of the clock bears no relation to the time announced by the characters. The dialogue between the Mr. and Mrs. Smith, the citations from the newspaper,

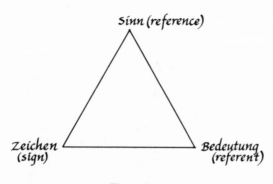

Figure 1

as well as the gratuitous statements of the characters contribute to this deceptive form of communication.

Lexis and *logos* are not linked to what is happening on stage, because the stage action no longer has any meaning. Without wishing to repeat the commentaries on the elements of the absurd in this play, let us sketch briefly what is "produced" in *The Bald Soprano*. Our interpretation will be based on Frege's triangle, the first attempt in modern philosophy to formulate the problem of communication by means of verbal signs.[6] Frege's triangle shows the mental and semiotic mechanisms which render human communication possible and meaningful. Each sign refers back to what it represents (its denotatum), not a particular object but rather, as Umberto Eco has remarked, a class of objects[7] (table, star). However, the *Sinn*, the meaning, is the mode of mental representation of the object, or rather the way in which the object referred to is understood. Frege's often cited example, "morning star" and "evening star," are two *Sinnen* of the same object, the planet Venus.

Frege's system (fig. 1) can help account for referential manipulation of verbal signs. This triangle and its variants in Ogden and Richards, Morris, or Carnap[8] allow us to observe the complexity of the mechanisms of encoding and decoding theatrical messages. Our focus here is confined to messages considered as *lexis* and *logos*, be they dialogical or monological, and related to a system of references which, in each case, requires definition.

V.

To return to *The Bald Soprano*, we observe that the characters speak. What they say does not contain referents common to the characters, readers, or spectators. The tripartite relation between sign, referent, and reference is constantly disrupted by statements which preclude reconstruction, or semantic linkage. Thus, the "dialogue" (in fact non-existent) is based on a series of monological, abrupt, and even laconic statements: a gratuitous verbal performance.

How can one formulate the problem of reference in this series of verbal, non-referential performances? The use of the semantic triangle for understanding what "occurs" in *The Bald Soprano* would have to be based not only on the unities of minimal dialogue, on phrases such as "the bald soprano," but also on the necessity of evaluating the "meaning" of Ionesco's use of the theater since, as we have already noted, the process of referential manipulation culminates in *The Bald Soprano*. It stems as much from a critique of language as from the limited autonomy of the dramatic text. It is comparable to other plays in which the referent and reference are specifically manipulated.

We shall examine the mechanism of this referential manipulation in the relation between title and text before looking at further examples in the play. The title implies a twofold relation: the referential constraint it imposes upon the text, and the title as a function of the text. In the first case, the conventions of production, as well as the habits of reader and spectator of drama, require the title to refer to the text and *vice versa*. This requirement may be due to an implied relation which can be thematic, pronominal, or nominal as in the case of *Antigone*, *Hamlet*, and *King Lear*, or generally thematic, as in the case of *The Tempest, Death of a Salesman*, and *Galileo*. The referential relation between title and text is broken in *The Bald Soprano*,[9] as there is no "bald soprano" referent. Reference is made to the title, though, when the Fire Chief asks Mr. and Mrs. Smith: "By the way, what about the Bald Prima Donna?" and Mrs. Smith's reply eliminates the referent through a disruption of the logical relation between "The *Bald* Prima Donna" and "She always wears her *hair* the same way." These contrastive expressions are mutually exclusive. One could contend that the soprano in question is wearing a wig and conclude that sopranos whose hair is not particularly attractive usually wear wigs. This hypothesis is shown to be wrong, as the title, the Fire Chief's question, and Mrs. Smith's reply suggest. An evaluation of the title by the spectator or reader is presupposed, however. Here, we may refer to Jakobson's metalinguistic function. What is the code implicit in the title? Does it supply the spectator or reader with a system of referents and reference which would permit its acceptance? The title is evaluated according to Ionesco's constant referential disruption of the relation between language and reality. The series of empty yet constantly manipulated referents in *The Bald Soprano* entail the creation of a certain referential "fullness." The empty referents such as the title, the statements about the Watson family, or even the running-on of dialogue where the characters haphazardly cite pseudo-proverbs, aphorisms, and sayings such as:

"Social progress is much better coated with sugar." (p. 116)
"I am looking for a monogynist priest to marry our maidservant." (p.116)
"I'd rather slaughter a rabbit than whistle in the garden." (p. 117)
"Sullivan Alfred" (p. 118)
"Tennyson Arthur" (p. 118)

stem from the disruption of a referential relation, neutralization of the referents, a textual positioning of the empty referents, as well as to what we have termed a referential "fullness" of the empty referents. The latter refers to the fact that the

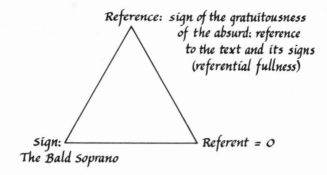

Figure 2

absurdity of the text (and its distorted referential systems) constitutes a new paradigm of the text, in which referential emptiness is functional. It will become re-referential by virtue of the metalinguistic code which the spectator reconstitutes from the theater of the absurd, a certain social function of language and, finally, from theatrical practice in the play itself. The title functions metalinguistically. It refers to a code which refers back to it via the text. The metalinguistic code is thus determined by the constraints of the text.

The Bald Soprano exemplifies a dramatic process, characteristic of the avant-garde text, which systematically disrupts referential and mimetic systems by "referential manipulation." The relation between the signs, referents, and references does not have a logical and referential stability which would permit the receiver to decode messages in terms of the triple elements of the triangles of Frege or of Ogden and Richards: sign, reference to the object of discourse (reality, the class of objects); meaning, as the limitative relation between the object and its differential, verbal representation ("morning star" = planet of Venus; "evening star" = planet of Venus). In Ionesco, this process of decoding can be represented as in figure 2. *The Bald Soprano* may thus be considered an autonomous and self-referential dramatic text. This is so because it uses the artifice of the referential fullness of a language, autonomous insofar as it systematically permits the improbable and the absurd.

Analyzing *The Bald Soprano* as a series of "semiotic experiments," Olga Karpinska and Izaak Revzin show how Ionesco subverts the basic principles of human communication. There are six such principles:

1. The sender and receiver refer to the same reality.
2. The sender and receiver refer to the same world-model.
3. The sender and receiver have a certain "common memory," that is, a certain fund of common information about the past.
4. The sender and receiver make more or less similar predictions about the future.
5. The sender must describe the world in a concise and elliptical manner.
6. The sender must communicate something new to the receiver.[10]

They govern what Karpinska and Revzin call "correct" human communication. They are applicable to the theatre if we assume that the disruption of human communication in *The Bald Soprano*, while eliminating the code, contact, and context according to Jakobson's categories, leaves the metalinguistic code intact. Thus, paradoxically, while human communication is rendered impossible and ironic in *The Bald Soprano*, its disruption focuses theatrical communication through the metalinguistic code.

VI.

Let us now consider some other principles of theatrical communication in the light of the specificity of the dramatic text and its evolution. The modern, dramatic text tends to be autonomous due to its metalinguistic code, which is contingent on referential manipulation and incongruity, a technique common to several of the textual strategies involved. The principle of incongruity, which subverts "correct communication," entails the use of shock, surprise, the improbable, the fantastic, and the absurd. It results in the destruction of mimetic referentiality and the autonomy of the dramatic text.

In examining plays by such authors as Jarry, Apollinaire, Pirandello, Witkiewicz, and Ionesco, we will offer a definition of the dramatic text based on Jakobson's concept of the poetic function. The latter projects a principle of equivalence from the axis of selection onto the axis of combination. The *autonomous* function of the dramatic text disrupts the axis of the mimetic and projects the principle of incongruity onto the axis of the autotelic. The mimetic axis presupposes a referential restriction of the dramatic plot and of the *logos*, *lexis*, actions, and systems of referents shared by dramatist and spectator. The autotelic axis entails disruption of the principles of "correct communication." It is coextensive with the performance, whose referents are manipulated by the text because of their emptiness.

These categories become clearer when applied to avant-garde authors cited earlier.

VII.

Thus, Jarry's *Ubu roi* (King Turd) exemplifies the principles of incongruity and referential manipulation. In *Ubu roi* we find:
1. The use of the empty referent: Poland.
2. The discursive manipulation of the elements specific to the empty referent.
3. Ubu-speak ("Le parler Ubu") as a referential manipulation.

Our concept of the empty referent can be compared to the position taken by Michel Arrivé, which maintains that the literary text has no referent, or rather that it has a "simulacrum of a referent":

A text such as *Ubu roi* is sandwiched between the comment that 'the scene takes place in Poland, that is, Nowhere' and the final sentence 'If there were no Poland, there would be no Poles,' where the word 'Poles' functions as a sign of the text whose subtitle it is (*Ubu roi ou les Polonais*).[11]

While "Poles" is indeed a sign, it entails textual and referential manipulation. That is to say, Jarry manipulates the referent "Poland" in order to disrupt its denotative (as opposed to connotative) reference. For *Ubu roi* to exist as a system of autonomous signs, the referent "Poland" must exist prior to the text. The empty referent is contingent on the full referent "Poland." For, when Jarry states: "As to the action which is about to begin, it takes place in Poland—that is to say, nowhere,"[12] he presupposes a system of reference which must account for 'Poland' as well as 'Poland = nowhere.' In the first case, he must manipulate the "Polish" elements both discursively and referentially. In the second, he must neutralize them. Thus he says:

> The curtain rises on a set which is supposed to represent Nowhere, with trees at the foot of beds and white snow in a summer sky; the action also takes place in Poland, a country so legendary, so dismembered that it is well qualified to be this particular Nowhere, or in terms of a putative Franco-German etymology, a distantly interrogative somewhere.[13]

And also

> Nowhere is everywhere, but most of all it is the country we happen to be in at the moment. And that is why Ubu speaks French. But his assorted vices are reinforced by Captain Bordure who speaks English, Queen Rosamund who gabbles away in double Dutch, and the Polish masses talking through their noses and all dressed in gray. Certain satirical elements may be evident, but the play's setting relieves its exponents from any responsibility.[14]

Hence the associative and connotative chain Poland → Nowhere → Distantly Interrogative Somewhere → Everywhere → the country one happens to be in at the moment. This connotative chain implies complete topological indeterminacy, yet it underscores the incongruity which has become the organizing principle of the text. Poland-as-Nowhere thus displaces geographical and historical "Poland."

We agree with Michel Arrivé that the literary and theatrical text has no referent, because Poland, which is the same as Nowhere, Somewhere, etc., does not exist. Yet, at the same time, Poland as referent makes referential manipulation possible. In *Ubu roi*, the principle of incongruity depends on referential manipulation. The continuity of drama and narrative in *Ubu roi* is provided by the exploits, deeds, and gestures of Ubu. Incongruity is a form of textual extravaganza that discards referents such as Poland or denotative language (whence "*merde et finance*" becomes "*merdre et phynance*").

The geographical and historical referent "Poland" is emptied of its own reference in *Ubu roi* by the confusion of names and facts. In the first case, we have a series of Polish or so-called Slavic names: King Wenceslaus, Queen Rosamunde, and their sons Boleslaus, Ladislaus, and Bougrelas. Neither Rosamunde nor Bougrelas are Polish names. Functionally they render everything absurd, unreal, and incongruous. Judith Cooper has aptly pointed out:

> The sound of the names seems to be of primary importance rather than any specific historical reference. Their foreign sound would automatically seem comic to French ears. And once more we notice the repetition of sounds in all four names which increase the comic effect. The most important character of the four is Bougrelas and his is the most unusual of the four names. It is nothing more than a derogatory epithet with the Slavic-sounding ending -las. A hero with such a name could not possibly be taken seriously, just as no audience could sympathize with a character named Bordure.[15]

The first name Bougrelas (Buggerlaus) is a sign without a referent, or rather a sign-index which feigns the existence of a referent. It thereby becomes an autonomous textual sign which evolves thus: empty referent → textual sign → referential fullness.

Besides these Polish or pseudo-Polish names, there are some historical Polish names in the play: Jan Sobieski, Stanislas Leczinski, Nicholas Rensky, General Lascy. The latter have human referents, but they contribute nonetheless to incongruity, given their historical and geographical context but unreal and absurd situation. Jan Sobieski, King of Poland (1673–1696), is one of King Ubu's soldiers, killed in the battle with the Russians. Stanislas Leczinski, King of Poland in the first half of the eighteenth century, is none other than the peasant from whom Ubu wants to extort taxes. We shall examine more closely the case of this peasant who bears the name of a king of Poland. At the time of his reign, Leczinski was well known in France, where he was governor of the duchies of Barrois and Lorraine. Leczinski lived in Nancy; Place Stanislas was named after him. Marie Leczinska, his daughter, was the wife of Louis XV. All these facts, familiar to the educated Frenchman, are references which Jarry manipulates and renders inoperative.

In act II scene iv, the following conversation takes place:

> Papa Turd: Which one of you is the oldest? (A PEASANT steps forward.) What's your name?
> The Peasant: Stanislas Leczinski.
> Papa Turd: Well then, hornstrumpet, listen carefully or these gentlemen will cut off your years. So are you going to listen to me?
> Stanislas: But Your Excellency hasn't said anything yet.[16]

Given the status of the referent "Leczinski," what is said can be analyzed in the two models shown (figs. 3 and 4).

The autonomy of the text is the result of referential manipulation emptying the normal referent of its verifiable, existential, and historical content, thereby displacing even the historical truth.

When in act III scene ii, Ubu requests that someone state his heritage, the following list is given:

> The Herald: Principality of Podolia, Grand Duchy of Posen, Duchy of Cortland,

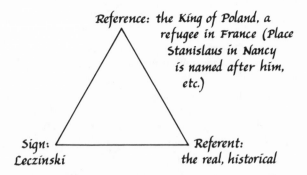

Figure 3: Semiosis I (historical, real)

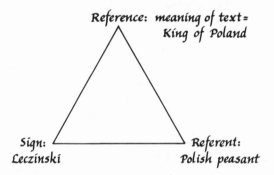

Figure 4: Semiosis II (textual autonomy)

Earldom of Sandomir, Earldom of Vitebsk, Palatinate of Polackia, Margraviate of Thorn.[17]

Given that the action of *Ubu roi* takes place in Poland as well as nowhere, this list must be construed as a referential manipulation of geographical and historical data, despite some correct references. No Poland, in fact, can serve as referent for this list, or match the geographical and administrative names or the historical Polish, Russian, and German references.

Because of the incongruous mixture, this list seems exotic to the French reader. Ubu-speak (*"Le Parler Ubu"*) creates incongruity insofar as it is repetitive, energetic, excessive, and vulgar, yet also fundamentally non-referential. It is composed of recurrent lexical items: *merdre, phynances, croc à merdre, cornebleu, cornegidouille*, etc. If they are connotative and nonreferential it is because they are composed of phonemes, syllables, and keywords whose referents are emptied of reality.[18] This mechanism produces textual autonomy. The action of *Ubu roi* does not take place in Poland or "Nowhere," but upon the stage where the drama is enacted.

VIII.

In *Les Mamelles de Tirésias*, Apollinaire also claims to create theatrical autonomy. His play bears a resemblance to Jarry's, though the text is more varied,
being a surrealistic theatrical scenario and a vaudeville. *Les Mamelles de Tirésias*
mingles the improbable with the comic, the surrealistic with music and farce. The
internal and external referentiality accentuates the essential theatricality of the characters, as well as the pomp of the stage-setting. The continuity of the text does not
seem to stem from the narrative but seems accidental and based on the mixture of
dialogue and song. *Les Mamelles de Tirésias* shows a twofold metamorphosis:
Thérèse becomes a man (Tirésias) and the husband becomes the wife. The result
is a series of *quid pro quo* that makes the stage performance self-referential due to
the displacement of the tripartite relation of sign, referent, and reference. The double
metamorphosis is linked to, or rather generated by, the metalinguistic code, which
can be defined in the exact terms of the Director of the Troupe in the Prologue:

> The great unfolding of our modern art can join, without any apparent connection as
> in life, sounds and gestures colours, cries, and clamour music, dance, acrobatics,
> poetry and painting, Chorus, action and varying decors
>
>> You will find here the actions which accompany the main drama and
>>   embellish it
>> The changes of tone from the pathetic to the burlesque
>> The prudent use of improbabilities
>> As well as the actors, collective or not,
>> Who are not necessarily part of Humanity
>> Nor of the whole universe
>> For the theater must not be an art of illusion
>>
>> It is fitting that the dramatist use
>> All the tricks at his disposal
>> ....
>> Right that he should make the hoard of inanimate
>> objects speak
>> If it pleases him and that
>> he should take no more account of time
>> Than space.[19]

In his preface, Apollinaire insists upon the autonomy of the theater whose goal is
"to amuse and interest." Yet he says of his play that "its aim is the highlighting
of a vital question for those who hear the language in which it is written: the problem
of repopulation."

There are thus two referential levels: 1) verifiable reality: France is becoming
depopulated, the number of births has diminished; and 2) stage "reality," which

is non-verifiable and surrealistic according to Apollinaire's definition. The text mixes the two levels in accordance with the principle of incongruity.

The double metamorphosis operates thus: Thérèse → Tirésias; husband → wife. In both cases there is a transition from a probable referent to an autonomous stage sign, which also serves as the pretext for the creation of a specific referent, namely the woman changed into a man and *vice versa*. In fact, this double metamorphosis also creates comic stage sequences, songs, and wordplay. The metamorphosis is thus a semiotic operation with syntactical and semantic consequences. Syntactically, it creates a series of actions and stage gestures; semantically, it transforms the real referent of the first level—a woman (Thérèse) and a husband, etc.—into stage signs. This transformation, then, is the outcome of referential manipulation. The transformation of real characters into stage signs is better illustrated by the breasts of Tirésias which need further examination.

Referentially, the breasts stand for the feminine attributes of Thérèse. They are represented somewhat negatively because Thérèse loses them and gradually changes into a man:

> Oh, now it seems a beard begins to appear?
> And now my bosom's disappearing.

> (She partially opens her blouse from which her breasts fly out, one red and the other blue, and as she loosens them they fly away. They are children's balloons which are held back by strings.)

> Fly fly away Oh birds of woman's weakness
> Aren't they lovely things such lovely lovely things?
> Sweet delicate charms
> Full delicate charms
> Aren't they lovely things
> Aren't they lovely things[20]

The sign-referent-reference triad is thus disrupted. The breasts represent femininity solely on condition that they form part of the woman's body, thereby serving as the referent for the sign "breasts."[21] The reference of the sign "breasts" is sexuality, attractiveness, and maternity. In *Les Mamelles de Tirésias*, the sign "breasts" is severed from its reference and referent. The text operates a stage materialization of the breasts, which change into children's balloons, a materialization which is, in fact, meta-textual. Thus, the breasts in the text are no longer those of a woman, or even of a man (Tirésias); they become autonomous stage sign-objects created through incongruity, and the paradoxical title. In fact, *Les Mamelles de Tirésias* is a sign which no longer corresponds to any real referent. Tirésias, a masculine name, cannot be given feminine attributes. Tirésias, in the play, is Thérèse changed into a man, but he is also a stage character. As such, Tirésias is a stage-sign, an empty referent (metamorphosed woman, deprived of her attributes, a man-woman) transformed and reequipped with referential fullness as the "*mamelles de Tirésias*," that is, as neither man nor woman, but text. Apollinaire's strategy is to detach the sign from its referent and reference and to allow the text its autonomy. This consists of a play upon words, leading to verbal breakdown, of song and gratuitously referential stage operations. Apollinaire thus creates an autotelic text through the use of incongruity.

An excerpt from scene vii of the first act illustrates the principle of incongruity as well as textual autonomy:

The People of Zanzibar, the Policeman, the Husband
(dressed as a woman)

The Policeman: The duellists of the landscape will not prevent me from saying that I find you
As pleasant to touch as a rubber ball.

The Husband: Ah choo. (A dish breaks.)

The Policeman: A cold is exquisite.

The Husband: Atchi. (Drums. The husband lifts up his skirt which is bothering him.)

The Policeman: Shameless woman. (He winks.)
What matter, she's a beautiful girl.

The Husband: My he's right
Since my wife's a man
I must be a woman (bashfully to the Policeman)
I am an honest woman-man
My wife is a man-woman
She has taken the piano, the violin, the butter-dish.

The Policeman: she is "*mère des cygnes*"
Ah! how they sing, those who are going to perish
Listen. (Bagpipes, sad air.)[22]

The device used is phonic echo which creates autotelic effect. The connecting elements are: caoutchouc → atchou → exquis → atchi → femme-monsieur → homme-madame → merdecin → mère des seins → merdecine → mère des cygnes. The stage signs have no real referent or simulacra. The breakdown of the mimetic coincides with the enhancement of the autotelic.

From Jarry to Apollinaire and Ionesco, the autonomy of the theatrical text is contingent on an intensified use of incongruity and the emptying of referents and references of their real content, a process culminating in *The Bald Soprano*. Two other theatrical processes should also be mentioned, and are exemplified by Pirandello and Witkiewicz. Both strive for theatrical autonomy, Pirandello through the subversion of the mimetic text, Witkiewicz through his theory of "Pure Form in the Theater."

IX.

Six Characters in Search of an Author is structured on various levels of reality,[23] which we shall call referential as in the case of *Les Mamelles de Tirésias*:

Level A: that of the characters. Here we must further distinguish sublevels, since each character represents an "idiosyncratic code."[24]

Level B: that of the author.

Level C: that of the actors.

Pirandello's play is generally taken to be "a play about the impossibility of drama."[25] It presupposes three referential levels and is based on a specific referential manipulation which consists of pushing "referential conflict" to its limit. This presupposition is a trap set by the dramatist, part of his semiotic strategy which allows him to dramatize and dedramatize the melodramatic situation of the characters. Pirandello's strategy is thus an attack upon the mimetic signs of Aristotelian theater of representation. These signs are: the characters representing personages or human beings, the actors signifying consonance between the roles they play and their referents, and, finally, the author (whose stage equivalent is the director). The latter functions in the text as a mimetic sign insofar as it is a textualization of the real; here the dramatic fable functions both as *muthos* and as *praxis*. Each of the referential levels thus corresponds to its mimetic sign, which Pirandello highlights, but also renders ineffectual.

The first referential conflict occurs between level A and level B. For the author, the characters seeking to be represented by the stage script are signs without fixed references. Moreover, they are psychologically unfathomable and, in the narrative, their accounts are confused and contradictory. The six characters are signs of a melodrama; their only referents are their bodily presence. If their confused and contradictory lines reflect the wish to identify the drama, the characters evidently cannot agree about its meaning. The discussion between the Father and the Beautiful Girl is a play on various references: who is the Father in relation to the whole family? Why has he come to Madam Pace's house? what relation exists between the Father and the Beautiful Girl? These questions are present, explicitly or implicitly. Their constant recurrence creates a tense conflict between the characters and levels B and C, precluding a mimetic representation of the conflict or of the story of the six characters. Nor can the actors perform something confused, exaggerated, and indeterminate. There is thus a referential struggle between the ideas which the characters have of themselves and the implicit postulates of mimetic theater as defined earlier.

The Father's soliloquy on consciousness ends with the conclusion of the impossibility of self-knowledge and even of communication among levels A, B, and C.

The Father: For the drama lies all in this—in the conscience that I have, that each one of us has. We believe this conscience to be a single thing, but it is many-sided. There is one for this person, and another for that. Diverse consciences. So we have this illusion of being one person for all, of having a personality that is unique in all our acts. But it is not true. We perceive this when tragically perhaps, in something we do, we are, as it were, suspended, caught up in the air on a kind of hook.[26]

This soliloquy allows us to define one of Pirandello's principal thematic structures; the multiplication of "I"'s and the dissolution of the stable personality. This can be linked to the sign-referent-reference triad as in the model shown (fig. 5).

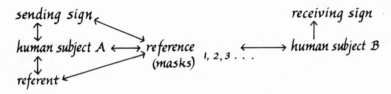

Figure 5

The same human subject A as the sending sign of his "I," in confrontation with human subject C as the receiving sign, will use other references (masks). Thus, the schema of failed communication is shown in figure 6.

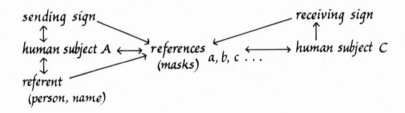

Figure 6

This model of failed communication can be applied to real human interaction and referential conflicts. Such as Pirandello's conclusion, despite the constant attempts of his drama to demythify human communication and the meaning of being for others.

The following dialogue excerpt exemplifies referential conflict (common in Pirandello) between level A and level C.

The Manager: Now, look here! On the stage, you as yourself, cannot exist. The actor here acts you, and that's an end to it!

The Father: I understand. And now I think I see why our author who conceived us as we are, all alive, did not want to put us on the stage after all. I have not the least desire to offend your actors. Far from it! But when I think that I am to be acted by . . . I don't know by whom . . .

Leading Man: (on his dignity). By me, if you have no objection!

The Father: (humbly, mellifluously). Honored, I assure you, sir. (Bows.) Still, I must say that try as this gentleman may, with all his good will and wonderful art, to absorb me into himself . . .

Leading Man: Oh chuck it! ''Wonderful art!'' Withdraw that, please!

The Father: The performance he will give, even doing his best with make-up to look like me. . . .

Leading Man: It will certainly be a bit difficult! (The actors laugh.)

The Father: Exactly! It will be difficult to act me as I really am. The effect will be rather—apart from the make-up according as to how he supposes I am, as he senses me—if he does sense me—and not as I inside of myself feel myself to be. It seems to me then that account should be taken of this by everyone whose duty it may become to criticize us.[27]

Two signs are at odds here: "to play" and "to represent." For the Father, "to play" and "to represent" refer to being unique, personal, unrepeatable. For the Leading Man, "to play" and "to represent" signify imitating, feigning.

In *Six Characters in Search of an Author* sending and receiving signs do not share common references. The play ironically reduces the problem of mimetic, Aristotelian drama to the sole function of signs (the soliloquies of the characters, the dialogue of the actors and director) involved in referential conflict. Mimetic theater's signs fail as vehicles of communication. It is not so much theatrical communication, as we saw in Jarry, Apollinaire, and Ionesco, that is at stake in the semiotic practice of Pirandello, as metatheatrical communication. Pirandello questions the stability of references in mimetic theater, whose premises are the permanency of character and personality, the linear development of plot, and the exchange and functional harmony of the textual roles, imitated reality, and the actor-agents of mimetic stage representation.

Six Characters in Search of an Author is thus a spectacle composed of signs which have been detached from the ordinary reference presupposed by the dialogue. The referents of the signs are there; they are the characters and actors in person. Yet this in no way insures referential solidarity between *logos* and *muthos*. What Pirandello calls *commedia da fare* therefore fails to occur. Pirandello's critical and ironic discourse is akin to a scalpel which dissects the living body of mimetic theater, revealing the artifice of mimetic communicaton, the basis of the narrativity and dramatic representation.

X.

The theoretical propositions of Witkiewicz center on his theory of "Pure Form in the Theater." This "Pure Form" must, by analogy with abstract painting, be an abstraction. That is to say, it must liberate itself from a dependency on reality or what Witkiewicz calls "vital meaning." However, Witkiewicz admits that this "vital meaning" can never totally disappear. He thus envisages a whole series of possibilities and combinations in which the actions and dialogue can exclude each other without depriving each action or statement of its "vital meaning." Witkiewicz proposes the following schema:

a) actions in accordance with the dialogue and having a vital meaning;

b) actions not in accordance with the dialogue;

c) actions in accordance with a dialogue which does not have a vital meaning;

d) a complete division between actions and dialogue without meaning, and dialogue without meaning.[28]

In this system, the semiotic triad reflects both the manipulation of the referent, the real (vital meaning), and the construction of a new formal referent, namely, the materiality of the stage signs as well as the development of the spectacle. The formal referent combines with the stage signs. In this combination, though, there is no reference other than that of "Pure Form." The problem of theatrical autonomy is therefore represented by Witkiewicz both as incongruity (referential "distortion," to use Witkiewicz's term) of empirical reality, and as the self-referent of the self-reflexive spectacle. It can be represented as in figure 7.

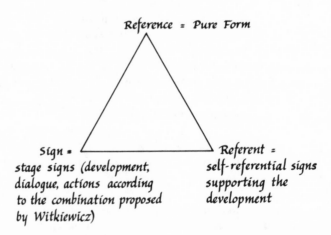

Figure 7

Crucial metalinguistic elements are in this way incorporated into the theory of "Pure Form." In modern theater, this theory, along with that of Artaud, is perhaps the most consistent and complete. It is not, however, devoid of ambiguity, and Witkiewicz himself implicitly acknowledges this. Theater, as he puts it, cannot divest itself of human presence or human speech. The development of the drama requires both gesture and narrative even though these may be presented as absurd.

The self-referentiality of the spectacle is contingent on signs which are, so to speak, semi-referential. The dialogue and actions may embody a "vital meaning," but not because of the development of the spectacle. "Pure Form" in Witkiewicz's theater is an obsessive caricature of the real on which it depends. There is a discrepancy between Witkiewicz's theory and practice insofar as he holds that the abstraction of painting can be realized upon the stage through the development of spectacle and through the combination of actions with referential and non-referential dialogue. Yet his theater, as caricature of the real, is particularly dependent upon verbal fullness. It is only in theory that the text of the spectacle attains a certain purity of stage signs which focus the spectacle through the incongruity of gesture, dialogue, and narrative. Witkiewicz's concept of "Pure Form in the theater" is exemplified by the following description:

> Three characters dressed in red enter the stage and greet one knows not whom. One of the characters recites a poem (which must appear at this moment as indispensable). An old man with a gentle appearance enters leading a cat on a leash. All this takes place in front of a black curtain. This opens and reveals an Italian landscape. Organ music is heard. The old man addresses one of the characters already on stage, saying something in line with what has already preceded. A glass falls from a table. Everyone drops on their knees and weeps. The old man changes then into a wild deer and assassinates a little girl who has just entered on stage from the side of the garden. At this, a handsome young man interrupts, thanking the old man for the crime he has just committed and the characters dressed in red begin to sing and dance. After this, the young man weeps near the corpse of the little girl, saying very funny and cheerful things. The old man assumes his original appearance of a mild and good man and laughs in a corner, saying things simple and sublime.[29]

Continuity is contingent on constant interchange of gesture and word, a series of discrete entities detached from all reference to a reality in which logically justifiable actions occur and in which words adhere to these actions.

XI.

In the modern dramatic text, therefore, reference to the real is manipulated, with the aim of subverting the latter or subordinating it to the principle of incongruity. The process stems in part from the use of empty referents as well as from their transformation on the stage, where they become self-referential signs.

The autonomous signs of drama, as defined above, are relational signs. They are the product of a distancing from reality, and of a conflict or series of conflicts among the signs, referents, and reference.

The modern drama script thus achieves autonomy through a modification of the semiotic triangle in which the tripartite solidarity and continuity are no longer determined by a reality understood according to logical and mimetic parameters.

NOTES

1. Cf. Aristotle's *Theory of Poetry and of Fine Art*, translated and with critical notes by S. H. Butcher and a New Introduction by John Gassner (New York: Dover Publications Inc., 1951), p. 29.

2. Op. cit., pp. 31 and 39.

3. Cf. op. cit., pp. 39–40: "A Complex action is one in which the change is accompanied by such Reversal, or by both. These last should arise from the internal structure of the plot, so that what follows should be the necessary or probable result of the preceding action. It makes all the difference whether any given event is a case of *propter hoc* or *post hoc.*"

4. See, for example, the series of studies collected in "Sur une dramaturgie non-aristotélicienne 1933–1941." References are to the French edition of Berthold Brecht's *Écrits sur le théâtre*, I (Paris: L'Arche, 1963), 1972.

5. The concept comes from A. J. Greimas and J. Courtès in their *Sémiotique, dictionnaire raisonné de la théorie du langage* (Paris: Hachette, Université, 1979). They define referentialization as follows: "The problem which arises when one considers the discourse from a generative point of view is not that of the referent given *a priori*, but of the referentialization of the statement which implies the examination of the procedures by which 'referential illusion'—the 'reality' or 'truth' meaning-effect proposed by R. Barthes, is established." Pp. 312–313; my translation.

6. See "Sinn und Bedeutung" written in 1892. We translate *Zeichen* by "sign," *Sinn* by "reference," and *Bedeutung* by "referent"; we are using this terminology in conformity with the practice of certain French semioticians, such as Michel Arrivé, to whom we refer in our analysis of *Ubu roi*.

7. Cf. Umberto Eco, *Segno* [Sign] (Milano: Enciclopedia filosofica ISEDI, 1973), p. 25.

8. In analysing the sign as an element in the process of communication, Umberto Eco (op. cit.) includes in the triangle the different terms which correspond to Peirce's use of Frege's sign, referent, and reference ('object' for referent, 'interpretant' for reference), in Ogden and Richards ('symbol' for sign and 'reference' for reference, that is, the *Sinn* of Frege), in Charles Morris ('signifying vehicle' for sign, 'denotatum' for referent, and 'designatum' or 'significatum' for reference). In Carnap's terminology 'extension' corresponds to referent and 'intension' to reference.

9. We cite *La Cantatrice chauve* [*The Bald Soprano*] in the translation of Donald Watson; Eugène Ionesco, *Plays*, volume I (London: John Calder, first published in 1958); the numbers in parentheses refer to this edition.

10. Cf. Olga Karpinska and Izaak Revzin, "Expérimentation sémiotique chez E. Ionesco (*La Cantatrice chauve* et *La Leçon*)," *Semiotica IV*, 3 (1971), 240–262.

11. Cf. Michel Arrivé, "Postulats pour la description linguistique des textes littéraires," *Langue française* 3, (septembre 1969), p. 6 (my translation).

12. Cf. Alfred Jarry, *King Turd* [*Ubu roi*], translated by Beverley Keith and G. Legman (New York: Boar's Head Books, 1953), p. 13.

13. Cf. *Ubu roi*, the article written by Jarry for the program issue of *La Critique* for the Théâtre de l'Oeuvre, and distributed to the audience on the first night. In *Selected Works of Alfred Jarry*, edited by Roger Shattuck and Simon Watson Taylor (New York: Grove Press Inc., 1965), p. 79.

14. Cf. ibid., p. 79.

15. Cf. Judith Cooper, *Ubu roi: An Analytical Study*, Tulane Studies in Romance Languages and Literatures, no. 6 (New Orleans: Tulane University Press, 1974), p. 47.

16. Cf. Jarry, *King Turd*, p. 47.

17. Op. cit., p. 42.

18. Cf. the very detailed analysis of "le parler Ubu" by Michel Arrivé in his *Les langages de Jarry: Essai de sémiotique littéraire* (Paris: Klincksieck, 1972); cf. especially "Essai de description du métalangage jarryque" and "Dictionnaire d'*Ubu roi*," pp. 43–113; 165–307.

19. Cf. Apollinaire, *L'Enchanteur pourrissant suivi de "Les mamelles de Tirésias" et de "Couleur du temps"* (Paris: Gallimard, 1972), p.114.

20. We cite, only for this passage, the English translation of Robert Goss in *Les Mamelles de Tirésias*, opéra-bouffe en deux actes et un prologue, Poème de Guillaume Apollinaire, Musique de Francis Poulenc (Paris: Au Ménestrel, Heugel et Cie., 1970), pp. 17–18.

21. We exclude, for the moment, the fact that in phantasmic structures of the libido and of fetishism the breasts can be regarded as what Freud calls a "partial object."

22. Cf. Apollinaire, *Les Mamelles de Tirésias*, Gallimard, pp. 130–132.

23. Cf. Gérard Genot's comments in his *Pirandello* (Paris: Seghers, 1970), pp. 59–60.

24. See W. Krysinski, "La dislocation des codes, l'accroissement des récits et la brisure de la représentation dans *Six personnages en quête d'auteur*," *Études littéraires*, No.3, 1980, p. 501 (my translation), in which the point was made that "The discourse of the Father and of the Beautiful Girl refer to the personal, subjective codes which one can call idiosyncratic codes which disrupt the stability of the 'sub-codes' such as those of *ethos, dianoia*, and *hamartia*."

25. Cf. the chapter "Speil von der Unmöglichkeit des Dramas" in *Theorie des modernen Dramas* by Peter Szondi (Frankfurt am Main: Suhrkamp Verlag, 1963).

26. Cf. Luigi Pirandello, *Six Characters in Search of an Author*, English Version by Edward Storer, in *Naked Masks; Five Plays by Luigi Pirandello*, edited by Eric Bentley (New York: Dutton, 1952), p. 231.

27. Cf. op. cit., pp. 244–245.

28. Cf. S. I. Witkiewicz, "Précisions sur la question de la Forme Pure au théâtre," in *S. I. Witkiewicz* (Paris, *Cahiers de la Compagnie Madeleine Renaud-Jean-Louis Barrault*, Gallimard, no. 73, 1970) tr. Koukou Chanska and Jacques Lacarrière; p. 56.

29. Cf. S. I. Witkiewicz, "Théorie de la Forme Pure au Théâtre", op. cit., pp. 27–28 (my translation).

XII.

THE REFERENTIAL ACT

Thomas E. Lewis

No one shall ever develop a theory of literary referentiality. The present renewal of concern with "referring in literature" promises less the possibility of explaining such a process than the creation of new reading practices that break with dominant twentieth-century assumptions in the West about the nature of literary textuality. Diversity of approach to this problem signals an eagerness on the part of critics professing various methodologies to enter a domain of inquiry that, until recently, they happily left to the occasional philosopher and a handful of Marxists. Indeed, the once welcome notion that "literary" texts identify themselves by being "self-referential" now appears overly to constrain critics in their accomplishment of scholarly and pedagogical goals. A legitimation of referential studies within the academy, therefore, may first be understood as a symptom of general dissatisfaction with a particular ideology of the aesthetic.

Attention to literary referentiality, however, should fully permit a break with aesthetics as such. In its present stage of elaboration, this attention will never succeed in doing so. Even as the aesthetic of self-referentiality is laid to rest, discussions of "referring in literature" widely reproduce the enabling premise of the older notion: namely, that processes of "literary" signification differ from other processes of signification. Despite the collapse, even within Russian Formalism, of distinctions between standard and poetic language, the idea that literature constitutes a mode of signification *sui generis* dies hard. Thus, at the same time as an understanding of literature as solipsistic is repudiated, inquiry into literary referentiality often preserves an assumption of literary essence. This assumption in fact hinders analysis of "referring in literature" because it imposes upon such effort the traditional concerns of epistemology.

I shall not rehearse here the arguments that have convinced me of both the impossibility of an intrinsic definition of literature and the unworkability of the epistemological categories upon which such definitions depend.[1] I can, however, illustrate how underlying epistemological interests muddle thinking about referentiality. When reading *The Odyssey*, for example, readers encounter the epic, a genre which, for Roman Jakobson, "strongly involves the referential function of language," even as it displays the dominance of the poetic function.[2] Significantly,

Jakobson does not attempt to collapse the poetic and referential functions of epic into one special function: that of "poetic referentiality." By implication, he considers that analysis of the referential function in texts dominated by the poetic function would follow the same semiotic procedures as analysis of referentiality in texts dominated by any of the functions, including the referential function itself. Despite his famous contribution to defining aesthetic function through its "self-referential" impulse—insofar as an essentially "self-focussing" message is constituted—Jakobson never suggests that, in poetic texts, the properly referential function of language undergoes metamorphoses so strange that it thereby acquires new methodological status.

But most of us today would tend to discuss the referential function of *The Odyssey* under the auspices of that mulish term, "literary referentiality," which Jakobson so carefully avoids. Here it happens that epistemology can begin to mislead analysis of referentiality in two ways: first, with respect to the object of representation, and second, with respect to the determinacy of representation. Assumptions about literary referentiality often extend so far as to posit a specifically "literary" referent, that is, a referent that differs from other possible kinds of referents as a result of the special use of language through which it is constructed. Implicitly or explicitly, a claim is made that there exists a unique *object*, to which only aesthetic perception affords adequate access; thus, aesthetics becomes a mode of cognition in its own right. When critics endorse the notion of a "literary" referent, therefore, they admit something important and deny it in the same instant. In the admission, literary signification is seen as an effect of reference to the world. In the denial, properly "literary" signification is seen as the effect of aesthetic cognition alone. Whereas cultural meaning constitutes the object of representation in the admission, intrinsically aesthetic meaning constitutes the object of representation in the denial. So it is that, from a referential point of view, an epistemological approach to the object of "literary" representation paradoxically recuperates textual meaning for aesthetics and throttles attempts to ascribe textual meaning to the world. Here arises a second understanding of the present interest in referentiality: while embodying the potential to inspire a vigorous cultural criticism, study of referentiality is often too readily accommodated to the institutional discourse of literary specialization.

Not everyone concerned with literary referentiality, however, upholds the existence of a specifically "literary" referent. Some critics acknowledge that referents signified by "literary" discourse may be signified by "nonliterary" discourses as well. Although all referents now enjoy the same methodological status, literary signification is still considered as a special semiotic; hence, the task of criticism is to distinguish a specific mode of referring in literature from other possible modes of referring. Pursuit of this task usually assumes a broadly tripartite division of signifying modes into denotative semiotic (standard language), connotative semiotic (literary language), and metasemiotic (scientific language).[3] Even this more moderate essentialism, however, can prompt an injudicious approach through epistemology to study of the determinacy of representation in literature. By "determinacy of representation," I do not mean consideration of specific techniques of sign production through which texts that are conventionally regarded as "aesthetic" manage to generate meanings. Classification of certain techniques as "aesthetic" varies historically and in relation to developments in several cultural spheres; "aesthetic" sign production can be, and often is, studied historically and not epistemologically. Rather, by "determinacy of representation," I mean consideration of the modality of a literary text taken as the sign of an object that it determines. For the moment, as in the preceding paragraph, I am equating the notion of the "referent" with that of an "object" that is determined by representation.

Epistemological concerns trouble this consideration when an *origin* is sought for the connotative meanings engendered by literature. Traditionally, critics have conceived of the literary text either as a connotative sign that is undercoded with respect to the object that it determines, or as a connotative sign that is overcoded with respect to the object that it determines.[4] In the first instance, the referent of literary representation surfaces as a social text that constitutes the conditions of literary *production*; in the second, the referent of literary representation surfaces as a social text that constitutes the conditions of literary *reception*, or interpretation. The referential text of *The Odyssey*, for example, may be considered either as a set of contemporary perceptions or representations in function of which Greeks lived the experience of an immense social revolution (ca. 750 B.C.) that powered the transition of their civilization from its Dark Age (1200–800 B.C.) to its Archaic period (800–500 B.C.), or it may be considered as a set of culturally coded representations of problems or values that persist into our own era and which comprise the basis, though not necessarily the identity, of modern apprehensions of the text. To the first manner of conceiving of the referent apply such terms of literary criticism as "conditions of possibility" (Macherey), "ground" (Peirce), "invention" (Eco), and "referential subtext" (Jameson). To the second manner of conceiving of the referent apply such terms as "resymbolization" (Bleich), "gap" (Iser), "interpretant" (Peirce), and "symbolic order" (Lacan).

No doubt this seeming exclusivity of referential perspectives is unwarranted. Conditions of both production and reception play a part in constituting the "object" that is determined by literary representation, and several of the critics whose vocabulary I have just cited take due notice of this phenomenon. Any epistemological approach to the determinacy of representation in literature, however, demands such exclusivity. To submit literary referentiality to a determinacy *of origin* requires predication of a denotative semiotic—a social text of either productive *or* interpretive conditions—in relation to which literature stands as a connotative semiotic. Now there is, of course, no such thing as a denotative semiotic, but this objection alone remains insufficient to restore deserved complexity to the question of the determinacy of literary representation. Indeed, only abandonment of the notion of origin can accomplish this end. Once origin has been abandoned, however, the notion of determinacy itself shifts perceptibly in the direction of that more fruitful notion of the *overdeterminacy* (or overdetermination) of representation in literature. Here a determinacy based on articulation of systematic relationships eventually replaces a determinacy based on predication of direct (whether mediate or immediate) causality. The referential text of *The Odyssey* may now be constructed as the site of a complex, even contradictory, conjuncture of multiple conditions of writing and reading.

To structure a theoretical terrain without recourse to origins does allow critics to account more adequately for the variety of objects determined by literary representation and their relations. It also suggests what an epistemological approach finally conceals about literary referentiality itself: "the function of the concept of origin, as in original sin, is to summarize in one word what has not to be thought in order to be able to think what one wants to think."[5] Most of us concerned with literary referentiality want to think that we can specify determinate referents for the literary texts we read. In order to do this, we often isolate one or another origin of literary signification that serves as ground and anchor of textual meaning. A third insight, therefore, into the present concern with referentiality is that, with the successive demises of authorial intention, decidable language, and competent readers as guarantors of literary intelligibility, we seek to discover still another inviolable sanctuary of literary meaning. Yet our search remains possible for only so long as we continue to think of literary referentiality as something that occurs, rather than as something that *is made* to occur. To abandon myths of origin makes analysis of referring in literature no longer an epistemological but an ideological and political enterprise.

Fulfillment of what I do not hesitate to call the political vocation of referential studies depends precisely on judgments made as to the nature of both the determinacy and the object of representation in literature. A notion that "literary" signs, like all signs, are governed by inference can foster an understanding of the determinacy of literary representation such that referentiality is perceived as an *activity* of intertextual inscription. A notion that "literary" meanings, like all meanings, are comprised by cultural units can suggest a definition of the object of literary representation such that referentiality is perceived to involve the social commerce of *ideologemes*.

The "literary" text, taken as a sign of an object that it determines, cannot be thought of as obeying its own rules of sign. The notion of an intrinsically "literary" sign rests on the spurious claim of being able to isolate specifically literary connotators in texts.

> The analysis of connotators may help describe a text, any text, but it could never ascertain that text's literariness, for we would search in vain for the specific connotators of literature. A text can be attributed to the category of literary objects only if one resorts to purport, to extralinguistic reality, which means to explanations of a sociological, psychological, and ethnological kind. In practice, I must again repeat, only a sociocultural investigation can tell us whether or not a text is to be considered literary in a given age and by a given audience. Naturally, this is so of all kinds of connotators because every connotator must be referred to a content-purport once the analysis has shifted to the metasemiotic of connotative semiotics. (Di Girolamo, p. 63)

In fact, the "literary" does not constitute a connotator at all. The appearance of those connotators that critics often consider as distinctive of literary discourse is by no means limited to texts that are said to belong to literature; rather, "the literary 'overtones' we might observe in some signs or sets of signs are the result of a combination of connotators which, when taken individually, do not qualify as 'literary,' but, for example, as 'archaic,' 'learned,' 'dialectal,' 'figural,' etc., which are connotators common to everyday speech, scientific language, and the like" (Di Girolamo, p. 63). Even consideration of styles and genres fails to provide sufficient reasons to establish the "literary" as a connotator. Various studies reveal that so-called "literary" structures inform as well the conventions of composition, and often of interpretation, of texts classified as historiographical, religious, philosophical, scientific, and political. No semiotic reasons exist, therefore, that warrant a view of the governance of "literary" signs as inherently different from the governance of signs in general.

Nevertheless, if the literary text, taken as a sign of an object that it determines, must obey the general rules of sign, it is erroneous to invoke a linguistic, or Saussurean, model of sign in order to explain the determinacy of representation in literature. The notions of the arbitrariness and biconditionality (signifier/signified) of sign finally construct signs as "bastions of identity, equivalence, and forced unifications."[6] Indeed, if the relation of signs to the world seems duly problematic for Saussure, the relation of signifiers to signifieds seems unduly secured:

> From this perspective, the sign, ruled by the law of definition and synonymy, represents the ideological construct of a metaphysics of identity in which signifier and signified are biconditionally linked. By opposition, textual practice would consist in a challenge, a denial, a dissolution of such a rigid and misleading identity. Texts are the necessary liturgical ceremony where signs are sacrificed at the altar of significance, of *la pratique signifiante*. (Eco, "Theory of Signs," p. 38)

Yet, in Eco's view, the polarity created here remains false; signs can be analyzed as texts, and texts can be analyzed as signs. The wedding of a theory of language to a theory of sign, which produces the polarity between signs and texts, is a historical, not an ontological, fact. The history of this rocky marriage has exercised a debilitating influence precisely on study of the determinacy of representation in literature. For the view promoted by the linguistic model (that signs and texts differ) is really only applied to alleged differences between linguistic signifiers and textual signifiers. The linguistic model still assumes that attribution of textual meanings to textual signifiers proceeds on the basis of relations of equivalence between textual signifiers and textual signifieds. Thus the effect of extratextual determinations of meaning is denied.

Far from entertaining relations with their objects that can be specified by a problematic of identity/nonidentity, however, texts maintain relations to their objects that are specified by an inferential model of sign based on abduction. Abductive signs do not depend on relations of equivalence with their own meanings ($p \equiv q$), but, from the point of view of a theory of communication, on inferences ($p \supset q$) anticipated as probable by sign producers, and, from the point of view of a theory of signification, on inferences actually made by sign interpreters. Like deduction and induction, abduction represents an activity of synthetic inference; it distinguishes itself from other inferential modes insofar as it involves reasoning from a specific result, to formulation of a law, and, finally, to formulation of a case.[7] With respect to literary texts taken as signs of referential objects, abduction suggests that readers infer from a given text the existence of a world whose laws and processes enable the text to be interpreted (or naturalized) as a statement about that world. Thus, any textual sign, or sememe, "must be analyzed and represented as a *set of instructions* for the correct co-textual insertion of a given term" (Eco, "Theory of Signs," p. 43). So it is that referentiality in literature, like referentiality in all types of discourse, surfaces as an activity of *intertextual inscription*.

Only through recognition that literary texts are governed by inferential rules of sign can discussion of the determinacy of representation in literature begin to take place without recourse to essentialist assumptions involving one or more metaphysics of identity. To pose the question of the determinacy of literary representation is also to ask, "How do texts constrain meaning?" Eco, of course, devotes much space in his writings to discussion of how texts attempt to program certain readings within themselves as part of their own process of production. That this concern betrays a residual essentialism becomes quickly evident in such phrases as "*the correct* co-textual insertion of a given term" (my emphasis). Yet the logic of an inferential model of sign, especially when elaborated through notions such as that of an "inferential walk," pushes beyond this position. According to Eco's own scheme, readerly inferences always involve ideological determinations that are spatially located outside or beyond the text.[8] Once such determinations have been admitted, however, it is no longer possible to maintain either that what readers confront is "the text" or that what constrains readerly inferences is "the text."

For the crucial concept here is not "constraint," but the very notion of "the text itself." As Tony Bennett argues, texts can be said to participate in the constraint of meaning only if what is meant is that

> the text that the reader or critic has in front of him or her is encountered as a resisting force, constraining the interpretive and analytical options that may be adopted in relation to it. . . . What most needs to be stressed, however, is that, whatever the material form or social context in which the text reaches the reader, it does so only as already covered by a pre-existing horizon of interpretive options, options which are encountered as limits, as a force which has to be reckoned with. . . . It is not some shadowy ideal text, a text hidden within the materiality of the text, but the text in its specific material form as inscribed within a definite set of social relations and as already covered by an accumulated history of readings that, in the present, exerts a determinacy over the modes of its consumption. It is the readings already produced in relation to a text, and not some . . . 'text itself,' which bear upon and limit present and future possible readings. It is for these historical and not at all essentialist reasons that texts are encountered as a resistance.[9]

A notion of "the text itself" remains an illusion because texts are only available as entities that are always already imbued with meanings through various practices

of interpretation, appropriation, distribution, and classification of texts.[10] The theoretical perspective implicit in Eco's logic, and explicit in Bennett's formulations,
thus becomes one of displacing "the text" from the center of focus in analysis of
the determinacy of literary representation. An inferential model of sign must finally
locate the site of such determinacy as a "reading formation, a set of intersecting
discourses which *productively activate* a given body of texts and the relation between
them in a specific way."[11]

On this view, already constructed, or culturally activated, readers confront already
constructed, or culturally activated, texts. Not only, therefore, is referentiality to
be conceived of as an activity of intertextual inscription, but also the determinacy
of such activity is to be conceived of as provided by operations of historically
variable ideological conjunctures. While these assertions in no way imply that
"new" readings may not issue from the encounters between readers and texts, they
do deny that "referring in literature" consists of a direct cue by "the text" of an
"hors-texte" of history, transcendental subjectivity, personal experience, or the
like. Here the problem of origins that plagues epistemological approaches to the
determinacy of literary representation disappears. For, instead of positing the literary
text as a sign that is to be played off against an "object" that it is said to determine,
the view afforded by an inferential model of sign suggests that a text is inseparable
from the determinations in which it is inscribed.

Any concept of the object of representation in literature, or what I shall begin
to call the "referent," must fulfill the conditions imposed by this understanding of
the determinacy of representation in literature. The referent of literary representation
should thus surface as an entity susceptible to construction such that it appears as
already inscribed within its determinations. Now the "referential fallacy," as pre-
mised by semiotics, eliminates "things" from the field of "objects" to be considered here. Because *"every attempt to establish what the referent of a sign is forces
us to define the referent in terms of an abstract entity which is only a cultural
convention,"* the meaning of a term can exist only in the form of a *cultural unit*;
the abstract entity through which a referent is defined, moreover, is itself "another
representation referred to the same 'object,' " or an interpretant.[12] Interpretants
guarantee the cultural validity of signs (for some group of interpreters) by displacing
signification into a series of further sign functions. The referents of literary texts,
therefore, are initially to be conceived of as determinate constellations of "cultural
units."[13]

In his discussion of aesthetic value, Jan Mukařovský offers an exemplary formulation of the object of representation in literature such that it appears as a cultural
unit already inscribed within its determinations.[14] While Mukařovský seeks ultimately to answer the question, "Is objective aesthetic value a reality or a false
illusion?" (Mukařovský, p. 70), his argument involves less a transitive use of the
notion of value, in the sense of "evaluation," than a substantive use of the notion
of value, in the sense of "values." Mukařovský first maintains that, because of its
nature as a sign, the work of art is a social fact. Yet the artistic sign differs socially
from the more frequent communicative sign in that the information it conveys is

no longer inflected toward empirical objects or events about which receivers may inquire as to their actual existence or occurrence. Rather,

> the change which the material relationship of the work—the sign—has undergone is thus simultaneously its weakening and its strengthening. It is weakened in the sense that the work does not refer to the reality which it directly depicts, and strengthened in that the work of art as a sign acquires an indirect (figurative) tie with realities that are vitally important to the perceiver, and through them to the entire universe of the perceiver, as a collection of values. Thus the work of art acquires the ability to refer to a reality which is totally different from the one which it depicts, and to systems of values other than the one from which it arose and on which it is founded. (Mukařovský, p. 75)

In Mukařovský's view, communicative signs situate sender and receiver in a signifying process for which a depicted reality, known to the one and about which the other is informed, serves as the source of the material connection between sender and receiver. In art, however, depicted reality does not constitute the source of the material connection in the signifying process, but rather, only its intermediary.

> The real tie in this situation is a variable one, and points to realities known to the viewer. They are not and can in no way be expressed or even indicated in the work itself, because it forms a component of the viewer's intimate experience. This cluster of realities may be very important and the material tie of the art work with each of them is indirect, figurative. The realities with which the art work can be confronted in the consciousness and subconsciousness of the viewer are squeezed into the general, intellectual, emotional and willful attitude which the viewer assumes toward reality in general. . . . Also, the attitude which the individual takes toward reality is not the exclusive property even of the strongest personalities, for it is to a considerable extent, and in weaker persons almost totally, determined by the social relationships in which the individual is involved. (Mukařovský, pp. 82–83)

Hence, artworks refer to that which Mukařovský calls "extra-aesthetic values." This assertion, moreover, derives its authority from analysis of the expression plane, as well as the content plane, of aesthetic sign functions. In a lengthy discussion, Mukařovský shows that, even for the most abstract styles of art, formal features acquire semantic value in the interpretive encounter. Indeed, he suggests that interpretation of nonrepresentational art becomes possible only after the perceiver has begun to ascribe certain extra-aesthetic values to such features as line and color, in painting, which themselves embody semantic potential. These notions—that aesthetic texts take extra-aesthetic values as their objects, and that interpretation proceeds from extra-aesthetic values toward perception of the internal organization of the artwork—eventually lead Mukařovský to a compelling conclusion about the nature of the aesthetic process.

> We said earlier that all elements of a work of art, in form and content, possess extra-

aesthetic values which, within the work, enter into mutual relationships. The work of art appears, in the final analysis, as an actual collection of extra-aesthetic values and nothing else. The material components of the artistic artifact, and the manner in which they are used as artistic means, assume the role of mere conductors of energies introduced by extra-aesthetic values. If we ask ourselves at this point what has happened to aesthetic value, it appears that it has dissolved into individual extra-aesthetic values, and is really nothing but a general term for the dynamic totality of their mutual interrelationships. . . . The influence of aesthetic value is not that it swallows up and represses all remaining values, but that it releases every one of them from direct contact with a corresponding life-value. It brings an entire assembly of values contained in the work as a dynamic whole into contact with a total system of those values which form the motive power of the life practice of the perceiving collective. (Mukařovský, pp. 88–89)

The referents of literature, or "extra-aesthetic values," therefore, are here already inscribed within their determinations. Mukařovský posits no distinct object that would qualify as an intrinsically "aesthetic" referent. As I have shown, to posit the existence of a properly "aesthetic" referent makes the object of representation in literature subject to an essentialist determination, even when so-called "extrinsic" factors are acknowledged to exercise determinations on this object as well. Yet the argument set forth by Mukařovský fully breaks with epistemological problematics structured by spatial metaphors of "inside" and "outside."[15] Precisely because his referents are already "extra-aesthetic," Mukařovský can consistently assert that textual meaning is an effect of reference to the world.

Mukařovský's formulations furnish the protocol by means of which the referent of literary representation may be analyzed as already inscribed within its determinations. Nevertheless, his definition of the referent as an "extra-aesthetic value" requires further precision. Indeed, Mukařovský's affirmation—that extra-aesthetic values involve "the general, intellectual, emotional, and willful attitude which the viewer assumes toward reality"—strongly anticipates a twentieth-century Marxist definition of ideology:

> Ideology, then, is the expression of the relation between men and their 'world,' that is, the (overdetermined) unity of the real relation and the imaginary relation between them and their real conditions of existence. In ideology the real relation is inevitably invested in the imaginary relation, a relation that *expresses* a *will* (conservative, conformist, reformist or revolutionary), a hope or nostalgia, rather than describing a reality.[16]

Furthermore, Mukařovský's notion that aesthetic processes release extra-aesthetic values "from direct contact with a corresponding life-value" itself anticipates a concept of the "pseudo-real" and implies recognition of the "contextual mobility" of fictive significations.

Terry Eagleton defines the "pseudo-real" as "the imaginary situations which the text is about."[17] Paralleling Mukařovský's distinction between the communicative sign and the artistic sign, he argues that signifieds within fiction refer not to concrete situations but to certain ideological formations that concrete situations have produced. The meaning of the imaginary events presented in a text, therefore, "lies not in their material reality but in how they contribute to fashioning and perpetuating a particular process of signification" (Eagleton, *Criticism and Ideology*, p. 74). As does Mukařovský, with respect to the distinction between "aesthetic" and "extra-aesthetic" value, Eagleton arrives at a bold elision of boundaries between the fictional and the ideological:

> It is useful in this respect to think of the text not merely as the *product* of ideology, but as a *necessity* of ideology—not in an empirical sense, since ideologies without literature have certainly existed, but theoretically, in that fiction is the term we would give to the fullest self-rendering of ideology, the only logical form that such a complete rendering could assume. And this is not, of course, because fiction is 'untrue,' and so a fit vehicle for 'false consciousness,' but rather that in order to reconstruct a society's self-representations we would finally encounter the need to cut them loose from particular 'reals' and mobilise them in the form of situations which, because imaginary, would allow for the range, permutation, economy and flexibility denied to a mere reproduction of the routinely lived. (Eagleton, *CI*, pp. 77–78)

Thus, for Eagleton, literature stands out as a vast enterprise of ideological representation in which multiple fictive strategies encode varying attitudes, or relations, of individuals to their experiential world. On this basis, moreover, Mukařovský's concern with depragmatized "extra-aesthetic values," as well as his concern with their articulation into social "systems of values," can be assimilated to Marxist theory:

> It could be claimed, indeed, that what constitutes a product as 'literary' is exactly [its] contextual mobility. . . . The 'literary' . . . is whatever is detached by a certain hermeneutic practice from its pragmatic context and subjected to a generalizing reinscription. Since such reinscription is always a particular gesture within determinate ideologies, 'literature' itself is always an ideological construct.[18]

Hence, in place of Mukařovský's notion of the referent as an "extra-aesthetic value," Marxist criticism substitutes the more enabling concept of the "ideologeme" to define the object of literary representation. According to Fredric Jameson,

> the ideologeme is an amphibious formation, whose essential structural characteristic may be described as its possibility to manifest itself either as a pseudoidea—a conceptual or belief system, an abstract value, an opinion or prejudice—or as a proto-narrative, a kind of ultimate class fantasy about the 'collective characters' which are the classes in opposition. This duality means that the basic requirement for the full description of the ideologeme is already given in advance: as a construct it must be susceptible to both a conceptual description and a narrative manifestation all at once.[19]

Thus the texts of literature may be said to consist of various unfoldings of the narrative potential embodied in the very ideologemes to which such texts refer.

Jameson understands what Eagleton calls the "pseudo-real" of individual texts as providing an imaginary solution to unresolvable social contradications; thus, from the outset, the aesthetic is here inscribed within the ideological by conceiving of the social as immanent to form (Jameson, p. 77). When the individual text is later "refocussed as a *parole*, or individual utterance, of that vaster system, or *langue*, of class discourse," then "this larger class discourse can be said to be organized around 'minimal units,' " or ideologemes (Jameson, pp. 85, 87). Finally, in a formulation that refines and resonates with Mukařovský's views, the individual text, now restructured through the ideologeme, emerges as "a field of force in which the dynamics of sign systems of several distinct modes of production can be registered and apprehended" (Jameson, p. 98). At every moment, therefore, this view of the object of representation in literature avoids the essentialist fallacy, for the referent defined as ideologeme remains wholly inscribed within its determinations.

What conclusions follow for the study of referentiality from a definition of the object of literary representation as an ideologeme and from a notion that the determinacy of literary representation is provided by activities of intertextual inscription? Analysis of referentiality in literature may be said to encourage repudiation of a narrow concern with aesthetics and augur the development of a vigorous cultural criticism. In conjunction with the referential fallacy, the essentialist fallacy deprives the referent of the fixity that is accorded to essences and things. Now subject to ongoing processes of the social determination of meaning, the referent can no longer stabilize the reading of texts. Referentiality, therefore, does not just happen. It *is made* to happen when a reading formation activates a particular inscription of texts into an ideological practice. Analysis of referentiality has little to do with the epistemological attempt to discover an absolute ground of textual meaning. It has everything to do with the political struggle over the forms of use and effectivity that texts enjoy within the broader social process.[20]

For Hispanists, the social destiny of Benito Pérez Galdós's *Fortunata y Jacinta* may perhaps prove illustrative of the foregoing arguments. What is the referent of this text? If I bracket consideration of popular readings of the novel, I feel confident in asserting that no critic today would progress very far toward an answer to this question before having to take account of the relevant debate carried on by Stephen Gilman and Carlo Blanco Aguinaga in three articles published in *Anales Galdosianos* between 1966 and 1970.[21] *Fortunata y Jacinta* comes before critics today as already carrying a political charge; no academic interpretation of this text currently can be circulated without its being evaluated and classified in light of the interpretive options that have accrued as a result of the polemical exchange between Gilman and Blanco. Yet, for my purposes, the exemplariness of *Fortunata y Jacinta* resides not only in that studies of the novel now enjoy explicitly political resonance, but also in that ideological decisions made in regard to the referents of the novel can be shown to inform how its structure is perceived by the critical discourses in question.

In 1981, quite independently of one another, there appeared two of the more recent attempts at describing a referent for *Fortunata y Jacinta*. One of these attempts was made again by Gilman in his *Galdós and the Art of the European Novel 1867–*

1887.[22] The other was made by me in an essay entitled "*Fortunata y Jacinta*: Galdós and the Production of the Literary Referent."[23] While I still endorse the major arguments of my article, the presence of the term "literary referent" in its title should indicate that I would today formulate somewhat differently the theoretical framework within which my analysis takes place. I do not want, however, to use this space as the occasion upon which to defend my reading of *Fortunata y Jacinta* as one that is "more something or other" than Gilman's reading. Rather, I want to examine aspects of both readings in order to suggest that the particular predication of referents enacted by each of us depends on the reading formations into which the text of *Fortunata y Jacinta*, and we ourselves, are inscribed.

In my essay, I consider that *Fortunata y Jacinta* produces as referents a set of progressive middle-class values that are addressed to the "vacío ideológico" created in Spain during the process of ideological assimilation of the landed and financial middle classes by the traditional nobility, 1875–1900. I argue that Galdós's *costumbrista* representation of lower-middle-class experience in *Fortunata y Jacinta* unfolds a narrative logic that remains at odds with the dominant tendency of the overall structure of the novel. For example, the social implications of the representations offered in "Costumbres turcas"(III, 1) resist the synthetic and reconciliatory movements of the plot and formal argument that govern the text generally. Based on descriptions that establish the *café* as a representational space informed by special psychological strategies of identification and aggression (Lacan's "Imaginary"), "Costumbres turcas" constructs an image of a possible form of subjective relation to Restoration society that counters the more conservative image of subjectivity represented through the Santa Cruz *tertulia*. Thus, Juan Pablo Rubín's eventual assimilation into the political machinery of the Restoration is portrayed as a disheartening, though unavoidable, repudiation of progressive values that seem embedded in the very texture of lower-middle-class life. Even in this chapter, therefore, I perceive that the narrative surface of *Fortunata y Jacinta* is traversed by various historical perspectives: the fictional return to the apparent possibility in 1875 of elaborating an effective ideological practice of the middle class, coupled with narrative awareness in 1887 of the impending integration of the landed and financial middle classes within the Restoration "bloque de poder." I claim, then, that it is the project of this novel to organize and to transform cultural representations available in the 1880s in a way that seeks to restore a specific kind of ideological presence to the middle class. In the form of a contradiction between its guiding structural premises and the representational logic of its textualization of the lower middle class, however, the work may be said to acknowledge its own failure to accomplish this task. It is through recognition of this structural dissonance that the full significance of the production of the referent in *Fortunata y Jacinta* may be grasped. For, by undertaking in the mode of the Imaginary to articulate elements of a progressive middle-class ideology, the novel constructs the referent in a manner that replenishes in consciousness the absence of such a practice from the ideological problematic of the Restoration.

Now, my perspective on the referents of *Fortunata y Jacinta* depends on a specific understanding of how the novel is structured; and my understanding of textual structure here depends on a series of more general assumptions that may be said to comprise my reading formation. Thus, my perception that the temporality represented in the novel surfaces as a peculiarly conflictive and uneven one, involves my own view that historical moments are best conceptualized through the categories of contradiction and overdetermination. My willingness to base so much of my reading on a "secondary" character such as Juan Pablo Rubín is owing to my view that characters can never be understood as adequate embodiments of qualities or attributes; therefore, marginal agents or *actants* in a text deserve special consideration, not as inadequate representations of a universal consciousness, but precisely as indexical components of an overall system of relations that represents determinate positions for subjectivity. My assertion that the novel reveals an internal dissonance depends on my convictions that literature does not present "reality" or express the author's intention, that it does not provide knowledge or truth (in an epistemological sense), and that certain of its significations always escape its dominant explanatory strategies. My location of this text in relation to the ideological problematic of Restoration Spain is motivated, of course, by my understanding of the place and function of literature within social formations generally. In other words, I construct the form of this text through a poststructuralist optics in which an Althusserian Marxism serves as the dominant factor. When I read this text, therefore, I productively activate it by inscribing it within a particular set of intersecting discourses that themselves constitute a specific ideological practice.

In *Galdós and the Art of the European Novel: 1867–1887*, Gilman seems to recognize that at least some acts of predication of referents for texts consist of the inscription of texts into an ideological practice by means of a reading formation.

> Once having aided us in posing the problem, . . . Marxist critics, at least in the case of *Fortunata y Jacinta*, offer an incorrect solution. Here is a story, in their view, of an innocent, proletarian victim caught in the "engrenage" of an immense and complex bourgeois society, which literally cries for a revolution. All of Galdós's social and historical "materias reunidas" are justifiable artistically because they are "socially realistic" and show us vividly the mechanisms of corruption and exploitation.
>
> Why is this, at first glance, apparently reasonable interpretation of our novel, . . . "incorrect"? (Gilman, p. 229)

It seems, then, that not all acts of predication of referents for texts are considered by Gilman to consist of an ideological inscription, for, as this passage illustrates, Gilman inscribes his own reading of *Fortunata y Jacinta* into the position of truth. I shall suggest, however, that Gilman's reading accomplishes the inscription of "our" text precisely into a determinate ideological practice.

Gilman's discussion of *Fortunata y Jacinta* is a lengthy and challenging one, so I must limit myself here to presentation of his argument largely as it appears in the opening chapter of Part III, the section devoted exclusively to *Fortunata y Jacinta*. Gilman argues that, as does Cervantes, Galdós exploits "the temporal paradox of fiction (or the fictional paradox of time) in order, not just to make us laugh or to attract our attention, but to make us aware of who we are and who we could be or should be, to lead us to become, as it were, working members of the 'Wortkunstwerk,' whose consciousness of society and self is heightened and changed by that membership'' (Gilman, p. 233). According to Gilman, the temporal paradox of fiction is that the past tense of the author's discourse becomes the present tense of the reader's experience: in fictional narrative, ''then'' becomes ''now.'' Nevertheless, ''in the greatest nineteenth-century novels (and *Fortunata y Jacinta* is surely one of them), after the scrupulous documentation of social illness and the poetic expression of intensely lived experience have been completed, 'then' and 'now' become 'forever' '' (Gilman, p. 245). I take this to mean that Gilman believes that great novels afford access to universal and transcendent truths about human nature that are immune to those conditional, transitory, and perhaps all too fragile phenomena that give concrete shape to the present and past of human beings. In *Fortunata y Jacinta*, then, it is ''the sheer health of Fortunata's consciousness'' (Gilman, p. 240) that becomes the vehicle through which readers accede to such truths. Unlike *all* the other characters, who ''fill the pages of the novel, but whose ample assortment of eccentric reactions to their metropolitan milieu amounts at best to 'costumbrismo' on a grand scale'' (Gilman, p. 239), Fortunata ''is or becomes a *presence*'' (p. 240): ''she may also be in her own novelistic way a savior'' (p. 240). According to Gilman, therefore, ''although it is not an argument that Marxist critics who do not live in Marxist societies are likely to agree with'' (p. 244), it is through the consciousness of Fortunata that ''Galdós intended to show us that salvation is possible'' (p. 244).

Hence, Gilman posits the referent of *Fortunata y Jacinta* as a transcendent consciousness that embodies awareness of a path to salvation. I now want to inquire further into the contours and motivations of this consciousness: who is to be saved? From what are they to be saved? What path do the elect follow? Except on rare occasions, answers to these questions are not directly forthcoming from Gilman; yet such answers would surely make explicit some aspects of Gilman's own reading formation. Since he praises in Galdós, and prescribes for Galdós's readers, the exercise of what he calls ''the art of listening,'' perhaps you and I should ''listen'' carefully to Gilman in the hope of discovering some indication of the ideological practice into which I shall allege that he inscribes this text.

> Discussion of what Galdós intended and what he in fact achieved in the creation of his masterpiece must wait until a step-by-step exploration, from style, through poetic imagery, into Fortunata's consciousness, is completed in the chapters to follow. Naturally, Marxist readers will not be convinced, insofar as they are committed to a definition of what novels are (and should be) antithetical to that of Galdós. (Gilman, p. 230)

Authorial intention; unity of intention, style, imagery, and subject matter: the assumptions about the nature of textuality that Gilman brings to his reading of *Fortunata y Jacinta* are here apparent. Masterpiece: also apparent are his evaluative interest in transcendent art and his institutional concern to demonstrate that *Fortunata y Jacinta* deserves recognition by non-Hispanists as one of ''the greatest

nineteenth-century novels.'' Consciousness: consistent with an emphasis on authorial intention, he makes the assumption that the possibility of discursive meaning
depends on identifying a source of self-aware expression (''the presence of Fortunata
as a perfect conductor of experience'' [Gilman, p. 243]). Even more telling, there
is here revealed Gilman's tendency to displace responsibility for his own assumptions and to give them author-ity by projecting them onto Galdós. Let us listen
again to the closing sentence of that quotation: ''Naturally, Marxist readers will
not be convinced, insofar as they are committed to a definition of what novels are
(and should be) antithetical to'': . . . ''mine''? No, ''antithetical to that of Galdós.''

This last tactic should be recognized for what it is: ''a political strategy for reading
in which the critic's own construction of authorial intention is mobilized in order
to bully other interpretations off the field.''[24] Gilman repeatedly indulges in dis-
guises and displacements of this sort that attempt to secure the truth of his position
by inscribing both the text, and Gilman's own readers, within the discourses of
quite specific ideologies. Let us listen again:

> For passionate readers and rereaders of *Fortunata y Jacinta*, Fortunata is the woman
> who, among all women, is the most profoundly known. We know her from within,
> and we know her at length, from spiritual birth to physical death and believed-in
> resurrection. We know her in a way we can never know women of flesh and blood—
> our mothers, our sisters, our wives. (Gilman, p. 320)

Who is included in the ''we'' here? Certainly not women, unless women are to be
judged incapable of coming to know themselves as intimately as they may come
to know a fictional character. Rather, it is ''we men'' who are supposed to know
Fortunata in this way. And, in Gilman's analysis, to know Fortunata is to know
and to possess the meaning of the text—the text as woman—just as Galdós knew
and possessed the meaning of the text. For, after all, the text *is* the masterful
expression and perfect representation of Fortunata's consciousness.

Who, then, is saved by Fortunata, and from what? I want to listen to Gilman
one last time as he writes the image of his own subjectivity, and perhaps ours, into
his discussion of the referent of this novel.

> Galdós is not trying to excuse nor does he still aspire (as does Zola) to cure the
> diseased society portrayed in the novel. Like Mark Twain's Mississippi shores, Sten-
> dhal's Parma, or Cervantes' ''la Mancha,'' it is both unjustifiable and in its own
> terms chronically ill, but Galdós does see, with the clear, distant vision with which
> great novelists are blessed, the ironical interdependence and interaction of society
> (sick almost by definition) with those rare incited souls who inhabit it but are immune
> to its debasement and who at the end find their individual paths to a reevaluation of
> the human condition. (Gilman, pp. 245–246)

Like great novelists, are perhaps literary critics blessed with ''clear, distant vision''?
Do literary critics stand in need these days of abandoning a society that is ''sick
almost by definition''? Are literary critics some of those ''rare incited souls''—the
elect—who find their individual and transcendent paths to salvation? It is Gilman's

own consciousness, and the image of subjectivity made possible by a complex ideological practice, that are saved by Gilman's Fortunata. And, in the end, by elevating themselves above those common unincited souls who also inhabit society, and yet who are not immune to its mechanisms of debasement, what these rare incited souls are saved from is any responsibility to or for a chronically ill society.

So it is that, when Gilman reads *Fortunata y Jacinta*, he productively activates the text by inscribing it within a reading formation that Catherine Belsey has called "expressive realism": "This is the theory that literature reflects the *reality* of experience as it is perceived by one (especially gifted) individual, who *expresses* it in a discourse which enables others to recognize it as true."[25] As a reading formation, expressive realism is constituted by the intersecting ideological discourses of humanism, empiricism, and idealism. Expressive realism holds "that 'man' is the origin and source of meaning, of action, and of history (*humanism*). Our concepts and our knowledge are held to be the product of experience (*empiricism*), and that this experience is preceded and interpreted by the mind, reason or thought, the property of a transcendent human nature whose essence is the attribute of each individual (*idealism*)" (Belsey, p. 7). Gilman's referents, therefore, arise from the intertextual inscription of *Fortunata y Jacinta* into these ideological practices by means of the reading formation of expressive realism.

The referents of *Fortunata y Jacinta* that I posit in my essay on the novel also arise from a process of inscribing the text into an ideological practice by means of a reading formation. Throughout his discussion, Gilman's constant assertions regarding what Marxist critics can or cannot do, and what they will or will not believe, suggest that, at least to some degree, he understands that his formulation of the referent of the novel is in struggle with alternative formulations, or, as I have tried to show, with rival referential acts. And so it is! This is what I meant when I wrote that analysis of referentiality has little to do with epistemological attempts to discover an absolute ground of textual meaning. Rather, it has everything to do with political struggles over the use and effectivity that texts enjoy within the broader social process.

NOTES

1. See especially Tony Bennett, *Formalism and Marxism* (New York and London: Methuen, 1979); Mary Louise Pratt, *Toward a Speech Act Theory of Literary Discourse* (Bloomington and London: Indiana University Press, 1977); Costanzo Di Girolamo, *A Critical Theory of Literature* (Madison and London: University of Wisconsin Press, 1981).

2. "Linguistics and Poetics," in *The Structuralists: From Marx to Lévi-Strauss*, ed. Richard and Fernande DeGeorge (Garden City, N.Y.: Doubleday, 1972), p. 94.

3. Di Girolamo, p. 6.

4. Overcoding occurs when, "on the basis of a pre-established rule, a new rule [is] proposed which govern[s] a rarer application of the previous rule"; undercoding represents "an operation by means of which in the absence of reliable pre-established rules, certain macroscopic portions of certain texts are provisionally assumed to be pertinent units of a

174 On Referring in Literature

code in formation, even though the combinatorial rules governing the more basic compositional items of the expressions, along with the corresponding content-units, remain unknown.'' Umberto Eco, *A Theory of Semiotics* (Bloomington and London: Indiana University Press, 1976), pp. 133, 135–136.

5. Louis Althusser and Etienne Balibar, *Reading Capital*, trans. Ben Brewster (London: New Left Books, 1970), p. 63.

6. Umberto Eco, "The Theory of Signs and the Role of the Reader," *Bulletin of the Midwest Modern Language Association* 14, 1 (Spring 1981), p. 38.

7. Deduction entails reasoning from a law, to a case, to a result; induction entails reasoning from many results and many cases to formulation of a law. See Eco, "Theory of Signs," pp. 44–45.

8. *The Role of the Reader* (Bloomington and London: Indiana University Press, 1979), pp. 22–23.

9. "Text and Social Processes: The Case of James Bond," *Screen Education* 41 (Winter/ Spring 1982).

10. "Texts come before us as the always-already-read; we apprehend them through sedimented layers of previous interpretations, or—if the text is brand-new—through the sedimented reading habits and categories developed by those inherited interpretive traditions." Fredric Jameson, *The Political Unconscious: Narrative as a Socially Symbolic Act* (Ithaca and London: Cornell University Press, 1981), p. 9.

11. Tony Bennett, "Texts, Readers, Reading Formations," *Bulletin of the Midwest Modern Language Association* 16, 1 (Spring 1983), p. 5.

12. Eco, *A Theory of Semiotics*, pp. 66, 68.

13. For more detailed discussion of the referent as cultural unit, see my "Notes toward a Theory of the Referent," *PMLA* 94, 3 (May 1979), pp. 459–475.

14. *Aesthetic Function, Norm and Value as Social Facts* (Ann Arbor: University of Michigan Press, 1970).

15. A problematic structured by spatial metaphors of "the inside" and "the outside" is common to both empiricist and idealist epistemologies. See Althusser and Balibar, *Reading Capital*, pp. 35–40.

16. Louis Althusser, *For Marx*, trans. Ben Brewster (New York: Random House, 1970), pp. 233–234.

17. *Criticism and Ideology* (London: New Left Books, 1976), p. 80.

18. Terry Eagleton, *Walter Benjamin, or Towards a Revolutionary Criticism* (London: Verso Editions and New Left Books, 1981), p. 123.

19. *The Political Unconscious: Narrative as a Socially Symbolic Act* (Ithaca and London: Cornell University Press, 1981), p. 87.

20. See Tony Bennett, *Formalism and Marxism* (New York and London: Methuen, 1979), pp. 167–168.

21. See Stephen Gilman, "The Birth of Fortunata," *Anales Galdosianos* I (1966), pp. 71–83; Carlos Blanco Aguinaga, "On 'The Birth of Fortunata,' " *Anales Galdosianos* III (1968), pp. 13–24; and Gilman, "The Consciousness of Fortunata," *Anales Galdosianos* V (1970), pp. 55–66.

22. (Princeton: Princeton University Press, 1981).

23. *MLN* 96, 2 (March 1981), pp. 316–339.

24. Bennett, "Texts, Readers, Reading Formations," p. 15.

25. *Critical Practice* (New York and London: Methuen, 1980), p. 7.

CONCLUSION

THEORIES OF REFERENCE

Anna Whiteside

I: The Frame of Reference

I, 1: Preamble

First, a word about what this essay is not about. Since the subject of this volume is *literary reference*, we shall not be dealing with the problems of truth or existence *per se*, for the simple reason, as Leonard Linsky and John Searle, amongst others, have pointed out, that successful reference is contingent on neither. On the whole the literary reader (as opposed to the historian, sociologist, anthropologist, philosopher, and all those who use literary texts as source material) and *a fortiori* the literary critic, are not particularly interested in the truth value of a literary text, or in the ontological status of the literary referent. These are rather the problems of logicians and a certain school of semanticists, and have been dealt with by such authors as Woods, in *The Logic of Fiction*, and Heintz (1979).[1] Nor shall I be dealing with the linguistic aspects of reference, except initially in as far as they contribute to literary pragmatics.

What this essay does hope to do, however, is to outline some of the specific ways reference functions in literary discourse as opposed to ordinary discourse. In so doing I will inevitably draw on the findings of both philosophers and linguists, since it is they who have so far formulated and described the concepts and processes of referring, thus providing the tools for this inquiry. In fact, now that the ontological issue—raised by Bertrand Russell, Ryle, Strawson (in his earlier works), and Quine, and largely evinced by Linsky, Searle, and Keith Donnellan—is no longer considered an essential part of referring, we find that philosophers and linguists present an increasingly complementary picture of what referring is. Broadly speaking, the philosopher is interested in the *relationship* obtaining between an expression and its referent, while the linguist's concern is with the act and process of referring—the *ways* we use language to draw attention to what we are talking about. In effect, then, both approaches necessarily consider 1) pragmatics, since the context of utterance determines the referent and thus reference, and 2) semantics, since meaning is contingent on the precise nature of the referent as established pragmatically. By the same token, this essay will examine both the relationships obtaining between literary discourse and its context-determined referent, and the ways in which the associated semantic evolution of literary referents work. This will entail some discussion of speech-act theory as propounded by philosophers such as Austin, Strawson, and Searle, and by linguists such as Emile Benveniste, and, obviously, Jakobson. For it is Jakobson's communication model which links the referential function to context and underscores the importance of a more complex referential function in literature, given the importance of speaker-receiver related context or contexts and the poetic function. Coincidentally, this discussion may induce a modest measure of Anglo-French semiotic *entente*, the aim being to show how it is possible to envisage fusion of Saussure's binary sign and the mainly Anglo-Saxon ternary one by combining their complementary functions—the former being strictly linguistic, the latter more philosophical.

But why this interest in referring in literature? Ever since Plato, and, somewhat more recently, since the discussion sparked by Frege's inquiry into the relation between sense and reference, followed by Russell's response in "On Denoting," philosophers and linguists have been debating the problems of reference. Relatively few, however, have turned their attention from ordinary discourse to *literary* discourse. Those who have (mainly logicians) are more interested in accounting for the fact that literary texts can indeed refer (to real or imagined things, states of affairs, etc.) than in discussing the specifics of literary referring: its pragmatic and socio-cultural dimensions, its modes, contexts, codes, types, levels, and, above all, the ways in which it functions and how these affect interpretation. Literary exegetes are no less to blame since few have tackled the problem. Yet surely, to claim to discuss the meaning or meanings of this or that text, as most of us do at some time or other, is necessarily to imply the whole question of reference. For though the signs of literary discourse constitute a text's linguistic dimension, its particular ideological significance lies beyond, and is determined by, the referent and all that this presupposes. Contrary to the belief of some latter-day structuralists and semioticians, literature does not and cannot live by signs alone—at least not in the Saussurean sense.

I, 2: Referring and Literary Theory

True, some aspects of literary reference have been dealt with separately; but though critics such as Woods (1974), Ihwe and Reiser ("Normative and Descriptive Theory of Fiction"), and Lewis ("Notes Towards a Literary Referent") have integrated many of them, no one, to our knowledge, has attempted to provide an overall theory of referring in literature. This volume is intended as a first step in that direction.

Let us briefly consider the individual referential issues already raised by literary critics and theorists, linguists, and philosophers. Glosses discreetly tell us what obscure archaic, or specialized terms, expressions, and names refer to—sometimes so discreetly that the referent lacks its socio-cultural frame of reference as well as its semantic and phonic connections and evolution. Unless the textual context is particularly enlightening, a gloss is not designed to provide complete reference, with the result that the text's full potential meaning may not be realized. But critical editions and the traditional *explication de texte* type of commentary spring into the breach explaining much of the rest, adding pre-textual (that is, from earlier drafts), intratextual, and intertexual references (in both the notional and structural sense of the latter).

Semiotics reinforces intratextual, and to some extent intertextual, reference by interpreting literary discourse as a series of interrelated signs: discover the scoto-mized code and the appropriate signs will reveal their meaning through their re-lationship to one another. Little codes breed bigger codes, and as sign-systems are decoded, so they form a macro-sign-system, a master-code to which, hindsight tells us, they had been pointing all along, and which, in this unscrambled text, spells out *meaning*. But if, for semioticians, signs refer syntagmatically to one another and hence to their code, if their decoded referent in turn becomes a sign and so, through the chain of semiosis, eventually refers to a particular literary form, and if form is meaning (as Patrice Pavis's chapter suggests), then there exists a strange paradox: the majority of literary semioticians in fact use the notion of referring while pretending to ignore the referent. Having adopted a linguistic model (Saus-sure's signifier-signified), they are caught referring without a referent—ever mindful that for Saussure the referent, being strictly extra-linguistic, was irrelevant. But Saussure, like many a philosopher, strangely enough, confused the referent with existence, and referring with affirmation of existence. Critics and literary theorists, however, be they semioticians or no, must deal with referents, contexts of reference, and thus reference itself if they are to refer, say, to *Anna Karenina*, to its heroine or to any other of the text's entities. Even Barthes or Foucault, who claim that form is the ultimate meaning, have, by so doing, acknowledged reference: reference to a particular form or consciousness of form.

Socio-criticism, from Dilthey to Goldmann, Althusser, Adorno, or Foucault (and to some extent structuralism and semiotics, as Patrice Pavis's chapter shows), pushes back referential horizons by examining texts in their sociological, cultural, his-torical, and thus, in their complete ideological context. They thereby transform the context of production into the referent itself—a referent variously coloured, as will be shown (see section II, 2) by the context of reception.

A narrower and more linguistic view of pragmatics has also contributed signifi-cantly to discussions of literary reference as an integral part of the speech-act, and thus of explicit and implicit speaker-addressee contexts of discourse. Reference-determining factors such as modalisors, spatio-temporal deixis, anaphora, and other related components certainly have their uses, but the pitfall of literary vivisection is to insist on treating the text as ordinary discourse, thereby disregarding its literary difference. (Michael Issacharoff's chapter examines the difference and shows how serious vs. non-serious discourse—see II, 3 "Modes"—can be a useful consid-eration when examining playscripts.) Jakobson's literary sensitivity has helped us avoid such dangers. His communication model provides an indispensable framework for our present discussion. Not only does he integrate sender, receiver, speech-acts, and context by defining the message in terms of its referential function to all four, he also examines the literary text's specifically aesthetic ("poetic") function in terms of textual self-reference.

In philosophy the debate has waxed wider and longer, but, being primarily concerned with logic (and modal logic), it has shed little light on the specifics of literary reference. Indeed many philosophers deny the possibility of a literary referent at all. Exceptions exist, however, as the issue of *Poetics* on reference and literature shows (Vol. 8, Nos. 1–2, 1979) and as the work of some speech-act theorists has demonstrated. John Searle's "The Logical Status of Fictional Discourse" is one such example. It is significant that his main argument deals more with the nature of the literary speech-act than with the different ways texts, or rather the "speakers" in and behind them, refer. Nevertheless, this discussion of the special status of the literary speech-act is useful and corroborates Linsky's and Strawson's views.

The logical status of the referent is one of the focal points of discussion on referring, and, latterly, on referring in literature. Frege dismissed the referent's logical status as having nothing to do with truth; Russell would not even countenance a non-existent referent, let alone a literary one. Meinong, however, opened the door to two types of existence: being and so-being (*Sein* and *So-sein*). It soon became clear that the heart of the matter lay not in things referred to, but in the act of referring itself—which brings us back to pragmatics. After all, the Golden Mountain, Cerberus, Mr. Pickwick, and Wells's time-machine may not exist, but we can still refer to them.

Indeed, as Linsky points out (1967) when discussing the question "Does Santa Claus live at the North Pole?" there are two possible answers: "Yes, he does," and "No, he does not really live at the North Pole. It is just make-believe." Now what is at issue here and in literary discourse is not so much the intrinsic status of the referent as the mode of the speech-act: the first reply respects the make-believe mode; the second rejects it for the existential mode. In literature the speaker (writer or character) pretends to perform illocutionary acts which are in turn perceived by the reader as what Searle calls "non-deceptive pseudo-performance." The difference between ordinary and literary speech-acts, then, is not so much that in one world things exist while in the other they do not, or that in one they are true, in the other not, or that meaning changes (after all "words still have their normal meanings" in fiction); but that the mode of performance and interpretation varies. As Blanchot remarks, the reader reading fiction reads with an altered attitude (Linda Hutcheon's chapter explores this problem).

In fact reference, far from having to be true, as Russell would have us believe, does not even have to be accurate. A speaker can use a definite or seemingly definite description to refer, according to Donnellan (1966) and Linsky (1967), even if 1) it does not fit the referent, that is, is false, or 2) if the presupposition of existence is not satisfied. In the first place, to use Linsky's example, a speaker who says of an unmarried lady enjoying the amiable company of some gentleman at a party, that her husband is nice to her, may successfully refer—as even a reply like "But that's not her husband" will confirm. Similarly, in literature, a writer or character may incorrectly describe New York, Napoleon, or the Holocaust, yet still refer . . .

initially to the entity in question, or rather to our image of it, but above all to the author's (re-)creation of it, that is, to his, and consequently the reader's, "secondary" referent; a hyphenated, doubly connoted writer-reader artifact. For example, Robbe-Grillet refers to New York in *Topologie d'une cité fantôme* precisely by disclaiming any intention of referring to the "real" New York—a disclaimer which, while implying, albeit tenuously, the very relationship it refutes, nevertheless attests to the supremacy of secondary reference in literary discourse. Similarly, when Stendhal refers to Napoleon, Baudelaire to Paris, Chekhov to Moscow, and Dickens, Mark Twain, Balzac, and Steinbeck to particular social conditions, however realist or naturalist their art (and there is a distinction as Gombrich [1960] shows), they refer not so much to the extratextual primary referent mentioned as to their own highly connoted intertextual and intratextual literary artifact (something Thomas, Chambers, Meltzer, Krysinski, and Issacharoff all explore in different ways). Barthes, talking of *"l'effet de réel"* (the reality effect), and Ricoeur corroborate the view that literary reference is existentially false reference, a referential illusion whose very force is the illusion it manages to create. Literary critics interested in the role of the reader have further undermined primary reference in literature by showing that from a single description readers construct fairly different imagined or secondary referents.

It would seem then that the distinction between primary and secondary reference in literature is a question of degree rather than of absolutes. For it is arguable that in literature their roles are perhaps reversed, that is, that the primary or "real" referent may actually be subordinated to the secondary referent which recreates and thus replaces it, that is to say, becomes primary by virtue of its literary foregrounding and immediacy. What then of the reader whose knowledge of the "real thing" is primarily second-hand? Where does one distinguish between primary and secondary reference? Although there are two criteria involved here, one existential (which is real, which not?), the other perceptual (which seems most immediate?), both are in fact inextricably intertwined, since from a materialist's (and probably many a reader's) point of view, existence is just as much an image in the mind's eye as in the beholder's. All this prompts one to wonder whether, in literary discourse, the distinction between referent and signified, or indeed between signifier and referent, where a text's form is its signifier, is as unambiguous as is commonly held.

Three self-evident conclusions stem from the discussion of literary reference by critics, theorists, and others: first, that literary critics and theorists, philosophers and linguists are all aware that referring in literature is possible; second, that they feel the need to account for it; third, that it is considerably more complex than referring in ordinary discourse. From these conclusions we derive an obvious fourth. An overall theory is needed which will both account for the specificity of literary reference and combine its apparently divergent facets and functions.

I, 3: Reference defined

Before going any further, it might be well to state what we mean by reference. Let us start with Lyons's definition, since it is one of the broadest. It is "the relationship which holds between an expression and what that expression stands for on particular occasions of its utterance" (1977, Vol. I, p. 174). Here, then, are the three basic considerations concerning reference: an *expression*, *what it stands for*, and the *context* of utterance. In a more Saussurean vein one might translate this trio as 1) signifier within the sign-system of a given *langue*, 2) referent, and 3) *parole*. But, as we hope to show, the highly connoted literary referent in fact tends to become an integral part of the literary sign.

The danger of this definition is that it presupposes an element which has too often been overlooked: the speaker. For an expression alone does not refer—or at least may not be deemed to do so in a very reliable way, despite the arguments (summarized by Linsky, 1967 and 1971, and Quine, 1966), of philosophers who, in any case, are primarily interested in non-literary discourse. Rather, it is the person using the expression who refers, as Lyons shows, and Strawson, Linsky, Donnellan, and Searle all emphasize. So we should perhaps read Lyons's definition bearing in mind Linsky's discussion of uniqueness of reference and the referring expression: "to secure uniqueness of reference through increased determination of the 'referring expression' is otiose, for what secures uniqueness is the user of the expression and the context in which it is used *together* with the expression" (Linsky, 1967, p. 117). If it seems obvious that "expression" and "context of utterance" imply both speaker (author or literary character) and addressee, it was not always so, and indeed much ink has been devoted from Russell to Ryle to the cause of uniquely referring expressions.

Life, let alone literature, would be somewhat problematic if we did not take these aspects of referring for granted: that is to say referring as an *act* (an aspect which Lewis's chapter develops), and its implied contextual (and thus illocutionary and perlocutionary) correlates. For example, if someone tells you he has just bought "a rabbit," reference (albeit indefinite), and thus the referent, are contingent on contextual definition. If the context is a) a visit to a toyshop, the rabbit in question could well be a pink polyester monstrosity; but if he has just returned from b) a Volkswagen dealership, we immediately visualise a car; if, however, the context is c) a pet-shop, presumably the rabbit would be alive; if d) a game and poultry shop, then it should be dead. Here context suggests both state (or mode): a) artificial, b) figurative, c) alive, d) recently dead; and type: c) one of the varieties sold in petshops, for example, a white angora, or d) one of the edible sort. Similarly, if you say to someone "I would like the rabbit," this referent (definite or indefinite) will vary considerably according to 1) the context, 2) the identity of the speaker and receiver, and 3) to the perlocutionary function. Should the addressee be a waiter, the perlocutionary function would be that of a hungry client ordering rabbit; here again the context allows you to assume that "the rabbit" will arrive not live, or frozen solid, but cooked—and in the style specified on the menu of the restaurant where the speaker has chosen to eat.

So in literature, context, speaker and addressee, mode, types of illocutionary acts, and their perlocutionary function all help determine reference and referents, as will be shown in more detail in the sections which follow. In a sense one might even say that literary discourse is more referentially biased than ordinary discourse, in that readers tend to assume the writer's intention to refer, however indirectly.

Contrary to ordinary discourse, literature thrives on the ambiguities of contextual mobility and disguised singular reference. Satires, parodies, and all forms of intertextuality depend upon them. Titles, too, exploit them. *The Old Man and the Sea* initially appears contradictory; its definite descriptions seem to refer, but to what old man, to which sea? *Une saison en enfer* (*A Season in Hell*), though apparently indefinite, refers, since one could say that it actually refers to a specific period in Rimbaud's life as interpreted by him, to a particular imagined construct as it appears in this literary creation—or both, the latter evoking the former. In fact titles always refer—to the texts they identify as well as to their own descriptive deictic function.

Before examining *contexts* (see II, 2), a word about the other two terms in Lyons's definition: the referring expression and its referent. Given literature's enormous contextual elasticity, duplicity, and multiplicity, the literary referent has an unusually protean and dynamic propensity. Describing the phenomenon thus leads to certain pitfalls. In the first place, a referent itself may act as a referring expression: the name Moby Dick refers to a whale which in turn is used to refer to, and thus comes to represent, certain concepts. Similarly characters such as Ahab or Scrooge refer to literary characters whose mere names, by evoking their literary context, come to refer symbolically to particular human qualities. Whether the referent is used as a symbolic or metaphoric referring expression, and regardless of how many stages it may evolve through (in poetry these can be particularly numerous), it is clear that some referents are more equal than others. Although the terms *primary* and *secondary* referent are useful in that they indicate derivation, their suggestion of hierarchy causes problems, given the constantly shifting nature of this hierarchy in literature. Some philosophers use the terms existentially; others, including linguists, anaphorically. To borrow Charles Chastain's example in "Reference and Context" (1975), the philosopher's primary referent when he speaks of "the house" is some "real" world house. From this evolves another referent: the memory image someone has of this house set in the context of his memory, that is, store of memories. In effect this is already a hypothetical intermediary referent, since it is unlikely to be the original memory image, but rather a remembered and thus modified memory image, set inevitably in an altered memory context. Still more removed is the related or so-called secondary referent, set this time, for example, in a literary context. So when I read of Marcel's family home in Combray in *À la recherche du temps perdu* (*In Search of Time Past*), my mental image refers back to a selection of associated memory images or to a conglomerate image of a suitable house or houses I have seen. This does not preclude the possibility of the house being Proust's house at Illiers-Combray, which I may have visited, since this cannot be identical to the one Marcel remembers, despite strong architectural similarities, for different eyes in a different age make a different world. How this memory selection takes place is in turn determined by context association and connotation; thus, here again, contexts not only determine reference, but become referents themselves, as Thomas

Lewis shows. As for connotation, it plays a far greater role in literary reference than has hitherto been admitted. The reader can continue this chain indefinitely; either intertextually, by using his Combray-connoted house to form the basis of another fictional house whose context reminds him of Proust's evoked one, or intratextually, by constantly referring back to the preceding image of Marcel's ever-modified home.

Linguists link referents too, but for them, secondary reference is anaphoric and therefore intratextual. Thus, apparently indefinite expressions may, in fact, refer when considered anaphorically—and in literary discourse, except for the opening sentences (and sometimes even then in the case of the *roman fleuve*, satire, parody, transposed myth, or history, for example), these indefinite expressions usually pre-suppose anaphoric links. Going beyond obvious pronominal anaphora, a literary character may speak of "a room with a view"; from the context it is clear that, in fact, this apparently indefinite and non-referring expression definitely refers . . . in a most specific way. Or again, in *A la recherche*, we may read that "a visitor" used to ring at the garden gate on summer evenings before dropping in for a talk, when clearly "a visitor," considered anaphorically, is a singular definite referring expression, the referent being Swann.

Literary texts play considerably on tension created between apparently referring and non-referring expressions. Jane Austen may speak of a house near or in the town of M., but subsequent description and narrative anaphorically subvert initially non-referring appearances. Legends or tales beginning "Once upon a time there lived a damsel, king, etc.," though they may not establish spatio-temporal reference, do create character or role reference. Such a damsel is never a mere damsel, but the one who is about to become the heroine, etc. Conversely, Balzac's lengthy definite descriptions may fail to refer, despite his and our intentions, if the reader's memory is defective, or he or she misses certain cues.

Although we should be aware of these two distinct uses of primary and secondary referent, they are not quite as different as they may appear. First, an anaphoric chain, and *a fortiori* its referent, relies on the perceived mental image which refers back to a given thing or event. Second, both anaphoric referents and perceptual or imagined referents, symbolic or otherwise, are at least similarly if not equally distorted by changing contexts and permeable memory images, which both lose and gain something each time. In a sense, symbolically invested referents display the same ambiguity as anaphoric ones, in that the concurrent referents of a given referring expression—be it a name, a pronoun, or, say, an indefinite noun—rely on readers' differing abilities to reconstruct and perceive changing reference. But here we anticipate reader-writer collaboration.

The distinction between referring in ordinary and in literary discourse, then, is rather one of degree; it presupposes greater elasticity in addressee (that is, reader) expectations and responses. It involves most of what is involved in ordinary dis-course reference; namely, pragmatic considerations including both addresser and addressee within and outside the text, types of speech-acts, multiple contexts, levels, and modes of reference, and ambiguous or changing perception of what constitutes the sign and thus its referent. But, here again, these concepts become considerably more elastic in literary discourse and the interplay between them more complex. So that the overall effect is what might be called the dynamics of "shifting" reference and referential identification (referents, like Mukarovsky's sign, being contingent on cultural—apperception—as Jean Alter and Thomas Lewis show).

In what follows I shall endeavor to present these interwoven aspects separately and then reassemble them in a two-tone semio-semantic view of the literary text.

I, 4: The Referent

Since referring inevitably presupposes discussion of what a referent is, let us consider, briefly, some of the ways in which this concept has been construed. (See fig. 1.) Although the conventional triangle is used throughout, this by no means implies that the different triads are synonymous—though in some cases it may enhance certain similarities.

The discrepancies among these triads require explanation. First the strictly linguistic points of view which separate sign and referent: Saussure divorces the sign (signifier and signified) from the extra-linguistic hypostatized referent (1916, p. 100). The second triad, Benveniste's correction or revised interpretation of Saussure (*Problèmes de linguistique générale*, II, p. 82), reinforces this split, as he remarks that it is not so much the relation between the signifier and the referent which is arbitrary, as that between the sign and the referent.[2]

Ogden and Richards's triad (in *The Meaning of Meaning*) contains the most concrete, behavioristic referent of all those formulated by the philosophers. For them it is an object or state of affairs in the external world, identified by means of a word or expression; reference is the mediating concept. This seems close to the way in which Umberto Eco interprets the referent within his "Theory of Codes" (in *A Theory of Semiotics*), where he appears to dismiss the referent as a "referential fallacy." "The referential fallacy," he says (p. 62), "consists in assuming that the meaning of a sign-vehicle has something to do with its corresponding object." He equates this referential fallacy with what he calls "the extensional fallacy" by relegating reference and extension to a theory of mentions and of sign production involving a truth-value which posits actual existence. Hence, when talking about *mentioning*, he says "The act of *referring* places a sentence (or corresponding proposition) in contact with an *actual circumstance* by means of an indexical device" (p. 163). Thus, in one fell swoop, his own, Ogden and Richards's, Saussure's, and Benveniste's referent, Carnap's extension, and Morris's denotatum appear to be relegated to the wastepaper basket as mere fallacy. But, in a sense, Eco is making much ado about ontological nothings, since here he is concerned with meaning and lies, or statements which do not refer to an actual thing or state of affairs. (Incidentally it should be noted that Morris's "denotatum," being the object which actually exists, corresponds to what is now usually called designatum; conversely his "designatum," evoking the "kind of thing or class of objects or the 'significatum' " [Morris, 1938], is now more commonly known as a denotatum.)

Although these positivist and rather narrow interpretations of the referent may at a first glance appear unsuitable for our purpose, they constitute the very spring-

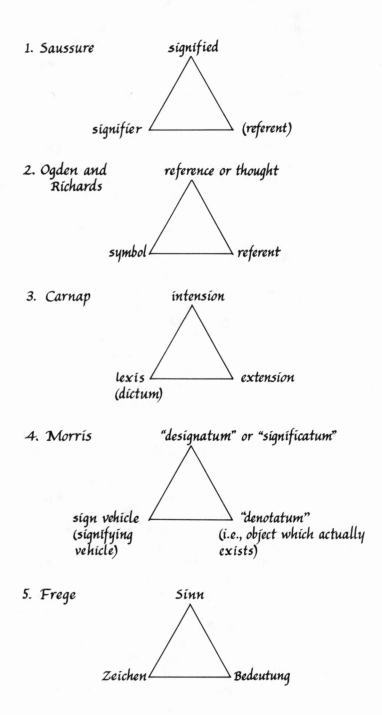

Figure 1

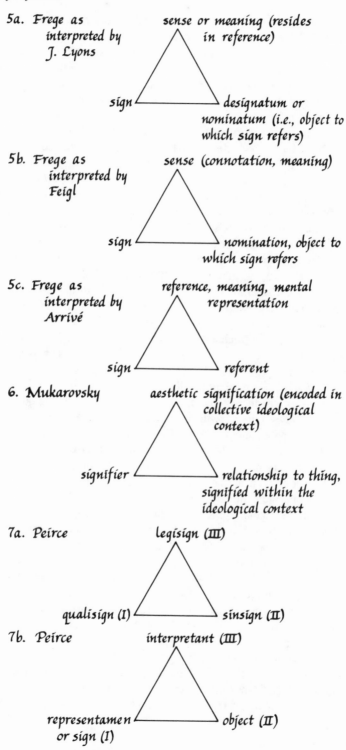

5a. Frege as
    interpreted by
    J. Lyons

sense or meaning (resides
in reference)

sign — designatum or
nominatum (i.e., object to
which sign refers)

5b. Frege as
    interpreted by
    Feigl

sense (connotation, meaning)

sign — nomination, object to
which sign refers

5c. Frege as
    interpreted by
    Arrivé

reference, meaning, mental
representation

sign — referent

6. Mukarovsky

aesthetic signification (encoded in
collective ideological
context)

signifier — relationship to thing,
signified within the
ideological context

7a. Peirce

legisign (III)

qualisign (I) — sinsign (II)

7b. Peirce

interpretant (III)

representamen — object (II)
or sign (I)

board for literature's less concrete referents, and are essential in that they express reference (relationship and act) in its simplest, most immediately recognizable form, which is reference to a thing. Incidentally, a materialist would claim that a mental image provoked by an expression, description, etc., is a thing, does exist as a particular brain activity, just as television images exist and are produced by an analogous electronic activity. This then makes the expression a referring expression and the image the referent.

But what of Frege, Mukařovský, and Peirce? Their views will take us up the primrose path to secondary reference—to the worlds within worlds, ideologies within ideologies, forms within forms, entities within entities, that are the stuff of referring in literature. Frege's theory has unfortunately fallen prey to misleading terminology—partly through translation into modern nomenclature, partly through translation from German into other languages. In his *Sinn und Bedeutung* (*Sense and Reference*, Geach and Black's 1960 translation) his use of *Bedeutung*, as Lyons points out in his discussion (in *Semantics*, Vol. I, p. 199), is in fact closer to *Beseichnung* (designation). So Lyons proposes translating Frege's *Zeichen-Sinn-Bedeutung* triad as sign, meaning, (that is, meaning which resides in reference), and designation. Feigl's earlier 1949 translation of Frege further clarifies the issue; here *Sinn* is "sense" (connotation, meaning) and *Bedeutung* is "nominatum" (the object to which the sign refers). This is roughly the same as the version used by such French transcribers as Michel Arrivé: sign, reference (that is, meaning, mental representation), and referent, as shown in Wladimir Krysinski's chapter. In a sense these cumulative interpretations of *Sinn* and *Bedeutung* help show, contrary to Saussure's claim and Eco's referential fallacy, that meaning and reference are indeed related. Frege raises a further problem, which takes us closer to the question of the literary referent, when dealing with the term "icons." As Françoise Meltzer's chapter points out, these are closer to the Greek meaning of "likeness," "image," "picture," than to their other object meaning. Thus we move from the referent as object to the referent as the literary image or imagined form of the object, so that the object referent is seen as the basis of the reader's individualized, imagined referent. So, in this more literary sense, the original "real" referent becomes a class or type, and the "iconic" referent, portrayed by description, narration, scenic representation, or shapes on a page (in concrete poetry) becomes a token. Frege puts it as follows: "It would be desirable to have an expression for signs which have *sense only*. If we call them 'icons,' then the words of an actor on the stage would be icons, even the actor himself would be an icon" ("On Sense and Nominatum," *Readings in Philosophical Analysis*). What is interesting in Frege's argument is that these icons, these mimetic images (to use Wladimir Krysinski's Aristotelian parallel) are directly concerned with the aesthetic, and, as Françoise Meltzer points out in her chapter, Frege opposes them to truth and existence. "In turning to the question of truth," says Frege, "we disregard the artistic appreciation and pursue scientific considerations." But even though Frege opts for the latter, his contribution is significant for a theory of the literary referent, since he reduces the gap between signified and referent and paves the way to their symbiotic relationship.

Mukařovský, dealing with the art object as a sign, further develops both the aesthetic dimension, briefly mentioned by Frege, and, in so doing, the signified-referent symbiosis. For him the signifier is the object to be perceived; the meaning or signified is the aesthetic signification (coded in collective consciousness), and the referent is interpreted as the relationship to a thing signified in the total cultural and historical (that is, ideological) context—an aspect which Patrice Pavis's, Jean Alter's, and Thomas Lewis's chapters elaborate.

Thus referring is shifting ever further from the concrete referent of the linguists and Ogden and Richards. Reference is now relative, encompassing both referent and signified, since it goes beyond specific meaning for a particular readership, to show that meaning is but one meaning in relation to many others.

I too have slipped from referent to reference, for at this level of symbiosis and ever-broadening horizons of context, it becomes increasingly difficult to limit discussion to the referent: the relationship between sign and referent becomes the dominating factor. Similarly, as we shall see in the next section, literary reference, viewed in its widening contexts, shifts from relatively concrete referents, having little obvious meaning or sense, to an increasingly Platonic ideal form, defined by relationships between forms which generate a dialectical synthesis of meaning and referent.

I have left Peirce's triads till last because his theory, integrated in his immense, all-encompassing semiotic scheme, is by far the most sophisticated—far more so than any diagram could ever suggest. Since, as David Savan's excellent monograph (1976) shows, Peirce's triad presupposes an understanding of his categories of Firstness, Secondness, and Thirdness, which govern his entire theory of semiotics, let us briefly consider these categories. Firstness is the possibility of some abstractable quality in what we perceive. Secondness is the state of what he calls "haecceity": being-there-ness, existence, or occurrence. Thirdness is the Hegelian or Kantian "synthesis"—a third entity connecting two others, a transforming or mediating law, a becoming, a process. The terms of the first and most familiar triad (qualisign, sinsign, and legisign) reflect these three categories. "A *Sinsign*," Peirce begins, "is an actual existent thing or event" (Buchler, p. 101). This then is our referent, and the legisign corresponds to reference. But the sinsign, as its name indicates, is also a sign, and the complete quotation runs as follows: "A *Sinsign* is an actual existent thing or event which is a sign." Thus we move beyond the signified-referent relationship, suggested by Mukařovský and Frege, to semiosis, the dynamics of the literary referent. For in literary discourse, as structuralists and semioticians have observed, literary elements (expressions, objects, roles, actions, units, structures) may themselves become signs, referring to and thus transforming other referents into more signs which in turn refer . . . and so on *ad infinitum*.

So this qualisign-legisign-sinsign triad is in turn contained in, and thus becomes, a single element of a more encompassing triad, made up of the sign (or Representamen, as Peirce often calls it), the Interpretant, and the Object. Peirce presents them according to his categories, so that once again, as its name indicates, the Interpretant (a Third; that is, in the category of thirdness) plays a mediating synthesising role, roughly the equivalent of reference, being between the Sign (a First) and the Object (a Second), comparable to the referent. Now what is interesting for us is that the Object, as Peirce sees it, is "much more than that to which a sign refers or purports to refer." Peirce is aiming at a conception of an object which will be adequate to the whole range of signs, from the "Jacquard loom . . . to the most advanced cosmological theories" (Savan, p. 18). Pursuing Peirce's thinking on the relation between object and context (for he did not resolve the problem), Savan has suggested that "the object might be defined as that part of the context which is common to the sign and all its interpretants" (p. 19). If this is the case, then the literary Object or Referent, as well as being *dynamic* in the way that Peirce's first triad suggests, also entails the possibility of *unlimited semiosis*: hyphenated sign-referents which refer to an ever-widening multitude of contexts. If this is so in the world of literature, and we hope to show that it is, then referring in literature is indeed a cumulatively semio-semantic process: a dynamic transcontextual linking of referents, as they evolve from referent to referent, from context to context. The logical extension of this, shown by Michael Riffaterre's work, is intertextuality, as Genette's *Palimpsestes* would seem to corroborate.

But here we are anticipating our conclusion. So let us first turn to more specifically literary considerations, to literary referents in particular, or rather the merging of these referents into reference and, ultimately, into the contexts that both identify and endow them with meaning.

II. LITERARY REFERENCE

II, 1: Construing the Literary Referent

The foregoing tentative conclusion that referring in literature is a dynamic, transcontextual, and ultimately semio-semantic process, leads me back to Lyons's definition of reference as a relationship. Indeed, this relationship between sign, referent, and context is so close-knit that it is hard to consider any single element separately. Thus, although this section will be dealing mainly with various *forms* of the literary referent (ranging from the most concrete to the most abstract), it will necessarily be considered in terms of a) the signs it evolves both from and into, and b) its defining context.

At the concrete end of the scale, what could seem more obvious than concrete poetry or futurist texts? The very tools of writing—letters, words, and sounds— are arranged in such a way that they draw attention to themselves. But, readers being what they are, even such apparently concrete self-referential referents tend to a double role and act as signifiers too. Thus, relatively concrete referents also refer to an identified form, sound, or process of signification—despite the manifestoes decrying this activity. Ideograms in fact use shape(s) to refer to the elements that create them and *vice versa* (Anna Whiteside's chapter develops this). Even pure sounds are strung together in an order, or orders, by the writer (however unconsciously) and the reader (however stochastic the composition), and so compose a form, forms, or possible sets. In all cases, form still leads beyond itself and, as in music, refers the interpreter to a structuring process which will enable him, ultimately, to make sense of the perceived form(s). (So, too, even nonsense rhymes refer—not to nothing, not to sense either, or at least not directly; but to nonsense as the denial of sense and to our need, albeit frustrated, as readers reading a text, to make sense. They refer, then, to themselves as contradiction and, indirectly, to reading as a structuring activity.)

Other putative tangible referents that come to mind include do-it-yourself poem or novel kits such as Queneau's *Mille et Un Poèmes* or Marc Saporta's *Composition No. 1*, each comprising a collection of discrete units (pages of individually cut lines in the first case, loose pages in the second) to be combined by the reader in any order or orders, and thus pointing, yet again, to compositional and reading processes.

The dramatic text can also be considered from this point of view. It "exists" both in its dramatized form and as a printed text whose typographical arrangement refers to the dramatic genre. Similarly, typographical page arrangements usually afford immediate recognition of verse or prose; and subsequently determine, or at least help determine, the reader's generic expectations by providing instant cues to a frame of reference. Genre, though, is not a particularly concrete referent (despite typography, which *is*), so let us return to literature's relatively concrete ones.

When a writer says to his Dear Reader (and he too can exist as a token, rather than always being the virtual reader, the represented type) that "this book" recounts the events which befell, let's say, Tristram Shandy, what book is it? the one the writer is writing or the one you, dear reader, hold in your hand as you read? Already contexts of reference lead us not just to other referents, but to different worlds: the writer's world, the reader's world, and the fictional worlds each and both create. (Of possible worlds, more later, since here we are already anticipating the question of modes to be dealt with in section II, 3.)

Obviously, stage objects and characters are also relatively concrete referents, though they have a double status. As Keir Elam (1980, p. 8) notes, they are referents *and* signs representing a thing. One might call them iconic or mimetic referents; they comprise props, scenery, costumes, and make-up, as perceived through various lighting effects; though, clearly, all do not have the same status. Some may be referred to in the dialogue, some by gestures, some only by the didascalia (Michael Issacharoff examines these different ways of referring in detail). Others may be perceived, but not mentioned in the text: costumes, lighting, make-up, accents, and prosody may be ancillary and used to direct attention to a particular referent at a given moment, enhancing a quality or qualities which help define it. Finery or rags refer to a character's assumed role or status within a given society—a dramatic cliché which has led to many a double dramatic referent (*dramatic* in the sense that it relies on audience participation and awareness, as opposed to *theatrical*—that which happens on stage, to use Keir Elam's nice distinction; *Semiotics of Theatre*, p. 2). A kilt, a period costume, or even an accent may do more for spatio-temporal reference than any decor—however elaborate. Malvolio's yellow stockings, though the rest of his body be hidden, refer to him and also to a particular culture's chromatic code, and so, metonymically, to his personality, with mirth and mockery. Moon-beams may help define the love-lorn hero or romantic heroine, just as garish make-up or talcum powder differentiate between the vamp and, say, the tuberculosis victim's impending exit.

Then there is the implied referent (discussed by Michael Issacharoff). A strange paradox, but nevertheless referred to (diegetically if not mimetically) in the dialogue or in the didascalia: Macbeth's dagger, which he sees and tries to clutch; Caliban's music so eloquently described, Ionesco's unseen Primadonna, or Beckett's Godot.

Nor should we forget the actors themselves who, however strong our powers of suspension of disbelief, are, nevertheless, there on stage in a very real way. For although mimesis refers back to what it imitates, it is simultaneously an event, as exemplified by Pirandello's *Sei personaggi in cerca d'autore* (*Six Characters in Search of an Author*; see Wladimir Krysinski's chapter). In our search for meaning, we see that these actors and their producer refer to the problems of dramatic creation. Of course, for the naïve spectator or reader (mentioned in Patrice Pavis's and Linda Hutcheon's chapters) there is no double or ambiguous referent, no referential chain, no dynamic reference. Jill playing Hedda Gabler is always Jill for Jack—so much so that reference is forever blocked within the immediate frame of reference.

Paradoxically the text an actor quotes is also a referent—a verbal referent (see Jean Alter's chapter). Indeed, a logical extension of this would be to say that any *actualized* text, be it a stage-production or individual reading of any type of text, both is referent and refers back to the written text. Thus the written text is both referent and referring expression (or sign) in that it is the virtual text lending itself to different "concretizations," to use Ingarden's term, and interpretations.

If each production is an actual event in its own right, coincidentally it is an ideological statement (see the chapters by Jean Alter, Patrice Pavis, and Michael Issacharoff) referring, mimetically, to dramatically appropriate socio-cultural phenomena in order to enhance meaning. The Vitez production of *Britannicus* in punk make-up and hair dyes, and Ariane Mnouchkine's *Richard II* in Japanese Kabuki style, are just two such ideological statements, suggesting that *Richard II* can be meaningful in the context of Japanese feudal power struggles and that *Britannicus* can be perceived as a play of our times. Incidentally, this flexible ideological referent revives an old controversy often linked to the use of proper names in literature (Thomas, Meltzer, Issacharoff, Alter, Krysinski, and Chambers all deal with this problem in their chapters). Which *Britannicus* or "*Britannicus*" are we referring to? Racine's seventeenth-century creation, depicting seventeenth-century ideals? Racine's hybrid classical ideology as seen through neo-classical eyes? A neo-classical interpretation of a decadent interpretation of a classic of Roman history or fable? Or a twentieth-century interpretation of one or all of these? Mukarovsky evokes "the total context of social phenomena" (science, philosophy, religion, politics, economics, etc.) "of a given milieu," as chapters by Lewis, Pavis, and Alter point out. So the dramatic referent becomes ever more elusive, ever less fixed.

But what of poetry and fiction? As well as obvious textual referents (characters, things, events, places, and so on) referred to in the text, many others are similar to those of plays. Visible signs, such as *Tristram Shandy's* marbled page and two blanks, are mimetic referents. In their diegetic context they also refer, rather like

Macbeth's unclutched dagger, to three implied abstract referents: the author's work (of which the marbled page is a "motley emblem"), a missing chapter, and paper for the reader to paint, in his own mind, Toby's lady love. Subsequently these same referents become the reader's concretizations, as is corroborated by the author's comment immediately after the second blank: "—Was ever anything in nature so sweet!—so exquisite!" Because these iconic signs are also self-referring, they are analogous to drama's sign-referents. Other visual signs (formal symmetry or anomalies) and phonetic ones (assonance, onomatopoeia, rhyme, rhythm) may also be discrete and, to some extent, self-referring, whilst also contributing to the text as a global concretized referent.

Form constitutes a more abstract referent. Baudelaire's *Tableaux parisiens* (see the chapter by Ross Chambers) refer beyond topology to the conventional form of the *tableau*, and so back to his particular use of it. Eluard's "La Victoire de Guernica" (Jean-Jacques Thomas's chapter) also reaches beyond topological reference by referring to implied opposition between the extratextual Guernica and this textual recreation, to the conflict between horror and callous acceptance, *and* to the very form chosen to describe it—one which plays on a system of internal opposition. So the poetic function refers to ideology as form, and the referent, whether fictional, poetic, or dramatic, becomes ever more elusive. As Barthes said, "The work of art is a form which history spends its time filling in."

We can perhaps go one stage further before toppling into nothingness and say with Foucault (discussing Barthes in *Pour une archéologie du savoir*, 1978) that this very form is the only reality, the only sure referent. Althusser's refinement of Marxist ideology corroborates this. He advocates stepping outside history to show that Marxist interpretation of realism was, in its own different way, as biased as the bias it was busy demonstrating. Even if a text is construed as an ideological Product, this product remains "symptomatically deformative of its historical reality" (Lewis, 1979, p. 459). It refers in the last instance to an ideological space, its own blind spot, defined as a dialectical absence deriving from an unrepresented relation to other non-identical cultural referents.

II, 2: Contexts

a) Intersecting Contexts

The referent is determined by contexts of production and reception. But literary context, like the referent it defines, is complex, protean, and elusive, given its several and often coexistent levels, which we will now examine. Before even discussing meaning, and *a fortiori* socially symbolic meaning, we need to show how reference is contingent on context. Jakobson's theory of communication raises this issue. It needs some expansion for our present purpose.

The three fundamental contexts which underlie all reference, both in the sense of reference as an act (see Thomas Lewis's chapter for a full development of this aspect), and as a relationship which establishes meaning are: the utterer's, the receiver's, and the so-called encyclopaedic context (see fig. 2).

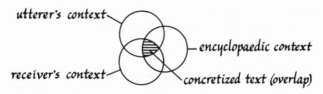

Figure 2

That these three overlapping contexts and their interaction are fundamental to reference is inevitable for, as Benveniste remarks, reference is an integral part of the speech-act and, thus, of the speaker's and receiver's literal, cultural, and ideological situation. This in turn implies the encyclopaedic context of available knowledge constituting their known world. Otherwise, how do we know what "I" or "you" or "his words" refer to, let alone "He" or "God" or "Rome" (to use a more obviously encyclopaedic-oriented context)? So this triad of contexts stands as the foundation for the second set of contexts—however wide or narrow these may be and regardless of their degree of coexistence.

This second set's three main contexts are 1) intratextual, 2) intertextual, and 3) extratextual, with metatextuality sitting on the fence between intra- and intertextuality. They lead to the interpretation of referents within 1) the "work-as-a-symbolic-act," 2) the work as *parole* or "*ideologeme*," 3) perceived "reality" as ideology of form (see Fredric Jameson, 1981). The boundaries between these three contexts are not fast, nor does one context preclude another. It is rather a question of interpretation and degree.

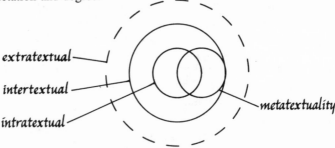

Figure 3: Expanding concentric circles of reference of a concretized text: i.e., secondary set of contexts. This figure represents in detail the shaded area of the fundamental contexts shown in fig. 2.

Since Althusser carries literary reference to its ultimate form by setting it in the widest context imaginable, I shall start from this Ultima Thule and work inwards, proceeding from extratextual to intertextual and, via metatextuality, to intratextual contexts (or "levels" of reference, as Linda Hutcheon calls them). All such contexts involve the interaction of utterer and receiver/reader contexts as well as a common encyclopaedic one. The reader has an image of the text as a "cracking tower of ideologies" (Holquist and Reed). According to these authors, texts provide, not photographs of societies, but "X-rays of the systems out of which they are constituted." Patrice Pavis likens the phenomenon to an iceberg whose vast and invisible base sustains the recent visible layers that rise above the water level. All three metaphors point to the coexistence of multiple layers and to the fact that they are, for the most part, hidden. The cracking tower affords a glimpse, the iceberg shows here and there a few of its numerous layers, the rest changes colour as seen dimly through the water. So too, X-rays are selective, making certain aspects visible, but obscuring or distorting others.

The reader's context, likewise, tends to obscure the writer's, even though it is the latter which originally created reference. When Verlaine says "Dans le vieux parc," whose "old park" is it? his, or one that we remember? Even if our park were the same as his, our impression of it would be different. Yet again, we stumble on another problem which has occupied philosophers and linguists: who or what is doing the referring? The answer, after much debate, is that though words alone may denote (in the linguistic sense), they do not refer. It follows that texts alone do not refer, although this seems nonsensical—and is . . . in a sense. Even an anonymous text is obviously *by* someone, so that directly or indirectly it refers to its context of creation (the literary equivalent of a context of utterance). If we did not know who wrote *La Jalousie* or when it was written, the text's very form would refer us indirectly to a particular extratextual context of creation—that of the *nouveau roman*, and thereby (intertextually speaking), to a literary reaction against so-called realist novels. At all levels reference is an integral part of the speech-act, so that what an author or character says refers directly or indirectly to the author's context of utterance. Dickens's writings refer explicitly to English nineteenth-century society, and so do his characters, their language, and their behaviour. Nabokov's *Lolita* and the lollipop heroine it depicts refer to his un-American view of an aspect of a particular American society; Dante's *Divine Comedy* to fourteenth-century Florentine socio-political conditions, beliefs, and prevailing ideology, and thus to himself as a writer defined by and against his times. John Barth's *The Sot-Weed Factor* refers anachronistically to eighteenth-century mores and literary conventions whose parodic effect relies on a twentieth-century perspective.

Barthes's autobiography, *Roland Barthes par Roland Barthes*, exemplifies a speech-act which fuses and confuses extratextual and intratextual speaker reference. By the title he chooses, Barthes admits extratextual reference; yet he tells his reader that the text "should be read as though it were a novel." He is "I" and "he," subject and object of his speech-act, "I" and "you," speaker and addressee, dialoguing intertextually with himself as author of previous texts of which this autobiography is but a rewriting, a metatext. Thus Barthes exploits reference among all contextual levels whilst enshrining the (polyvalent) speech-act as the necessary means to his referential end: self depicted as a kaleidoscope of *personae*.

Intratextual and extratextual contexts are, in fact, related in all texts, since a literary *microcosm*, or *heterocosm*, is defined as just that: a partial reflexion (and ideological deflexion) of the extratextual *macrocosm*. So, for the reader, the intratextual context is contained in the outer extratextual one, as indeed are metatextuality and intertextuality. The dotted line of the extratextual context represents the expanding and contracting horizons of the latter in the reader's ideological eye. From Althusser and Barthes's standpoint, all the second set's contexts (extra-, inter-, meta-, and intratextual) share this centrifugally biased protean quality (as chapters by Alter and Lewis show). Conversely, chapters by Prince, Thomas, Chambers, Krysinski, Hutcheon and Whiteside all emphasize a centripetal focus, thereby implying a heightened metatextual awareness of text *qua* text in current writing and reader reception.

b) Shifting Contexts

Thus, neither fundamental nor secondary sets of contexts are fixed in a rigid pattern. Just as the secondary set of reader-construed reference moves outwards *and* inwards between contexts, so the focussing of the fundamental overlapping reader, writer, and encyclopaedic contextual lenses enhances first one, then another aspect. Like the lenses of a telescope (or microscope) they focus differentially, enhancing any one of the three ways of seeing, in any combination. For example, when reading a historical play, we can privilege the encyclopaedic contextual lens so as to emphasize historical "facts." Alternatively, we may prefer to construe it as a writer's or society's biased version, and so bring to the fore the utterer's context. By identifying with this utterer's context or dissociating himself from it, a reader may also focus on his own context. A stage-production can emphasize a particular receiver's (reader's, producer's, or culture's) context, in which case, the interaction between utterer, receiver, and encyclopaedic contexts again shifts. In fact, as we shall see later, the relationship between this fundamental contextual triad and the superimposed frames of intra-, inter-, and extratextual reference is one of inevitable interdependence, since, in any text, both sets are automatically implied in their different permutations.

For example, the Babiyar massacre in D. M. White's *The White Hotel* refers, at the level of fundamental contexts, to a particular utterer's transposition of encyclopaedic reality. The problem is to define the utterer. Do we mean the author, the psychoanalytic narrator, his tortured and hysterical female protagonist, or some other narrator? The answer is probably the whole gamut, its shifting hierarchy depending on their roles, and on the receiver's (that is, character's and reader's) conscious or unconscious perspective—and this too is protean and complex. Moving into the second set of contexts, we construe this episode extratextually by relating it to the documented 1941 massacre outside Kiev, and intratextually by linking it to other events and elements in the novel. The hotel fire could thus be construed as a premonition of the holocaust, or as a re-enacting of the original or derived meanings of "holocaust" (whose etymology goes back to the Hebraic sacrificial burning and thence to the Greek *holos kaustos*,"burnt whole"), or perhaps all of these. Thus the episode may also be seen as referring to the text's attempt at Freudian analysis and portrayal of a particular (Jewish) collective unconscious. This same death camp episode also provides a text (and context) for the other chapters by metatextually relating their versions of the protagonist's hysteria to her experience of this catastrophe. Indeed metatextual commentary seems to condition interpretation from the outset of *The White Hotel*: the opening letters' comment on the poem in chapter 1, chapter 2 is a parallel prose version of the poem, then poem and journal form the basis of the Freudian analysis "Frau Anna G." in chapter 3.

This Freudian account also refers intertextually to Freud's famous case history of Anna O., and the chapter on Babiyar to Yevtushenko's *Babi-Yar*. The maze of interwoven contexts compound the *illusion* of confusion between extratextual and all other reference, for ultimately intratextuality subsumes all other contexts.

For the literary reader then, as chapters by Hutcheon, Prince, and Chambers show, there is no "real" referent—since the referent is first and foremost a textually created, that is, an imagined construct. Thus all levels of this secondary set's contexts imply the interaction of various contrasting ideologies, making the reader a reader of ideologies *qua* ideologies.

One of the distinctive features of the literary text is the play on multiple and equivocal contexts, leading inevitably to simultaneous levels of reference and to what is in fact a *polyreferent*. As we have seen, Barthes's autobiography, like other examples cited, exploits polyreference by presenting the subject's different facets and *personae*. In poetry, the tradition of multiple contexts is so taken for granted that it defines the very way the genre is read. Thus the coexistence of literal (extratextual) and symbolic (that is, intratextual, and sometimes intertextual) levels, in a text other than poetry, is often deemed to lend it a "poetic" quality. In theatre, as Wladimir Krysinski shows, reference shifts from "historical" or "real" extratextuality to intratextuality. Apollinaire's *Les Mamelles de Tirésias* (*The Breasts of Tiresias*) is meant to refer, as the author's prologue tells us, to France's need for repopulation. The play also refers to the scriptural and theatrical creation of a dramatic text whilst being played. Even the floating balloons, once theatrical breasts, ultimately corroborate the predominance of intratextuality by referring to dramatic creation *within* the play.

Modern literature, particularly, plays on plurality and equivocation of contexts (termed "opacity" by Quine, 1976; "obliqueness" by Frege) because of an apparent perfusion and concerted confusion or lack of context. As Gerald Prince points out (see chapter 3), bad (confused or contradictory) references make it impossible for the reader to interpret the numerous examples of intratextual spatio-temporal deixis. However seemingly precise, "now," "next," "here," etc. do not refer, or rather they refer to themselves: "here" is here in the novel; "now," at this moment in the novel. In other words, they refer to fiction, namely the reading and writing processes. So context is deferred until finally it is seen to surround the invisible central speaker. This referential hide-and-seek in turn refers intertextually to the *nouveau roman's* refusal of the realist novel's referential practice, and, hence, to reader expectations relating to ideology, period, school, genre, form, and conventions.

Thus, when Robbe-Grillet, in *Glissements progressifs du plaisir*, refers intertextually to the thematic and structural materials of pop culture (folklore, detective stories, pornography, horror films and stories), he intentionally misleads the reader. For having established this context of codes, he destroys them by slipping into another set of codes. These eventually refer, metatextually, to the process of the creation (and destruction) of reference *and* meaning in terms of reference to particular contexts (see Bruce Morrissette's chapter). This self-referential device again signals the official bankruptcy and illusion of absolute or "real" extratextual fictional reference. In so doing it stresses the integral role of the reader in the creative and recreative process of imagined, or rather reconstructed, reference.

So, whether texts, and thus writers and readers, in fact refer (or should one say writers and thus texts and readers?) extratextually, intertextually, intratextually, or metatextually ultimately depends on the reader's recognition of reference. Now the potential variety of contexts and ensuing divergent referents are considerable. My mental images of Emma Bovary, of Henry James's Paris, or the events in *War and Peace* will not necessarily match someone else's, because, in spite of the same descriptions, we bring different contexts to our construction of them. Furthermore, the way we construe and construct the text's created context is a dynamic semiotic process. Referents become hyphenated referent-signifiers as contexts shift and meaning blurs. If signs fail to refer in one context, they are reinterpreted in another. In fact, one of the pleasures of reading (and rereading) is that reference, and thus meaning, is never complete. The referent can always be reoriented, refocussed, and redefined, as Robbe-Grillet's *Glissements* illustrate, and Krysinski's and Pavis's chapters explain: the former tracing the metamorphosis of the historical referent into the autotelic one, the latter its ideological translations.

The reader constructs a mutually defining referent-signified dipole within a given context (his own, alias the text's) and so arrives at a tentative meaning. This meaning then modifies, enhances, or deflects some other aspect (or aspects) of the referent, and so on in a never-ceasing hermeneutic spiral, similar to those postulated by Iser and Ingarden.

So too, intratextually, a text's characters, places, events, conversations, descriptions, narrators, narratees, speakers, pronouns, symbols, significant narrative and structural entities, are all defined in terms of their reference to one another. The links between them constitute units which in turn refer to and fit into larger and larger units. And so the intratextual, multilayered construct is, rather like the extratextual context, constantly referring to ever-widening contextual spheres.

Thus we have gone full circle, and the ideology or ideological space which was the text's ultimate referent for Althusser has become the context which defines reference. This is hardly surprising—after all, ordinary discourse too, though to a lesser degree, links the sign, not directly with real things, but with a world perceived within the ideological framework of a given culture. Biographers and autobiographers, chroniclers, realists, and naturalists, however scrupulously honest their intentions, are, and ever shall be, interpreters. Inevitably the line separating referent and context appears increasingly fuzzy, and the distinction becomes one of degree rather than of absolutes.

In fact one can say, without being unduly Platonic, that even the most apparently absolute (that is, "primary") referents are only relatively so. "The page" may well be the page a writer writes, or writes upon, in his authorial context; but it cannot be unequivocally so, as it is also your page as you read in your context and, in a secondary way, your image of the writer's page as he wrote those words at his writing desk. The question of which is real is superfluous; all are, in a sense, and we accept the convention of this referential multiplicity, knowing that literary reference obtains by virtue of the contexts we, the readers, bring to it (an aspect dealt with in Bruce Morrissette's chapter). Inevitably, then, literary reference assumes its own phenomenological implications, and increasingly "reality" or extratextual reference is replaced by the concept of validity. Nevertheless, because the notion of the referent as extratextual reality has enjoyed wide credence (despite Althusser's, Foucault's, and Barthes's insistence that it too is relatively artificial, being an ideological construct), and because this notion has somehow infiltrated literary exegesis, it is worth considering the implications of the two modes which the notion of contexts of reference apparently suggests, namely: the *"real" mode* (derived from the extratextual context) and the *fictitious* or *imaginary mode* (derived primarily from the intratextual context).

II, 3: Modes of Reference

How do we reconcile a statement such as Michel Arrivé's that "there is no literary referent," with the assumption which underwrites literary creation (and, *a fortiori*, the reader's recreation): namely, that we can indeed refer—as can literary characters (Heintz, 1979)—to Mr. Pickwick, Anna Karenina, Pegasus, Banquo's ghost, Macbeth's perturbed state of mind, Lilliput, Picrochole's war, Achilles' shield, Ulysses, and so on? Clearly, Arrivé would side with Russell (1905) and Strawson (1950), in claiming that because literature does not deal with "real" entities, it fails to refer. And yet, as Linsky points out in *Referring* ("Reference and Referents"), fiction has a reality of its own. It exists, after all! It constitutes an important part of our extratextual context.

All agree with Searle who says, in "The Logical Status of Fictional Discourse," that in fiction words have their normal meanings (p. 319), since there are no special dictionaries for fictional discourse (Gale, 1971). The difference between ordinary and fictional discourse (and I extend Searle's "fictional" to include all literary discourse) lies rather in the way readers interpret and writers perform (or have fictional characters perform) their fictional speech-acts. This is a difference not of meaning but of discursive mode. In normal discourse it is assumed that we mean, more or less, what we say—any deviation from this norm is marked by prefatory or postfatory riders such as "let's imagine that . . . ," hypothetical riders such as "perhaps . . . ," and disclaimers, "she says that . . . ," "that's his version," "but that's not what really happened," "but no one believes it," "Have you heard the joke, story, etc. about . . . ," "I was inventing," "I didn't really mean that," and so on. Deviations not marked by a spoken or situational disclaimer (story-telling, acting, postulating, etc.) are considered violations of the assumption that we mean what we say (Grice, 1957), and are interpreted as lies (Grice, 1968), that is, intentionally deceptive discourse.

In fictional discourse, writers indulge in "nondeceptive pseudo-performance," to use Searle's expression. In other words, there exists between writer and reader an unwritten pact that the writer is referring, not to the real world, but to his own interpretation of the real world, or to his own created world, or both. This does not mean that the reader will not recognize many aspects of it—character types, objects, general truths, place descriptions and events or proper names, etc. He certainly will, and this recognition, or as Patrice Pavis calls it, this "referential illusion," is one of the sources of the reader's pleasure. Carried further, this referential illusion may cause referential confusion. Such an extreme case would be Ricardou's naïve reader, mentioned by Linda Hutcheon, who talks of a fictitious character as though he were real, saying "If I were so-and-so I would have done such-and-such"—or better still, "X should have done this, not that."

So, although we can say that literature refers, we should be careful to distinguish the two modes of reference. On the one hand the "real" or indicative ordinary discourse mode (that is, meaning what we say or meaning to deceive) ranges from concrete to ideological to abstract referents in a world that exists, or is assumed to have existed; on the other, a fictional or subjunctive mode posits possible worlds and their story-related referents (see Thomas Pavel, 1975, and Kripke, Quine, and Linsky in Linsky, 1971). Since the second mode presupposes the first, it is hard to know where to draw the line. Yet there is a difference, and it constitutes one of the important idiosyncracies of literary reference. The literary referent is a construct which both relies on an affirmative, recognizably plausible or "real" entity (or a negative one as in science fiction, fantasy, utopic, or dystopic writings), and modifies our awareness of it, making it "more real" by removing the patina of use and habit (Schklovskii, 1965; Barthes, 1968) and by iconic augmentation (Ricoeur, 1976). As such, it reinvests the text with its particular enhanced meaning, so that, in fact, the relationship between "real" and "make-believe" is symbiotic, each lending meaning and referential potential to the other.

A brief comparison of "real" and literary referents will show this, as well as help define the literary referent's role and the way it functions within the text. A chair in a play such as Ionesco's *Les Chaises* (*The Chairs*) is, as Anne Ubersfeld remarks when discussing stage props, both a real and a make-believe chair: a referent, in the most concrete sense, and a representation of a chair, that is, a sign (1977, p. 37). Eco, for whom performance is a sophisticated form of ostension (1977, p. 110), corroborates this by remarking that one uses the concrete object as "the expression of the class of which it is a member" (1976, p. 225), while Keir Elam (p. 21–27) stresses the iconic quality of a dramatic referent of this sort, thereby treating it as a sign too (p. 21–27). Ionesco's chair is also a literary symbol, evoking the absence of people, of God, and of material presence (Ionesco, 1962), and, as such, far exceeds its initial reference. In so doing, it underlines the use of words, naming, and the relationship of a referring expression to its referent, or indeed of a sign to what it represents—to its denotata, and to its contextually determined designatum.

Instead of comparing a real chair and a fictional one, let us compare Ionesco's ,double signifier-referent chairs with, say, a unicorn, (Snark, or other fantastic creation).[3] The fact that unicorns have only secondary denotation (Goodman, 1952) is irrelevant to considering them as literary referents. It is not so much a question of what their existential status is as of how they are used and how this use is effective in endowing them with referential status, that is, by providing solid contextual backing and an identifying definite description. Indeed the more "memorable" the entity, the more readily subsequent reference may be established; and memorability is usually determined by events or context-related factors. Curiously enough, and precisely because unicorns are odd, our mental image of a unicorn is probably more memorable than that evoked by the word "chair."

For those concerned with referring in literature, all this talk of unicorns, states of disembodiment, Utopias, and other fictional entities is a referential red herring started by Russell and continued by Lavis (in "Le Texte littéraire, le référent, le réel, le vrai," 1971). It is now deemed to have little to do with referring, in the sense that once a definite description has been provided, once the mental image exists, then, even if none of us has actually seen or experienced the real thing, we can refer to it. For referring, as Thomas Lewis's chapter insists, is something we do, an act, and a link we establish between an expression (verbal or gestural) and what we thereby refer to, whatever its ontological status. After all, a writer or character (and thus a reader) may refer to Cleopatra, as did Shaw and Shakespeare, without having seen her. This does not mean that they have not really referred to her, or to someone's description of her. It merely means that, as in most literature, they refer to their interpretation, and ensuing mental representation, of someone else's description. Now this version may also be second- or third-hand—as in Shakespeare's use of North's second-hand translation (from Amyot's French version) of Plutarch's *Bioi paralleloi* (*Parallel Lives*). It is a question of degree, but not, and especially not in literature, one of existence or reality.[4]

In fictional discourse, a writer or heterodiegetic story-teller can also set the action in a period or place that he has never known, in the same way that you or I can refer to a time or place that neither we (nor, perhaps, the reader) have ever actually experienced. In fact, sometimes we simply do not know what is meant to be real or imagined. But again, the question of reality is irrelevant, for reference is nevertheless established, first and foremost, within the literary construct and fictional mode. Victor Hugo, when writing about Villequier in "A Villequier," deals with this problem. He juxtaposes his mental image of a bygone Villequier and a more recent one which, for him, in no way resembles the first, completely shattering not only many of its remembered denotations, but also its concomitant connotations. So which Villequier is Hugo's referent? Is it one of these, or both, or the geographical entity of that village in Seine-Maritime? (Ross Chambers's chapter on Baudelaire's *Tableaux Parisiens* and Jean-Jacques Thomas's chapter raise similar questions about Paris and Guernica respectively, as do the chapters by Krysinski, Meltzer, and Issacharoff about Poland and historical figures used and quoted in fiction.) One might also ask which Hugo do we mean? The father whose daughter was drowned near Villequier, or the older Hugo returning there years later to visit his daughter's tomb? If we were interested in the ontological status of either Villequier or Hugo in this poem, we might say, contrary to Frege, that though the referent (and the name) Villequier is the same, the sense of Villequier past and Villequier present is different (even if this sameness is perhaps more disputable than the sameness of Venus alias The Morning Star and The Evening Star, to Frege's stargazers). But this sameness is of little use in a literary discussion. Rather, we would draw the conclusion that reference in the two cases is different, since the context of reception (taking Hugo to be the observer, the person who experienced the situation) is different. Both mental images—even if the denotata had been identical—are surprisingly different because of the vital role connotation plays in literary reference.

In other words, mere designatum is not enough here; for literary reference relies on and is created, primarily, by intratextual linkings and connotation, so that the similarity between a literary referent such as Robbe-Grillet's New York in *Projet pour une révolution à New York* and our New York is merely a realistic illusion. In fact he has tricked us into interpreting a proper name in the real mode and trying to construe fiction as reality. This trick merely serves to remind us that, in fiction, all constructs are fictional within the fictional mode (however "real" or fantastic they may seem), and that the reader's readiness to draw parallels with his known world, to "identify" or to "recognize" fictional elements, by situating them in his own mental context, is unremitting.

Jarry, as Wladimir Krysinski's chapter shows, goes one stage further than Hugo, Baudelaire, or Robbe-Grillet, in that, having established a pseudo-"real" mode (Poland), he makes it entirely fictional. He then proceeds to transform this nowhere into a somewhere—the somewhere of his literary creation. But by calling it Poland when it is not Poland, he insists on the illusion of literary "real" reference and on the autonomy of the literary sign which can, in fact, refer to whatever the writer will, be it a substitute referent or the very process of creating reference.

If we move on from things, periods, and places to a comparison between "real" and make-believe *qualities*—avarice and ubiquity (to use Lavis's example) or disembodiment, the difference between the modes of ordinary and literary discourse becomes more apparent. Avarice, taken out of context, is something we can experience; ubiquity or disembodiment is not (not in our normal state anyway). Yet Scrooge's or Harpagon's avarice is no easier to refer to than Ariel's or Satan's ubiquity, or Banquo's ghost: the question is irrelevant. All can be referred to, providing we have the necessary context, in the make-believe mode (just as all qualities can be referred to in a non-fictional mode by our speaking about them). In fact it would seem, yet again, that the fictional referent, because so tightly bound to its context, is more memorable than the non-fictional one, for Scrooge has passed into "real" mode discourse as a metonymical expression of extreme avarice. So rather than saying that there are two types of referents, it is generally more useful to say that there are two modes of discourse: the serious and the make-believe.

Obviously this pretence of mode-mixing is a common literary device and relies on the assumption that proper names are the purest and most readily recognized referring expressions.[5] This mixing of modes not only enhances fiction's putative realism, it also works the other way around and imbues transposed home truths of real events with a fictional aura. Satire relies on it, and so too do moralistic or socially relevant *tranche de vie* writings such as those Diderot advocated for the theatre.

Michael Issacharoff and Françoise Meltzer deal at length with mode mixing in playscripts and novels, as does Wladimir Krysinski, using (amongst others) what is probably one of literature's most sophisticated crossing of modes: Pirandello's *Six Characters in Search of an Author*. Within the fictional mode, it shows the play as a *single* text created by author, characters, producer, and spectators, and also as *several* simultaneous interpretations. Thus combined, they debunk any claims that in theatre (or other literary forms), real and fictional modes are separable, by fusing the two into a single fictional entity. Probably the only case in which modes are consistently distinct is the playscript: here the traditional type of didascalia is in the serious mode and the dialogue in the non-serious mode (see Michael Issa-charoff's chapter).

Fiction thus points ultimately beyond modes to the processes of literary creation and interpretation—that is, interpretation as recreation. Distinguishing between the different contextual horizons of the secondary set (fig. 3) depends on interpretation in the fictional mode, which may pretend to mix serious and non-serious modes. The "reality" of fiction's extratextual referents is a question of *degree of illusion*, of this or that literary referent *seeming* more real than another. In other words, it seems real because we are the better able to fill in the skeleton the text's construct provides—the form which is literature's only constant. So, we have come full circle back to Plato, Foucault, and Barthes, for whom form is the only literary reality. Perhaps, then, metatextuality (see Linda Hutcheon's chapter) is the closest thing to a real mode in literature, since its object, being a text, must, like some overt poetic function, inevitably refer to the text's form.

II, 4: Dynamics of Referring in Literature

If form is the ultimate referent, our apperception of it necessarily depends on the process of filling and emptying it. For it is this very process which delineates form. Reference as a deictic process is thus essential to our recognition of form, so that the linguist's focus (reference as process) and the philosopher's (reference as a relationship) are contingent on each other and mutually defining. It would seem that one of the differences between ordinary discourse and literary discourse is precisely the latter's propensity to sustain the dynamics of this process. By way of conclusion, we will briefly summarize these dynamics.

Literary reference is forever protean. It evolves with the reader's (and, to some extent, the writer's) constantly changing perception, whilst developing within a given textual context, itself being shaped by the symbiosis of all contextual spheres. Furthermore, a constantly fluctuating contextual hierarchy forever keeps us reas-sessing and refining our perception of the referent and the evolving act of reference. For reference, seen as a relationship, is not suddenly established and immutably maintained. Being, rather, a question of perception, it depends on the reader's interpretational strategies, and on his constant testing and reappraisal of reference. At the same time, he is also measuring the validity of his interpretation by elaborating parallel complex coreferential systems, which constitute both a tentative interpre-tation and a means to interpretation.

As Mary Louise Pratt shows, in *Towards a Speech Act Theory of Literary Dis-course* (p. 3–37), the literary text is not to be viewed so much as an object possessing special properties, as "an *act* performed in a context." It is performed, ultimately, by the reader who brings out unending subjects and countersubjects as they evolve in this polyphonic fugue, first in one voice then in another, variously colouring, reshaping or inverting, enhancing or subduing them, as all play together in evolving contrapuntal combinations. Nor are any two performances identical, so that, while the text provides referring expressions or signs, it is the reader who ultimately makes them refer, makes them refer within the text and without, and thus creates meaning. "Never ask for the meaning of a word in isolation, but only in the context

of a sentence," warns Frege (see Quine, 1953, pp. 20–46). "Reference," adds
Benveniste, "is an integral part of the speech act," and only when this sentence
or text is seen as a speech act, and thus in a particular framework (that is, textual
and related to both speaker and reader), that reference obtains and meaning is
possible. Otherwise the signs remain empty; no sign-systems or contingent
meaning(s) coalesce.

Fortunately for the posterity of the literary text, as already suggested, the reader
looks for meaning, and thus reference, behind every bush—literal and metaphoric.
(In fact, of course, the order is the reverse, since he must first establish some sort
of reference for there to be meaning). It matters little to him that what he reads is
in the fictional mode, or indeed in mixed modes, since neither precludes the possibility of reference, even though referential status is altered. In fact mode-mixing
is a trigger which propels reference towards a dialectically enhanced dynamics. If
all other reference fails, the fictional mode will merely refer to itself as fiction, as
Gerald Prince shows. Or, caught between the two modes, like the balloon-breasts
in Wladimir Krysinski's chapter, referents may refer to their own transformation:
to the very creation, destruction, and recreation of reference before our very eyes.
Even such startlingly non-referring texts as Surrealist writings, which systematically
(but in asystematic fashion) cut coreferential bonds, refer . . . to themselves as
innovation, to new para-syntactic strategies. In a similar way, as Riffaterre remarks
(1979, pp. 199–234), many metaphorically overloaded and referentially contradictory texts point, like a boomerang, to themselves as semiotic structure.

It is interesting to note that often the triggers which propel signifiers to refer,
and thereby to signify specifically, are either the overfull or the empty sign.
Grojnowski, analysing literary decadence and its discourse (1978),[6] shows how the
aesthetically overcrowded sign, ceasing to refer coherently and thus to mean, turns
in upon itself till it reaches an altered state of reference by referring to the very
nature of the decadent sign, which, like the work of art, refers ultimately to itself.
Moving from the high-piled paradigms of decadent, poetic, and highly metaphoric
discourse to empty paradigms, such as "Poland of Nowhere," this very emptiness
seems to display an irresistible referential attraction for the reader, who, in his
"performance," seeks to fill it. Often referential or semantic opacity will simultaneously empty and trigger a text's signifiers to polyvalent referential contexts.
For instance, in Apollinaire's poem "Fête" ["Celebration"], the poet-soldier describes fireworks and roses. Looking down he suddenly mentions his cocked revolver. Though a soldier, this barely provides sufficient context for meaningful
reference. So what "revolver" is he speaking of, and why? Reference, now blocked,
floats in a vacuum, forcing us to cast around for a new context, and, in this case,
to switch to a latent erotic context. Thus we discover a speech act far more sub-
jectively and symbolically oriented than the bucolic third-person description initially
implied. The deictic function of the typographical arrangement (capitalized key
words such as "TO LOVE," ambiguous indented lines, and the artifice they explicitly mention), reveals new reference within a new code, and, thereby, converts
diegesis into referential mimesis. Here, then, as in many such cases, referential
blocking points to hidden reference, breeds polyreference, and unleashes semiosis,

allowing different interpretations to enhance one another. For subsequently these exotic flowers, like the pointing revolver, are not as innocent as first they seemed, now that a hidden trigger has reforged and interwoven the text's anaphoric and cataphoric referential chains.

Indeed, referential subversion and diversion, and the semiosis they engender, are instrumental in creating and weaving the many strands of the textual cloth. Our awareness, and thus performance of the text's perlocutionary function, triggered by our awareness of its predominantly fictional illocutionary force, is probably one of the most important factors in literature's referential dynamics. Thus we see, through the surface, other inferred levels of reference, as we perceive, for example, the perlocutionary referential function of symbolism, irony, or "historical" recreations. Irony, parody, *mise en abyme*, covert intertextuality (as when Nabokov's opening lines in *Ada* refer to Dostoievsky's world), metaphor, symbolism, and allegory are just some examples of the text's deictic role in the reader's boundless perlocutionary referential and semiotic enthusiasm. By the same token, we also see inferred concretizations, both diachronic and synchronic, mutually reinforcing one another, as emphasis shifts with the text's unfolding and the reader's constant adjustments to his recreation.

In literature, unlike most ordinary discourse, no one level ever precludes another: they all coexist, and in a constantly shifting hierarchy. It is perhaps this very coexistence of contexts, of modes, and of diverse illocutionary and perlocutionary acts which makes literary reference essentially an *act*, a dynamic self-referential process; one which never ceases and never shall. For in literary discourse the referential function encompasses far more than mere context (though this, too, is complex): it implies the metalinguistic, conative, emotive, and, above all, the poetic functions.

In literature, reference creates the tension that propels the dialectic movement of interpretation between reader and text. For this dialectic is contingent upon that of the text's double referential function. Form (as perceived by virtue of its metamorphic content) *and* process are the two poles, the two dynamic generators of this referential dialectic in literature. As such, they are its ultimate and necessarily symbiotic referents, the very foundation of literary creation and reader recreation. For referring, in literature, is the *sine qua non* of the literary act; and literature, in the last analysis, must be literary *praxis*.

NOTES

1. All references are to be found in the bibliography at the end of this volume.

2. We have already commented on the non-referential semantic and semiosical fallacy this leads to. Since it will also be dealt with in the next section, and since the purpose of the present section is to present the referent, and thereby reference, in relation to the sign and meaning, our remarks will be limited to 1) the separation of the sign (and apparently of meaning) from the referent, and 2) the latter's perceived degree of concreteness.

3. Unicorns have come under fire from Russell who, refusing anything but the real mode, would not admit that unicorns can exist in any form or shape—not even in heraldry. But what is the precise nature of their "existence"? They are fictional entities, just as Ionesco's chairs are fictional entities for the reader. We can represent both by drawing them or including them in fictional discourse, and both representations will refer to some previous image of them. Whether the source of this image is secondhand (seeing a painting of a unicorn) or real (sitting on a chair) matters little—literature is rarely concerned with referring to the real thing—and we are able to refer equally well to the mental image of both: looking at paintings and sitting on chairs are both events, and mental images of both exist in our minds.

4. The same problem also applies to ordinary discourse. Am I to say that before we knew Troy was where Hissarlik now stands, or before the mound called Cadbury Castle was identified as one of King Arthur's castles, no one could refer to these places? For the untravelled or ignorant reader, the possibility of referring to these places is no less than for the initiated. For centuries people have been referring to Troy; does it make a qualitative difference to the validity of their referring act that they can now add, to their erstwhile historico-literary referent, layer upon layer of archeological rubble? The answer must be no, for the act itself is not changed, even if the widening context, which now includes both the fictional and real mode, has enhanced our mental image by the archeological proof of what one suspected all along.

5. Some have argued the only ones—see Plato's *Theaetetus*, Russell's "Philosophy of Logical Atomism," and Wittgenstein's earlier writings in the *Tractatus*; Frege, and Wittgenstein in *Philosophical Investigations*, para. 40, represent the opposite point of view, i.e., that names necessarily have meaning, but only contingently reference, and are like disguised definite descriptions; more recently both views have been debated by Strawson (1950 and 1959), Kripke (1972), Donnellan (1970 and 1974), and Pavel (1979), to mention but a few.

6. *Littérature* 29 (1978): 75–89.

BIBLIOGRAPHY

Only basic and seminal works on reference and closely related problems are listed. Writings on specific literary texts and genres are not included.

Adorno, T.
1970 *Aesthetic Theory* (tr. C. Lenhardt). London & Boston: Routledge & Kegan Paul.
Althusser, L., & Balibar, E.
1970 *Reading Capital* (tr. B. Brewster). London: New Left Books.
Arrivé, M.
1969 Postulats pour la description linguistique des textes littéraires. *Langue Française* 3:3–13.
Balibar, E., & Macherey, P.
1974 Sur la littérature comme forme idéologique: Quelques hypothèses marxistes. *Littérature* 13:29–48.
Barthes, R.
1964 Eléments de sémiologie. *Communications* 4:91–135. (Tr. A. Lavers & C. Smith, *Elements of Semiology*. London: Cape, 1967 & New York: Hill & Wang, 1968).
1968 L' Effet de réel, *Communications* 11:84–89.
Benveniste, E.
1966 *Problèmes de linguistique générale* I. Paris: Gallimard. (Tr. M. E. Meek, *Problems in General Linguistics*. Coral Gables: University of Miami Press, 1971).
1974 *Problèmes de linguistique générale* II. Paris: Gallimard.
Buchler, J. (ed.)
1955 *Philosophical Writings of Peirce*. New York: Dover.
Carnap, R.
1942 *Introduction to Semantics*. Cambridge, Mass.: M.I.T. Press.
1947 *Meaning and Necessity*. Chicago: University of Chicago Press.
Chastain, C.
1975 Reference and Context, in K. Gunderson (ed.), *Language, Mind and Knowledge*. Minneapolis: University of Minnesota Press, pp.194–269.
Donnellan, K.
1966 Reference and Definite Descriptions. *The Philosophical Review* LXXV:282–304.
1970 Proper Names and Identifying Descriptions. *Synthèse* 21:335–358.
1974 Speaking of Nothing. *The Philosophical Review* LXXXIII:3–32.
1978 Speaker Reference, Descriptions and Anaphora, in *Pragmatics,* vol. 9 of P. Cole (ed.), *Syntax and Semantics*. New York: Academic Press, pp.47–68.
Eco, U.
1973 Langage artistique, segmentation du contenu et référents. *Degrés* 3:b–b15.
1976 *A Theory of Semiotics*. Bloomington & London: Indiana University Press.
Elam, K.
1980 *The Semiotics of Theatre and Drama*. London & New York: Methuen.
Feigl, H. & Sellars, W. (eds.)
1949 *Readings in Philosophical Analysis*. New York: Appleton-Century-Crofts.
Foucault, M.
1969 *L'Archéologie du savoir*. Paris: Gallimard. (*The Archeology of Knowledge*, Tr. A. M. S. Smith. New York: Pantheon and London: Tavistock Publications, 1972).

Frege, G.
    1892 Über Sinn und Bedeutung. *Zeitschrift für Philosophie und philosophische Kritik*
    100:25–50.
    (Tr.: 1) On Sense and Reference, in Geach & Black, 1960, pp. 56–78; 2) Feigl &
    Sellars, 1949, pp. 82–102.)
Gale, R. M.
    1971 The Fictive Use of Language. *Philosophy* 46:324–40.
Geach, P. T.
    1962 *Reference and Generality*. Ithaca: Cornell University Press.
Geach, P. T., & Black, M. (eds.)
    1960 *Translations from the Philosophical Writings of Gottlob Frege*. Oxford: Black-
    well.
Gombrich, E. H.
    1960 *Art and Illusion*. Princeton: Princeton University Press.
Goodman, N.
    1952 On Likeness of Meaning, in Linsky, 1952.
Grice, H. P.
    1957 Meaning. *The Philosophical Review* LXVI:377–88.
    1968 Utterer's Meaning, Sentence Meaning and Word Meaning. *Foundations of Lan-
    guage* 4:225–42.
Halliday, M. A. K., & Hasan, R.
    1976 *Cohesion in English*. London: Longman.
Heintz, J.
    1979 Reference and Inference in Fiction. *Poetics* Vol. 8, Nos 1–2:85–99.
Holquist, M., & Reed, W.
    1980 Six Theses on the Novel—and Some Metaphors. *New Literary History*, Vol.
    XI, No. 3:413–23.
Ihwe, J. F., & Rieser, H.
    1979 Normative and Descriptive Theory of Fiction: Some Contemporary Issues. *Po-
    etics* Vol. 8, Nos. 1–2:63–84.
Ingarden, R.
    1973 *The Literary Work of Art: An Investigation on the Borderlines of Ontology,
    Logic and Theory of Literature* (1965). Evanston: Northwestern University Press.
Iser, W.
    1978 *The Act of Reading: A Theory of Aesthetic Response*. Baltimore: Johns Hopkins
    University Press.
Jakobson, R.
    1960 Closing Statement: Linguistics and Poetics, in T. Sebeok (ed.), *Style in Lan-
    guage*. Cambridge, Mass.: M.I.T. Press.
Jameson, F.
    1981 *The Political Unconscious: Narrative as a Socially Symbolic Act*. Ithaca: Cornell
    University Press.
Kripke, S.
    1963 Semantical Considerations on Modal Logic. *Acta Philosophica Fennica* 16:83–
    94. [Reprinted in Linsky, 1971, pp.63–72].
    1972 Naming and Necessity, in D. Davidson & G. Harman (eds.), *Semantics of
    Natural Languages*. Dordrecht: Reidel, pp. 253–355.
Lavis, G.
    1971 Le Texte littéraire, le référent, le réel. *Cahiers d'Analyse Textuelle* 13:8–22.
Lemon, L. T., & Reis, M. J. (eds.)
    1965 *Russian Formalist Criticism: Four Essays*. Lincoln: University of Nebraska
    Press.
Lewis, T. E.
    1979 Notes Toward a Theory of the Referent. *PMLA* Vol. 94, No. 3:459–75.

Linsky, L.
　　1967 *Referring*. London: Routledge & Kegan Paul.
　　1977 *Names and Descriptions*. Chicago: University of Chicago Press.
Linsky, L. (ed.)
　　1952 *Semantics and the Philosophy of Language*. Urbana: University of Illinois Press.
　　1971 *Reference and Modality*. London: Oxford University Press.
Lyons, J.
　　1977 *Semantics* (Vol. 1). Cambridge: Cambridge University Press.
Morris, C.
　　1938 Foundation of the Theory of Signs. *International Encyclopedia of Unified Science*, Vol. 1, No. 1. Chicago: University of Chicago Press.
　　1946 *Signs, Language and Behavior*. New York: Prentice Hall. (Reprinted in Morris, 1971).
　　1971 *Writings on the General Theory of Signs*. The Hague: Mouton.
Mukarovsky, J.
　　1977a Art as a Semiotic Fact, in J. Burbank & P. Steiner (eds.), *Structure, Sign and Function: Selected Essays by Jan Mukarovsky*. New Haven & London: Yale University Press, pp. 82–88. (Originally published as "L'Art comme fait sémiologique," in Actes du huitième Congrès international de philosophie à Prague, 2–7 septembre 1934, Prague, 1936, pp. 1065–72; and reprinted in *Poétique* 3: 1970).
　　1977b *The Word and Verbal Art* (tr. and ed. J. Burbank & P. Steiner). New Haven & London: Yale University Press.
Ogden, C. K., & Richards, I. A.
　　1923 *The Meaning of Meaning*. London: Routledge & Kegan Paul.
Pavel, T.
　　1975 'Possible Worlds' in Literary Semantics. *Journal of Aesthetics and Art Criticism* Vol. 34, No.2.
　　1979 Fiction and the Causal Theory of Names. *Poetics* Vol. 8, Nos. 1–2:179–191.
Peirce, C. S.
　　1932 *The Collected Papers of Charles Sanders Peirce* (eds. C. Hartshorne & P. Weiss). Cambridge, Mass.: Harvard University Press.
　　1982 (*Writings of Charles S. Peirce: A Chronological Edition* is currently being prepared by the Peirce Edition Project at Indiana University–Purdue University at Indianapolis. Volumes 1 (1857–1866), 2 (1867–1871), and 3 (1872–1878) have appeared as of 1987. [Bloomington: Indiana University Press, 1982–.])
Piaget, J.
　　1961 *Les Mécanismes perceptifs*. Paris: Presses Universitaires de France.
Plato
　　(1973) *Theaetetus* (tr. J. McDowell), Oxford: Clarendon Press.
Poetics Vol. 8, Nos. 1–2 (Special issue on reference in fiction).
Pratt, M. L.
　　1977 *Toward a Speech Act Theory of Literary Discourse*. Bloomington & London: Indiana University Press.
Quine, W. V. O.
　　1953 *From a Logical Point of View*. Cambridge, Mass.: Harvard University Press.
　　1960 *Word and Object*. Cambridge, Mass.: M.I.T. Press.
　　1971 Reference and Modality (reprint of Quine, 1953, pp. 139–157), in Linsky, 1971.
　　1976 *The Ways of Parodox and Other Essays*. Cambridge, Mass.: Harvard University Press.
Ricoeur, P.
　　1976 *Interpretation Theory: Discourse and the Surplus of Meaning*. Fort Worth: Texas Christian University Press.
Riffaterre, M.
　　1978 *Semiotics of Poetry*. Bloomington & London: Indiana University Press.

1979 *La Production du texte*. Paris: Seuil. (*Text Production*, tr. T. Lyons; Columbia University Press, 1983).

Russell, B.
1905 On Denoting. *Mind* XIV:479–93. (Reprinted in Russell, *Logic and Knowledge*; London: Allen & Unwin, 1956, pp. 41–56).
1940 *An Inquiry into Meaning and Truth*. London: Allen & Unwin.

Ryle, G.
1957 The Theory of Meaning, in C. A. Mace (ed.), *British Philosophy in the Mid-Century* London: Allen & Unwin. (Reprinted in F. Zabeeh, E. D. Klemke, & A. Jacobson [eds.], *Readings in Semantics*; Urbana: University of Illinois Press, 1974).

Saussure, F. de
1916 *Cours de linguistique générale*. Paris: Payot. (*Course in General Linguistics*, tr. and annotated by R. Harris; London: Duckworth, 1983).

Savan, D.
1976 *An Introduction to Peirce's Semiotics: Part One*. Toronto Semiotic Circle Monographs, Working Papers & Prepublications, Toronto: Victoria University.

Searle, J.
1969 *Speech Acts: An Essay in the Philosophy of Language*. Cambridge: Cambridge University Press.
1975 The Logical Status of Fictional Discourse. *New Literary History*, Vol. 6:319–32. (Reprinted in Searle, *Expression and Meaning*; Cambridge: Cambridge University Press, 1979, pp.58–75).

Shklovsky, V.
1917 Art as Technique, in L. T. Lemon & M. J. Reis, eds., 1965, pp. 3–24.

Strawson, P. F.
1950 On Referring. *Mind* LIX:320–44. (Reprinted in Strawson, *Logico-Linguistic Papers*; London: Methuen, 1971, pp. 1–27).
1959 *Individuals: An Essay in Descriptive Metaphysics*. London: Methuen.
1964 Intention and Convention in Speech Acts. *The Philosophical Review* LXXIII:439–60. (Reprinted in Strawson, 1971).

Wittgenstein, L.
[1921] *Tractatus Logico-Philosophicus* (tr. D. F. Pears & B. F. McGuiness). London: Routledge & Kegan Paul, 1961 & 1974.
1968 *Philosophical Investigations* (tr. G. E. M. Anscombe). Oxford: Blackwell.

Woods, J. H.
1974 *The Logic of Fiction*. The Hague & Paris: Mouton.
1979 *Soundings of Deviant Logic*. The Hague & Paris: Mouton.

NOTES ON CONTRIBUTORS

JEAN ALTER, Professor of Romance Languages, University of Pennsylvania, is author of *La Vision du monde d'Alain Robbe-Grillet, Les Origines de la satire anti-bourgeoise*, and *L'Esprit anti-bourgeois sous l'ancien régime*. He is founding editor of *Forum*, an international newsletter for the semiotics of theatre.

ROSS CHAMBERS, who is Marvin Felheim Distinguished University Professor of French and Comparative Literature at the University of Michigan, recently published *Story and Situation: Narrative Seduction and the Power of Fiction* and is working on two new books, *Narrative in Opposition* and *Mélancolie historique, textualité moderne* (on the 1850s in France).

LINDA HUTCHEON is Professor of English at McMaster University (Canada) and a member of the Associate Faculty of the Center for Comparative Literature, University of Toronto. She is author of *Narcissistic Narrative, Formalism and the Freudian Aesthetic, A Theory of Parody* and articles in *Diacritics, Contemporary Literature, Poétique*, and others.

MICHAEL ISSACHAROFF is Professor of French at the University of Western Ontario. His most recent books include *L'Espace et la nouvelle, Le Spectacle du discours*, and *Discourse as Performance*. He is editor of *Langages de Flaubert* and co-editor of *Sartre et la mise en signe* and *Performing Texts*.

WLADIMIR KRYSINSKI is Professor of Comparative Literature and Slavic Literature at the University of Montreal. He is author of *Carrefours de signes* and numerous articles on comparative literature and literary theory.

THOMAS E. LEWIS, Associate Professor of Spanish and Comparative Literature, is Chairman of the Department of Spanish and Portuguese at the University of Iowa. He is author of *Fiction and Reference* and has published several essays on reference and literature in such journals as *Diacritics, PMLA*, and *MLN*.

FRANÇOISE MELTZER, Associate Professor of French and Comparative Literature, University of Chicago, is author of *Salomé and the Dance of Writing: Portraits of Mimesis in Literature* (forthcoming).

BRUCE MORRISSETTE is Sunny Distinguished Service Professor Emeritus of Romance Languages at the University of Chicago. His recent books include *The Novels of Robbe-Grillet, Intertextual Assemblage in Robbe-Grillet: From Topology to the Golden Triangle*, and *Novel and Film*.

PATRICE PAVIS teaches drama at the Institut d'Etudes Théâtrales, Université de Paris III. He is author of *Problèmes de sémiologie théâtrale, Voix et images de la scène, Dictionnaire du théâtre*, and *Marivaux à l'épreuve de la scène*.

GERALD PRINCE is Professor of Romance Languages and Chair of the Program of Comparative Literature and Literary Theory at the University of Pennsylvania. His *Dictionary of Narratology* is forthcoming from the University of Nebraska Press.

JEAN-JACQUES THOMAS is Associate Professor of Romance Languages and

Linguistics at Duke University. He has written widely on literary theory and linguistics, edited special issues of *Langages* and *Sub-stance*, and translated Michael Riffaterre's *Semiotics of Poetry*. His *La Langue la poésie*, just completed, is soon to appear.

ANNA WHITESIDE is Associate Professor of French and Comparative Literature at McMaster University (Canada). She is the author of works on autobiography, semiotics, speech act theory, and reference in *Semiotica, Neophilologus, Romanic Review, French Forum, Revue des Lettres Modernes*, and others. She is currently writing a book on Apollinaire's *Calligrammes* and visual poetics.

INDEX